T0214317

Lecture Notes in Computer Science 9704

Commenced Publication in 1973
Founding and Former Series Editors:
Gerhard Goos, Juris Hartmanis, and Jan van Leeuwen

More information about this series at http://www.springer.com/series/7409

Enrique Alba · Francisco Chicano
Gabriel Luque (Eds.)

Smart Cities

First International Conference, Smart-CT 2016
Málaga, Spain, June 15–17, 2016
Proceedings

 Springer

Editors
Enrique Alba
Universidad de Málaga
Málaga
Spain

Gabriel Luque
Universidad de Málaga
Málaga
Spain

Francisco Chicano
Universidad de Málaga
Málaga
Spain

ISSN 0302-9743   ISSN 1611-3349   (electronic)
Lecture Notes in Computer Science
ISBN 978-3-319-39594-4   ISBN 978-3-319-39595-1   (eBook)
DOI 10.1007/978-3-319-39595-1

Library of Congress Control Number: 2016939927

LNCS Sublibrary: SL3 – Information Systems and Applications, incl. Internet/Web, and HCI

Printed on acid-free paper

This Springer imprint is published by Springer Nature
The registered company is Springer International Publishing AG Switzerland

Preface

This volume presents the proceedings of the International Conference on Smart Cities 2016, which was held in Malaga during June 15–17, 2016. Research in smart cities is undoubtedly a very important topic. In fact, it is a topic of the future. Indeed many articles are starting to appear in a few other similar conferences and journals, but the field still needs some time to become established and recognized.

Some of the open issues are very basic: what is the meaning of *smart* in smart city? Is any paper on, for example, routes between two points a smart city paper? The number of open questions is great. However, some things are clear: there are many topics regarding the city (mobility, energy, construction, citizens, social implications, economy, technology, tourism) and studies on smart cities should have a corresponding holistic vision in their content. Studies on only one of these topics, typical in research to date, need to grow to consider the city and several of its aspects. As to the *smart* part, well, who knows what is smart in the first place? The definition is fuzzy at present, and, again, we need to go beyond the mere use of a sensor or a smartphone to make applications *intelligent*.

With this conference, we hope to advance our knowledge on these and other questions. Our expectations are large in the sense that, at the very least, we are trying to find the correct questions. With this conference we wish to start a long-lasting series of annual meetings in Málaga (Spain) where researchers, companies, and even municipal authorities can find answers and advances for the benefit of citizens and local economies. With a clear scientific focus, we also hold industrial talks and demonstrations, and promote bold thinking.

The topics of the papers in this volume include studies and tools to improve road traffic, energy consumption, logistics, frameworks providing new services for holistic decisions, driving assistance, electric vehicles, public transport, and surveys on smart city concepts.

We thank Springer for helping with these proceedings, as well as the Universidad de Málaga for their continuous support in the organization. We also thank the Spanish project moveON (TIN2014-57341-R) for endorsing this kind of activity, and the members of the NEO research group in Málaga for their enthusiasm.

June 2016

Enrique Alba
Francisco Chicano
Gabriel Luque

Organization

Organizing Committee

General Chair

Enrique Alba   University of Málaga, Spain

Program Chair

Gabriel Luque   University of Málaga, Spain

Publication Chair

Francisco Chicano   University of Málaga, Spain

Local Organization

Jamal Toutouh   University of Málaga, Spain
Javier Ferrer   University of Málaga, Spain
Daniel Stolfi   University of Málaga, Spain
Yesnier Bravo   University of Málaga, Spain
Christian Cintrano   University of Málaga, Spain

Publicity Chair

Francisco Aragón   University of Málaga, Spain

Program Committee

Enrique Alba   University of Málaga, Spain
J.A. Alvarez-García   University of Seville, Spain
Pierfrancesco Bellini   University of Florence, DINFO, Italy
Juergen Branke   University of Warwick, UK
Nelio Cacho   Universidade Federal do Rio Grande do Norte,
                                Brazil
Miriam Capretz   University of Western Ontario, Canada
Jose M. Carmona   Andata GmbH, Austria
J. Marcos Castro   Universidad de Málaga, Spain
María Rosa Cervera Sarda   Universidad de Alcalá, Spain
Francisco Chicano   University of Málaga, Spain
Javier Faulin   Universidad Pública de Navarra, Spain
Manuel Fernández-Utrilla   Universidad Europea, Spain
Javier Ferrer   University of Málaga, Spain
Luis A. Garcia   University Jaume I, Spain

Contents

X   Contents

A Holistic, Interdisciplinary Decision Support System for Sustainable Smart City Design

Johannes M. Schleicher[1(✉)], Michael Vögler[1], Christian Inzinger[2], Sara Fritz[1],
Manuel Ziegler[1], Thomas Kaufmann[1], Dominik Bothe[1], Julia Forster[1],
and Schahram Dustdar[1]

[1] TU Wien, Wien, Austria
{johannes.schleicher,michael.vogler,sara.fritz,manuel.ziegler,
thomas.kaufmann,dominik.bothe,julia.forster,
schahram.dustdar}@tuwien.ac.at
[2] University of Zurich, Zurich, Switzerland
christian.inzinger@uzh.ch

Abstract. With the advent of the smart city paradigm, modern cities
have become complex systems of systems with a host of increasingly
entangled dependencies and interactions among systems as well as stakeholders from multiple different domains. Efficient design, engineering,
and operation of such systems is challenging due to the large number of
involved stakeholders and their requirements, which might be conflicting
and will change over time. In this paper, we present results from our
ongoing efforts towards engineering next-generation smart city applications to provide stakeholders with a holistic and tailored view on their
problem domain to support them in managing relevant aspects of the
city, and furthermore provide effective assistance for important decision
processes. We introduce the URBEM Smart City Application (USCA),
an interdisciplinary decision support system, and present different views
on its use by involved experts from four central smart city domains in
the context of a smart city research initiative in the city of Vienna.

Keywords: Smart cities · Data analytics · Smart city application
engineering · Smart city applications

1 Introduction

Todays cities are evolving into complex behemoths consisting of a myriad of
sophisticated entangled systems. The recent advent and rapid adoption of the
smart city paradigm that enables vital new possibilities, also has significantly
contributed to the intrinsic complexity [1] of such systems. Complex systems and
models from multiple domains, such as e-government, traffic and transportation
management, logistics, building management, smart health care, and smart grids,
have become essential drivers for sustained innovation and improvement of citizen wellbeing. In order to enable sustainable, supply-secure, and future-proof
planning that can keep up with today's rapid city growth and urbanization,

© Springer International Publishing Switzerland 2016
E. Alba et al. (Eds.): Smart-CT 2016, LNCS 9704, pp. 1–10, 2016.
DOI: 10.1007/978-3-319-39595-1_1

it is vital to enable stakeholders to make well-informed decisions. To achieve this they rely on the expertise of domain experts who in turn use complex models for analyzing and simulating various aspects of a city ranging from building physics, energy and mobility systems, to sociological and behavior models.

The most vital part, however, is the ability to effectively integrate these models, allowing them to stimulate each other, which presents the enabling key for creating the foundation for sustainable and future-proof smart city design.

In this paper, we present results from our work in the context of the URBEM[1] smart city research initiative. URBEM is a joint initiative between Wiener Stadtwerke Holding AG (Vienna's biggest energy and mobility provider), TU Wien, and the City of Vienna. Its aim is to research and develop an interactive environment for analyzing scenarios for enabling "a sustainable, supply-secure, affordable, and livable city" in a holistic and interdisciplinary manner. We implement this by enabling a reactive Smart City Loop [2] that allows to integrate multiple domain expert models with each other and enrich them with accurate and timely smart city data in order to provide a solid basis for well-informed stakeholder decisions.

Additionally, we identify the following intrinsic requirements that need to be addressed to fully enable the crucial collaboration of stakeholders and domain experts in URBEM. First, we need the ability to integrate heterogenous, multidimensional data sources that are omnipresent when operating applications in smart city ecosystems. Second, since in smart cities and especially in URBEM, there are various stakeholders involved that enforce and must respect a plethora of different compliance and privacy regulations, we need mechanisms that allow for respecting these constraints, without impeding stakeholder interaction. Finally, to fully support domain experts in URBEM, we can not only provide them with pre-built services and applications, but must allow them to integrate and facilitate their own established and well-known heterogenous tool stacks.

Based on these identified requirements, we show how we achieve this vital integration by developing the URBEM Smart City Application (USCA) and outline how this has benefited involved domain experts and stakeholders.

The remainder of this paper is structured as follows.

In Sect. 2, we present USCA, a representative smart city application that emerged as a result of the URBEM research initiative, and discuss how it tackles the identified challenges. In Sect. 3, we outline how domain experts and stakeholders use and benefit from USCA, followed by a conclusion in Sect. 4.

2   The URBEM Smart City Application

In this section we present the URBEM Smart City Application (USCA). USCA allows for integrating models of multiple domain experts that operate in domains such as building physics, electrical and thermal energy, energy demand modeling, as well as mobility and sociological behavior modeling to provide an interactive,

---

[1] http://urbem.tuwien.ac.at/.

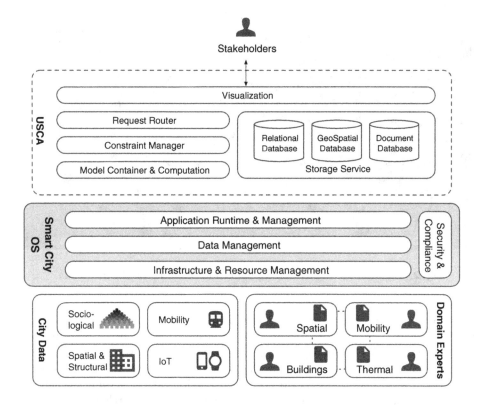

Fig. 1. URBEM cloud overview

explorable, and dynamic visualization for stakeholders. It is an application within the Smart City Application Ecosystem (SCALE), as introduced in [3]. Figure 1 shows an overview of USCA in the context of SCALE.

In USCA, stakeholders interact with a dynamic, web-based, geo-spatial *Visualization* that allows them to freely explore the city as well as different evolving aspects in the context of multiple scenarios with predictions up to the year 2050. Stakeholders can not only explore the city as a whole, but also inspect it in varying levels of detail, from districts, over blocks, down to individual buildings. They can enrich their view with the results of domain expert models by dynamically adding and removing additional layers. This enables them to get a detailed look at various aspects of the city in a dynamic and integrated fashion. Figure 2 shows an example where specific natural gas uplinks for several building blocks in Vienna are explored.

Each of these model interactions spawns specific requests, which are handled by the *Request Router*. The Request Router acts as a smart request proxy and is responsible for elastically scaling up and down the necessary infrastructure resources based on the request patterns of USCA. To achieve this it utilizes the capabilities provided by the *Infrastructure & Resource Management Layer* of the

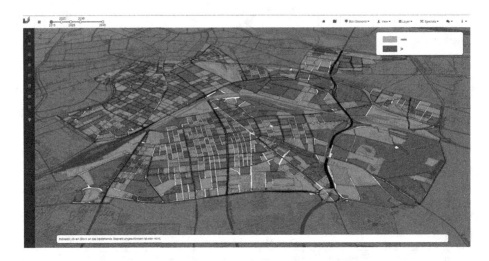

Fig. 2. Visualization of gas heating uplinks for building blocks in Vienna.

Smart City Operating System (SCOS) and the SYBL [4] language. This allows USCA to maintain a small footprint as it can ensure that resources are only consumed when needed. Additionally, the *Infrastructure & Resource Management Layer* enables infrastructure-agnostic deployments [5] so that USCA can be executed on a variety of different platforms, which is an important factor in the heterogeneous infrastructure landscape of current smart cities. It is further able to manage and operate edge infrastructure resources using LEONORE [6] and DIANE [7]. The Request Router then passes each request to the *Constraint Manager*, which in turn is responsible for ensuring that USCA meets the aforementioned complex compliance and privacy regulations. The Constraint Manager inspects each request to check which data sources and domain experts' models are needed to fulfill the requests. Based on this information it ensures that no privacy or compliance constraints are violated and forwards the specific requests to the *Model Container & Computation* component. If constraints are violated, the Constraint Manager can in turn utilize SCOS's *Security & Compliance Layer* to offer ad hoc compensations using capability migrations provided by Nomads [8]. The Model Container & Computation component ensures that the domain experts' models are correctly executed and are supplied with all necessary data. Along with the *Storage Service*, these components represent the core elements of USCA and are key to enabling a holistic, integrated city view. The Model Container & Computation component provides means for provisioning and executing containers. We currently support two popular container formats, Docker[2] and Rkt[3]. This allows domain experts to continue using their well-known and established tool stacks without sacrificing the ability to integrate them into USCA. The containers are packaged to include

---

[2] https://www.docker.com.
[3] https://github.com/coreos/rkt.

all necessary runtime artifacts. Additionally, they can be checked and verified to ensure that compliance and privacy constraints are not violated. This vital feature is enabled via the *Application Runtime & Management Layer* of SCOS. To give models access to required data, data containers are transparently integrated by injecting necessary container links. This mechanism enables a minimally invasive approach that allows domain experts to integrate provided capabilities into their own tools. Domain experts then simply access data in the data container via the established link and store the results of their models in the same container. In the background the *Storage Service* is used to provide necessary data via these links, as well as to store the model results in the appropriate data store. Additionally, the Constraint Manager can check at all times if data in transit can be consumed by the respective domain expert, which ensures that all compliance and privacy constraints are also met on the data level. The final element in empowering the Storage Service is the ability to utilize the *Data Management Layer* of SCOS. It enables the Storage Service to access a wide range of city data in various formats ranging from traditional relational data and documents, to live streaming data from the Internet of Things. All this data in turn can be incorporated into domain models as well as directly into the visualization.

3   Domain Expert Perspectives

In this section, we discuss the use of USCA by experts and their models from four different smart city domains. We briefly outline the specifics of each model, how it utilizes and benefits from USCA, and conclude with the observed benefits from the stakeholder's perspective.

3.1   Building Models

One of the key elements in urban city planning is to develop a proper method that allows simulating the effects of different urban development strategies (e.g., for 2020, 2030, and 2050) focusing on all buildings within a district or even an entire city. Therefore, different urban development scenarios are used as initial parameters to run building simulations for the focused building stock. Individual indicators (e.g., heating demand or refurbishment rates) are usually insufficient to run commercial building simulation tools. In order to maintain good performance and a time-efficient calculation period to simulate an entire urban environment, the simulation efforts for single buildings must be as low as possible. This model generates scalable density functions for both, residential and non-residential buildings by considering particular construction periods, different HVAC[4] technologies as well as individual occupancies in the course of a social milieu-based approach. The result is a comprehensive matrix of simulated density functions consisting of all possible combinations of the parameters mentioned above. The ability to expose this model within USCA allows the electrical

---

[4] Heating, ventilating, and air conditioning.

and thermal grid models to utilize generated results that enable them to use hourly load profiles, which in turn are required for the technical simulations. In order to generate high-resolution load profiles (both temporal and geographic) for each building, only the input of the urban development scenarios generated within the energy demand model and the number of buildings is needed. This significantly increases the possible level of detail for planning decision support in this domain.

3.2   Energy Demand Models

The model concerning the perspectives of building energy demand and supply mainly handles the long-term development of heating and cooling demands. Additionally, it is concerned with the demand for domestic hot water (DHW) in buildings and the interactions with grid-bound heating supply, specifically focusing on gas and district heating. Since the building stock causes a large part of the energy demand of modern cities and the realization of the European energy targets[5] require a decrease in this demand, a reduction of fossil fuels (e.g., gas and oil), as well as the integration of renewable energy sources. This can be achieved by thermal refurbishments of buildings, by changing the heating systems, and by using a different energy carrier. The used model simulates the long-term investments in the building sector and optimizes the investments in the expansion of the district heating and/or gas infrastructure. This model not only considers the current legislative and policies, but also assumptions for the future development of them [9]. The emerging results are spatially resolved. As this analysis is from an economic point of view, the integrated approach within USCA allows enriching the model with more technical details. Based on a thermal grid analysis of the status quo for the base year, information about the spatial heat losses or remaining capacities without expansion can be pointed out and are used as input for the economic model. Subsequently, the long-term results regarding heating and cooling demand, and the expansion of the district heating network for several years within the considered horizon, are the basis for thermal grid analysis. The results of the analysis allow finding appropriate measures regarding the grid to react to these changes.

3.3   Electrical Grid Models

The model of electric supply networks can predict reliability, overloads, and network utilization considering the limits of operational equipment used inside the network. In addition, the model is capable of making statements about which requirements will arise for future power grids through increasing integration of decentralized energy resources, decentralized storage, and energy combined supply networks (energy hubs), while considering demographic change. Modeling and simulating an electric supply network for urban areas requires an approach that

---

[5] http://eur-lex.europa.eu/LexUriServ/LexUriServ.do?uri=OJ:L:2013:178:0107:0108: EN:PDF.

allows for incorporating large amounts of network data. Therefore, power flow studies [10] for distribution areas fed by substations are performed. Transmission areas inside an urban area are neglected. Furthermore, energy and infrastructure (heat, gas, and electrical) combined systems are simulated by direct current power flow calculations within an optimization using an energy hub approach [11]. Possible objective functions of the optimization are the minimization of CO_2 emissions, or the minimization of line utilization, with the explicit constraint that network capacities (electricity, gas and district heating) should not be overloaded. Results from the energy demand and building models inside USCA form the framework conditions and input parameters for the electric supply network model. Based on a technical analysis for a base year, scenarios with increasing integration of renewables and cooling demand that are mainly covered by electric energy reveal the limits of currently used network equipment (lines, transformers, etc.). The obtained results affect future investment decisions in network utilities to address changing requirements within the electric supply networks.

3.4   Thermal Grid Models

Current developments of the European energy market are influencing the operational strategy of heat suppliers. Especially providers of district heating systems fed by conventional heat production have to react with appropriate measures to these changes. The integration of thermal storages, decentralization of heat production, changing heating technologies or adjusting the temperature of district heating networks make it necessary to simulate and analyze existing and future designs of district heating systems. In order to achieve comparable conclusions about operating behavior of district heating systems, it is essential to create a corresponding model including main components like pipes, pumps, storages, and valves. The basic idea of the created numerical model is the combination of a steady state hydraulic and a transient thermal calculation of the district heating network. The results of the iterative hydraulic calculation are the pressure and velocity distribution of the pipe network [12]. These results serve as input parameter for the thermal calculation. To simulate the thermal behavior of the district heating network a discretized one-dimensional pipe model is used. The discretization is done using the finite-volume method and the resulting equation system can be solved explicitly or implicitly. A common way to define the topology of networks is the usage of a node-edge matrix. This so-called incidence matrix is generated automatically from given GIS data. The usage of the simulation model within USCA increases the capability in terms of interactions with more detailed data provided by other models that are integrated in USCA. The output of the model can be used to support economic analysis from a technical point of view or serve as additional input for analysis of energy combined systems. The possibility to link models of different disciplines extends the scope of the overall application.

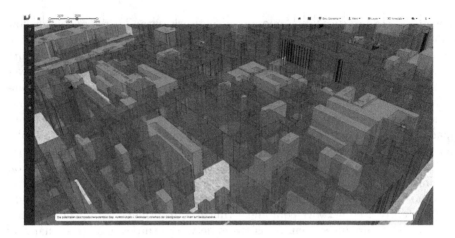

Fig. 3. Floor-space potentials for individual buildings up to the year 2030.

3.5   Spatial Modeling and Visualization

The visualization aspect represents a vital instrument to communicate the results of, as well as to interact with, the models of the domain experts via a simple and intuitive interface. The ability to spatially resolve the results of the models and to evolve them over time is an essential factor in understanding the impacts of complex systems on the city. USCA allows to seamlessly incorporate and combine city data with the results of domain expert models, which enable novel ways for illustrating vital elements for city design. In Fig. 3 we see a spacial placement of forecasted floor-space potentials for individual buildings in the year 2030. Through USCA it is possible to incorporate various city data sources to get an accurate picture of specific development potentials, which is an important factor for spatial modeling.

The development of smart cities requires the integration of multiple stake-holders from different fields. Therefore, USCA provides an easy to manage tool for displaying all relevant information, whereas the visualization enables all involved entities to get an overview about the complexity of the system and to gain an understanding about the main influences and challenges within other disciplines. The consequences of decisions (e.g., investment decisions, legislation, definition of subsidies) within other fields and additional required measures can be highlighted using the visualization. A representative example that illustrates these integration benefits can be seen in Figs. 4 and 5. Figure 4 illustrates detailed district heating demands of all blocks within Vienna's 11th district. The foundation for this is the energy demand model in combination with city data enriched by the building models, which in turn provides detailed load profiles. These high-resolution load profiles are then used by the electrical and thermal grid models to deliver specific grid impacts, which can be visualized at varying spatial detail levels via simply zooming in or out in the Visualization (Fig. 5).

Fig. 4. Energy demand visualization for the 11th district of Vienna

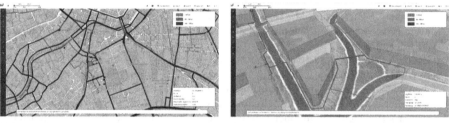

(a) Energy Grid High Level Overview for a district

(b) Detailed Energy Grid for a specific set of buildings

Fig. 5. Energy grid visualizations

4 Conclusion

The smart city paradigm led to a transformation of today's cities to complex systems of systems with a plethora of increasingly complex dependencies and interactions. A large number of stakeholders from multiple different domains pose complex requirements on these systems that might be conflicting and will change over time. Efficient design, engineering, and operation of such systems is increasingly challenging but represents an essential ingredient in supporting stakeholders to make well-informed decisions.

In this paper, we presented results from our ongoing efforts towards engineering and operating next-generation smart city applications that aim to provide stakeholders with a holistic as well as customized view on their problem domain. Such smart city applications must be designed to support stakeholders from different domains in managing and affecting relevant aspects of the city and provide effective assistance for important decision processes. To address these challenges, we introduced USCA, an interdisciplinary decision support system for holistic city planning and management. USCA is a cloud-based application built upon our recent work on smart city application ecosystems that uses a smart city operating system as its foundation. The application provides a holistic, integrated view on multiple complex domains based on models provided by different domain experts to support complex decision processes, while rigorously respecting relevant confidentiality and security constraints. We furthermore reported on the use of USCA by stakeholders from four central smart city domains in the context of a smart city research initiative in the city of Vienna.

References

1. Naphade, M., Banavar, G., Harrison, C., Paraszczak, J., Morris, R.: Smarter cities and their innovation challenges. Computer **44**(6), 32–39 (2011)
2. Schleicher, J.M., Vögler, M., Inzinger, C., Dustdar, S.: Towards the internet of cities: a research roadmap for next-generation smart cities. In: Understanding the City with Urban Informatics Workshop Colocated with CIKM, pp. 3–6. ACM (2015)
3. Schleicher, J.M., Vögler, M., Dustdar, S., Inzinger, C.: Enabling a smart city application ecosystem: requirements and architectural aspects. IEEE Internet Comput. (2016, to appear)
4. Copil, G., Moldovan, D., Truong, H.L., Dustdar, S.: SYBL: an extensible language for controlling elasticity in cloud applications. In: International Symposium on Cluster, Cloud, and Grid Computing, pp. 112–119. IEEE (2013)
5. Schleicher, J.M., Vögler, M., Inzinger, C., Dustdar, S.: Smart Fabric - an infrastructure-agnostic artifact topology deployment framework. In: International Conference on Mobile Services, pp. 320–327. IEEE (2015)
6. Vögler, M., Schleicher, J.M., Inzinger, C., Nastic, S., Sehic, S., Dustdar, S.: LEONORE - large-scale provisioning of resource-constrained IoT deployments. In: International Symposium on Service-Oriented System Engineering, pp. 78–87. IEEE (2015)
7. Vögler, M., Schleicher, J.M., Inzinger, C., Dustdar, S.: DIANE - dynamic IoT application deployment. In: International Conference on Mobile Services, pp. 298–305 (2015)
8. Schleicher, J.M., Vögler, M., Inzinger, C., Hummer, W., Dustdar, S.: Nomads-enabling distributed analytical service environments for the smart city domain. In: International Conference on Web Services, pp. 679–685. IEEE (2015)
9. Fritz, S.: How public interventions in buildings energy efficiency affect the economic feasibility of a district heating network - a case study for Vienna. In: 38th IAEE International Conference, May 2015
10. Gotham, D.J., Heydt, G.T.: Power flow control and power flow studies for systems with facts devices. IEEE Trans. Power Syst. **13**(1), 60–65 (1998)
11. Geidl, M., Koeppel, G., Favre-Perrod, P., Klockl, B., Andersson, G., Frohlich, K.: Energy hubs for the future. IEEE Power Energ. Mag. **5**(1), 24 (2007)
12. Walter, H., Glaninger, A.: Berechnung von rohrnetzwerken mit baumstruktur. KI Luft-und Kältetechnik **40**(11), 460–464 (2004)

A Status of Energy Efficient LED Based Traffic Lamps in Istanbul

Yusuf Dursun$^{(\boxtimes)}$, Moayed Almobaied, and Burcu Buyukkinaci

R&D Department at ISBAK Inc., Istanbul Metropolitan Municipality,
Seyrantepe Mah. Cendere Caddesi No:56, Kagithane/Istanbul, Turkey
{Ydursun,Malmobaied,Bbuyukkinaci}@isbak.com.tr
http://www.isbak.com.tr

Abstract. Recently, the energy resources have been decreased while the global energy demand is expected to grow rapidly. This has led the authorities associated with traffic management to seek various solutions for enhancing energy efficiency of the huge numbers of lamps used in traffic light systems. Hence, many metropolitan areas, like Istanbul, have started using traffic lights equipped with LEDs instead of the conventional incandescent bulbs. The energy saving, low maintenance costs, traffic and road security improvements all contribute to an environment friendly and economical configuration. In this paper, the (R&D) department at ISBAK Inc., demonstrates the benefits of switching the old-style incandescent bulbs to the LED based lamps in traffic signalization system at Istanbul as a case study that will may be useful for other municipalities and researchers. The comparison tables for power consumption show the contribution of LED based traffic lights in Istanbul to the national economy and environment.

Keywords: Energy savings · LED based traffic lamps · Incandescent bulbs · Traffic safety

1 Introduction

Over the last few years, the global energy shortages have been rapidly increased; where, on the other hand, the global energy demand is set to grow by 37 % by 2040 as the International Energy Agency (IEA) mentioned in world energy outlook 2014 [1]. Conventional traffic lights contain bulky and powerful lamps where these lamps consume a lot of amount of electrical power that are not efficient enough according to the currently energy saving standards. Recently, important governmental policies and standards were announced in order to efficiently utilize the electricity during the design process of the lighting equipment [2,3]. In order to save energy, cities switched the conventional bulbs in traffic lights to LED based traffic lamps.

LED is a solid state optoelectronic semiconductor which converts most of the input electrical power directly to light. Historically, in 1907, the British electrical engineer and experimenter Captain Henry J. Round published his observations

© Springer International Publishing Switzerland 2016
E. Alba et al. (Eds.): Smart-CT 2016, LNCS 9704, pp. 11–21, 2016.
DOI: 10.1007/978-3-319-39595-1_2

on a curious phenomenon where a yellowish light was emitted when he applied a certain voltage on the carborundum or Silicon Carbide (SIC) crystals [4,5]. In 1962, the first red luminescence diode (type GaAsP), developed by American Nick Holonyak, enters the market where it has been remarked as the birth of the industrially-produced LED. Indeed, Energy efficiency, long life, resistance to shock and vibration, less heat production and design flexibility are the main outstanding features of LEDs. LED technology was first used in traffic light at 1990 in the United States as the red lights in foggy road conditions for truck routes. At 1994 in Japan, the bluish-green LED was produced and the traffic applications, which based on LED technology, have been established in 1995 [5].

In 1998, the research and development department at ISBAK Inc. (Istanbul Telecommunication Transportation and Security Technologies), which is an affiliated company to Istanbul Metropolitan Municipality, started to follow this new technology in the designing process of the traffic lamps. The early products based on LED technology for road intersections at Istanbul had been achieved in 2000. Based on the European standard for Traffic_Control_Equipment_Signal_Heads EN 12368:2000 and the revised versions in 2006 and 2015 [6–8], Turkish Standards Institute (TSE) published the Traffic_Control_Equipment_Signal_Lamps Standard TS EN 12368 with the up-to-date version in October 2015 [9]. The R&D group at ISBAK Inc. follows this standard during the developing and fabricating process of the LED based traffic signal lamps. Actually, European standard EN 12368 includes all types of lamps used in traffic control equipment (incandescent, halogen, LED) where some issues related to the LED based traffic lamps are not specified at this standard. For this reason, the R&D department in ISBAK Inc. used some rules, in addition to European standard, from the American Standard ITE (Institute of Transportation Engineers) that focus only on LED based traffic lamps [10]. At the end of 2006, the all traditional traffic bulbs in Istanbul have been switched to LED based lamps. ISBAK Inc. successfully developed and produced 200–300 mm diameter LED based traffic lamps within a TEYDEB (Technology and Innovation Funding Programs Directorate) Project in 2006.

From the literature, the authors in [2] at 2002 introduce the expected economic effects, energy saving, and the main features in rep. of Korea when the conventional traffic signal lamps will be replaced by the Korean-type LED traffic signal; they expected an energy saving effect of 85 % and drop of 75 % in maintenance fee. In 2001, the City of Portland, USA, replaced most of its incandescent traffic signal lights with highly efficient LED based lamps. Using an innovative leasing arrangement to amortize the investment costs, Portlands Signal and Street Lighting Division was able to replace 13,382 red and green existing incandescent lamps with LED based lamps. The project resulted in 4.9 million kilowatt-hours (kWh) of annual savings in energy consumption (representing an 80 % reduction in energy usage), and a reduction of about 2,880 tons of annual CO_2 emissions [11]. In this paper, the contributions of 76869 traffic signal modules in 2101 signalized intersections in Istanbul(February 2016) to the national economy, energy saving and environmental protection are analyzed. The rest of

Fig. 1. The yellow incandescent bulbs and LED based lamps produced by ISBAK Inc. (Color figure online)

Table 1. Features and advantages of LEDs.

Feature	Advantages
Semiconductor light source	Cost-effective solutions
	Design flexibility
	Bright and strong light
Low power consumption	Electrical power savings
	Low heat generation
	Applicable to the use of solar energy
High reliability	Wide MTBF (mean time between possible failure)
	Wide operating temperature range
	Not deteriorate by burning
Long operating life	low light loss in long-term operation
	No need for frequently lamp replacement
	Low maintenances

this paper is organized as follows. In Sect. 2, a brief comparison between the LED based traffic lamps and the old-style incandescent bulbs is illustrated. The contributions of LED based traffic lamps to energy saving are explained in Sect. 3. Section 4 describes the other contributions in road safety and environmental protection; then the disadvantages of LED based traffic lamps are discussed. Finally, some conclusions are drawn in Sect. 5.

2   Comparison of LED Based Traffic Lights with Incandescent Bulbs

LED based traffic lights use 80 to 90 percent less energy and last around ten times longer than traditional incandescent bulbs that put out the same amount of light [12]. Furthermore, LEDs resist the mechanical shocks and vibrations due to their robust and non-glass outer covers which made of plastic capsule material. For vibration resist, there are no copper Fleming wires inside LEDs as in incandescent bulbs. Moreover, LED superior the incandescent bulb in that it

Table 2. Differences in power consumption between the yellow old-style incandescent and LED based traffic lamps.

Function	Yellow Incandescent	Yellow LED
300 mm Yellow Ball	100 W	12.500 W
300 mm Yellow Flash	100 W	12.500 W
300 mm Yellow Arrow	100 W	8.170 W

has the resistance capability to the most weather conditions as heat, humidity and winds. A general list of features and advantages of LEDs light sources are given in Table 1. Table 2 illustrates the difference in power consumption between the 300 mm yellow old-style incandescent bulbs and the 300 mm LEDs based lamps for various products. Figure 1 shows the bulb and LEDs based lamp which produced by ISBAK Inc.

Conventional incandescent lamps require color filters to provide the desired color of light, which causes a large amount of wasted electricity that is not used in light producing. In contrast, LED based traffic lamps can be designed to directly produce light as the required color. Another important advance for LEDs is the long-term effects; for 5 mm LEDs, which used in traffic lamps, the forward current should be between 10 mA and 30 mA in order to obtain a long-term and good performance working hours. In AlInGaP LEDs, operating 10,000 h under 30 mA current value leads to approximately 20 % reduction of starting luminous flux while this reduction of luminous flux will be 10 % in case of 20mA operating current. After 50000 operating hours there will be approximately 25 % reduction of luminous flux in case of 20mA forward current. For same case, the luminous flux will reduces to the half of the starting one after 100,000 h (about 11 years). On the other hand, the luminous flux of incandescent traffic bulbs, which have a life time of 8–10 thousand hours, reduces to the half of the starting value

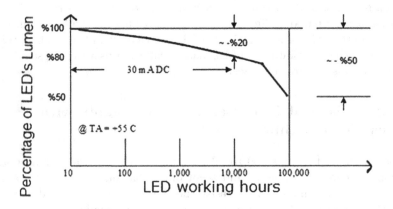

Fig. 2. LED lumen depreciation.

after only 1500 h of operating. Because the lumen depreciation is very little for LED based lamps, there is no need to change the lamps as much as in old-style incandescent ones which leads to a remarkable minimization in the maintenance costs. Figure 2 illustrates the lumen depreciation phenomenon of LED. The Min. Light intensity (cd) of LEDs used in traffic light and their light wave length (nm) are demonstrated in Table 3.

Table 3. Technical data of LEDs based traffic lamps designed in ISBAK Inc.

Operating voltage (230 VAC)	200 mm.			300 mm.		
Signal color	Red	Yellow	Green	Red	Yellow	Green
Min. Light intensity (cd)	200	200	200	400	400	400
Typ. Light wave length (nm)	630	592	505	630	592	505

3 Contributions of LED Based Traffic Lamps to Energy Saving

In the light of these benefits of LEDs, which mentioned at previous section, the ministry of transportation in Turkey has prepared a regulation based on Article 7 of the Law of Energy Efficiency No. 5627 dated 18.04.2007 for the improvement of energy efficiency. According to this regulation, it was reported that LED based systems will be given priority for traffic signalization to regulate the flow of traffic and to reduce the energy consumption in the signaling system and these lamps should be designed in accordance with TS EN 12368 standard [3]. Furthermore, within the framework of "Improvement of Energy Efficiency in Turkey Matching Project Twinning Project", which started in July 2005, studies carried out with the energy efficiency of organizations at France and Netherlands, ADEME and SenterNovem in order to establish energy efficiency concept in Turkey which is appropriate to their counterparts in Europe. In this context, project activities are conducted under the three main components; strengthening the legal and institutional structures, determination of potential energy savings and identifying barriers [13]. In 2006, the R&D group in ISBAK Inc. replaced all the old-style bulbs for the traffic light system with new LED based traffic lamps version. Figure 3 shows some of ISBAK Inc. products that currently used in Istanbul. Power consumption and energy saving comparison case study has been done at the R&D department in ISBAK Inc. between the LED based traffic lamps and the incandescent bulbs which used in Istanbul traffic light intersection. The average operating times for traffic lamps of the intersections in Istanbul is illustrated in Table 4. Tables 5, 6 and 7 summarize the results of this study.

Notes:

- 1 kWh energy = 0,311494 Turkish Lira (₺) with the taxes are excluded from this price; this energy cost is taken from the list of TEDAS-Turkish electric distribution company for 2016 [14].

Fig. 3. LED based lamps produced by ISBAK Inc at Istanbul city.

Table 4. Average operating times for traffic lamps of the intersections in Istanbul.

Traffic unit	Red lamp	Yellow lamp	Green lamp	Flash lamp	Red pedestrian	Green pedestrian
Operating time percentage	53.9%	2.2%	43.9%	50%	59.1%	40.9%

Table 5. Energy consumption of incandescent bulbs previously used in Istanbul.

Lamp type	Pow. cons. (watt)	Number of modules in Istanbul	Average operating time per hour (hours)	Annual pow. Cons. (kWh)	Annual cost(₺)
300 mm Red Lamp	100	5664	0.539	2,674,336.90	833,039.90
300 mm Yellow Lamp	100	5664	0.022	109,156.61	34,001.63
300 mm Green Lamp	100	5664	0.439	2,178,170.50	678,487.04
300 mm Flash Lamp	100	1399	0.50	612,762.00	190,871.69
200 mm Red Lamp	75	9789	0.539	3,466,510.05	1,079,797.08
200 mm Yellow Lamp	75	9789	0.022	141,490.21	44,073.35
200 mm Green Lamp	75	9789	0.439	2,823,372.75	879,463.67
200 mm Flash Lamp	75	228	0.50	74,898.00	23,330.28
200 mm Red Pedestrian	75	11221	0.591	4,356,968.43	1,357,169.52
200 mm Green Pedestrian	75	11221	0.409	3,015,228.57	939,225.61
300 mm Red Arrow	100	292	0.539	137,871.89	42,946.27
300 mm Yellow Arrow	100	292	0.022	5,627.42	1,752.91
300 mm Green Arrow	100	292	0.439	112,292.69	34,978.50
200 mm Red Arrow	75	1855	0.539	656,898.17	204,619.84
200 mm Yellow Arrow	75	1855	0.022	26,812.17	8,351.83
200 mm Green Arrow	75	1855	0.439	535,024.67	166,656.97
Total		76869		20,927,421.00	6,518,766.08

- The currency exchange rate between dollar and Turkish Lira (Turkish Central Bank 09.02.2016) is 1\$ = 2,9471₺
- Pow. Cons. Is the abbreviation of Power Consumption factor.

From Table 7, the total annual Energy Savings is about 89 %. Hence, approximately two million dollars of annual energy savings were achieved by switching

Table 6. Energy consumption of LEDs based Traffic lamps in Istanbul.

Lamp type	Pow. cons. (watt)	Number of modules in Istanbul	Average operating time per hour (hours)	Annual pow. Cons. (kWh)	Annual cost(₺)
300 mm Red Lamp	14.440	5664	0.539	386,174.25	120,290.96
300 mm Yellow Lamp	12.500	5664	0.022	13,644.58	4,250.20
300 mm Green Lamp	10.420	5664	0.439	226,965.37	70,698.35
300 mm Flash Lamp	12.500	1399	0.50	76,595.25	23,858.96
200 mm Red Lamp	7.964	9789	0.539	368,097.15	114,660.05
200 mm Yellow Lamp	7.608	9789	0.022	14,352.77	4,470.80
200 mm Green Lamp	7.854	9789	0.439	295,663.59	92,097.44
200 mm Flash Lamp	7.608	228	0.50	7,597.65	2,366.62
200 mm Red Pedestrian	8.202	11221	0.591	476,478.07	148,420.06
200 mm Green Pedestrian	8.062	11221	0.409	324,116.97	100,960.49
300 mm Red Arrow	7.440	292	0.539	10,257.67	3,195.20
300 mm Yellow Arrow	8.170	292	0.022	459.76	143.21
300 mm Green Arrow	8.610	292	0.439	9,668.40	3,011.65
200 mm Red Arrow	6.180	1855	0.539	54,128.41	16,860.67
200 mm Yellow Arrow	6.570	1855	0.022	2,348.75	731.62
200 mm Green Arrow	6.580	1855	0.439	46,939.50	14,621.37
Total		76869		2,313,488.12	720,637.67

Table 7. Annual energy savings with LED lamps.

	Incandescent lamps	LED lamps	Annual savings
Annual Pow. Cons. kWh	20,927,421.00	2,313,488.12	18,613,932.88 kWh
Annual Energy Costs ($)	2,211,925.65	244,524.34	1,967,401.31 ($)

all incandescent traffic bulbs in Istanbul to LED based traffic lamps. Moreover, the maintenance costs reduce by 91 % with LED based traffic lamps due to the statistics result which show that just only 5 % of LED based lamps are broken down once a year; on the other hand, the incandescent lamps are changed due to breaking or due to the loss of luminous flux in every 6 months for overhead traffic lamps. When only the energy costs are considered, the amortization period is 2.2 years for an LED based lamps. However, this period will reduce to be 1.5 years in case of the maintenance costs are supplemented.

4 Other Properties for LED Based Traffic Lamps

4.1 Contributions of LED Based Traffic Lights to Traffic and Road Safety

Indeed, the human eyes have best response to light sources with saturated color. Hence, the drivers can effectively distinguish the saturated color LED based light in comparing to the other light sources under the bright sunlight. Moreover, LED based lamp has the best light source which can be seen by the drivers in adverse

Fig. 4. CO_2 emissions of Istanbul [17].

weather conditions and can easily recognize other distracting light sources on the opposite road lane. Furthermore, the color of the LED light source does not change due to dimming. Previously, reflectors and colored lenses are used in the signal units with conventional signal lamps. But the sunrays are coming with horizontal angles especially in the morning and evening rush-hours; hence, drivers cannot easily perceive the color of the traffic light due to the reflections from the reflector of the traffic lights (phantom light) in east-west direction. LED traffic signal lights get their colors from LEDs where the colored lenses and reflectors are not used.Hence, these advantages of LED based traffic lights will decrease the numbers of accidents in the cities.

4.2   Contribution of LED Based Traffic Lights to the Environmental Protection

Turkey, taking part in some activities related to environmental protection, such as the Kyoto Protocol which is taking steps to ensure the international fight against global warming and climate change. Countries that signed the Kyoto Protocol in scope of United Nations Climate Change Framework Agreement, promised to reduce the re-lease of carbon dioxide and five other gases that cause the greenhouse effect or if they cannot they promised to improve their rights through emissions trade. The protocol was signed in 1997 and came into force in 2005. The Kyoto Protocol currently includes 160 countries on Earth and more than 55 % of their greenhouse gas emissions. Turkey has been included in the protocol on February 5th 2009 [15]. LED based traffic lights can be considered to be environmental solutions for their energy saving potential. According to statistics of International Energy Agency (IES) in 2013, 459.582 grams of CO_2 emissions are released to produce 1 kWh electric energy in Turkey. 8555 tons/year of CO_2 emissions are prevented by 18614 MWh energy savings. Figure 4 show the CO_2 emissions of Istanbul. For comparison, when the most frequently used automobiles in Turkey are taken into consideration, an average automobile releases 2725 kg CO_2 when it travels averagely 15000 Km per year [16]. Which means

Fig. 5. Heavy snow conditions cover the LED based traffic lamps.

green-house gas emissions would be prevented equivalent to 3139 automobiles withdrawn from traffic.

4.3   Disadvantages of LED Based Traffic Lamps

Nowadays, LEDs are more expensive than conventional lighting source technologies due to their initial cost. Although the payback time for the LED based traffic lamps (about 1.5 years) decreases every passing year, the initial cost of LEDs based traffic lamps is still higher comparing to incandescent/halogen bulbs. Historically, payback time was 3, 3.5 years due to the leakages in technology at the early LED based traffic lamps at 1995. In areas with heavy snow conditions, another disadvantage for the LED based lamps is appeared; Since LEDs produce a very little amount of heat which is not enough to melt the snow accumulated on lamps outer lens. In this case, drivers cant recognize clearly the state of lamps which cause to somehow a case of traffic chaos as shown in Fig. 5. Moreover, some electronics expertise is needed to design electronic drivers in order to supply the correct polarity, voltage and current at a constant flow.

5   Conclusion

Usage of LED based signal lamps is rapidly increasing all over the world due to the noticeable increase in the light efficiency of LEDs, energy-saving, ease of maintenance, their long life times and other benefits. Indeed, installation costs of LEDs are higher than incandescent lamps; however, the energy consumption is decreased by 89 %, the maintenance costs are decreased by 91 % and the payback time for the LED based traffic lamps is about 1.5 years. In this paper, The research and development department (R&D) at ISBAK Inc. (Istanbul Telecommunication Transportation and Security Technologies), which is an affiliated company to Istanbul Metropolitan Municipality, demonstrates the benefits of switching the old-style incandescent bulbs to the LED based lamps in traffic signalization system at Istanbul. Contribution of total 76869 traffic signal modules in 2101 signalized intersections in Istanbul (February 2016) to the national economy is explained. Approximately two million dollars of annual energy savings were achieved by switching all incandescent traffic bulbs in Istanbul to LEDs based traffic lamps and 8555 tons/year of CO_2 emissions are prevented by 18614 MWh energy saving. In Turkey, which has approximately 9,000 intersections, if all traffic signal lights are switched to LED based lamps systems then it is clear that significant energy savings, environmental protection and the maximum safety in traffic will be provided. Furthermore, within the context of government policy and energy-saving practice, the transition to LED lighting with remote control and automation applications to reduce the level of illuminance in urban and general lighting, is on the agenda of ISBAK Inc. For that, ISBAK inc. and Istanbul Technical University (ITU), developing a common project, with the support of Ministry of Science Industry and Technology (MoSIT), established a test road in Istanbul, ITU Ayazaga Campus where different road conditions and scenarios can be practiced in order to assess and measure the visual performance of drivers. According to the measurements and experimental results which will be held on the test road, it is aimed to develop a road lighting automation system working with correct dimming scenarios [18]. As a future work, we will also constraint on the low voltage systems (< 42 VAC)for traffic light which provide an important feature of traffic signaling due to the better monitoring and the increased safety for the engineers working on the traffic signals at the street.

References

1. International Energy Agency (IEA): World Energy Outlook 2014 (2014). http://www.iea.org/textbase/npsum/weo2014sum.pdf
2. Jung, B.M., Jeong, H.G., Han, S.B.: A status of energy efficient led traffic signals in korea. In: Right Light 5, Proceedings of the 5th International Conference on Energy Efficient Lighting, Nice, France (2002)
3. Ministry of Transportation in Turkey: Energy efficiency law: Law no. 5627 (2007). www.eie.gov.tr/eie-web/../EnVer_kanunu_tercume_revize2707.doc
4. Khanna, V.: Fundamentals of Solid-State Lighting: LEDs, OLEDs, and Their Applications in Illumination and Displays. Taylor & Francis, New York (2014)
5. OSRAM: The history of the led (2016). http://www.osram.com/osram_com/news-and-knowledge/led-home/professional-knowledge/led-basics/led-history/index.jsp
6. British Standards Institution (BSI): BS EN 12368: 2000, Traffic Control Equipment-Signal Heads (2000). http://shop.bsigroup.com/ProductDetail/?pid=000000000019996686
7. British Standards Institution(BSI):BS EN 12368:2006, Traffic Control Equipment-Signal Heads (2006). http://shop.bsigroup.com/ProductDetail/?pid=000000000030099722
8. British Standards Institution (BSI): BS EN 12368: 2015, Traffic Control Equipment-Signal Heads (2015). http://shop.bsigroup.com/ProductDetail/?pid=000000000030266574
9. Turkish Standards Institute (TSI): TS EN 12368: 2015, Traffic Control Equipment-Signal Heads (2015). http://intweb.tse.org.tr

10. Institute of Transportation Engineers (ITE): Equipment and Material Standards (1998). http://library.ite.org/pub/e26a6f93-2354-d714-51c9-7fc16b2c6082
11. IEnergy Sector Management Assistance Program (ESMAP): GOOD PRACTICES IN CITY ENERGY EFFICIENCY Portland, United States - LEDs for Traffic Signalss (2010). https://www.esmap.org/sites/esmap.org/files/CS_EECIPortland_final.pdf
12. Levin, M.: Leds: the economical lighting choice. Summit Canadas magazine on public sector purchasing (2005)
13. Ministry of Energy & Natural Resources:Improvement of energy efficiency in turkey. (http://www.eie.gov.tr/projeler/twinning_projesi.aspx)
14. TEDAS-TURKISH ELECTRIC DISTRIBUTION COMPANY: 2016 Ocak Tarifeleri (2016). http://www.tedas.gov.tr/#!tedas_tarifeler
15. UNITED NATIONS:The kyoto protocol (1998). http://unfccc.int/resource/docs/convkp/kpeng.pdf
16. Gocen, I.: Kara ulam aralarnn karbondioksit (co 2) emisyonlarna eko-verimlilik yaklam. https://anahtar.sanayi.gov.tr/tr/news/
17. Elbir, T., Mangir, N., Kara, M., Simsir, S., Eren, T., Ozdemir, S.: Development of a gis-based decision support system for urban air quality management in the city of istanbul. Atmospheric Environ. **44**, 441–454 (2010)
18. Buyukkinaci, B., Onaygil, S., Guler, O., Yurtseven, M.B.: Analysis of road lighting automation scenarios according to visibility performance. In: CIE Lighting Quality and Energy Efficiency Conference Proceedings (2016)

An ICT-Based Reference Model for E-grocery in Smart Cities

Roberto Tadei[1](✉), Edoardo Fadda[1], Luca Gobbato[1], Guido Perboli[1,2], and Mariangela Rosano[1]

[1] DAUIN, Politecnico di Torino, Turin, Italy
roberto.tadei@polito.it
[2] CIRRELT, Montreal, Canada

Abstract. *E-grocery is a new emerging and challenging business channel for the food and beverage market, enabling consumers to purchase grocery products online. It combines the issues of last mile distribution with those related to the perishability of foods, affecting the success and profitability of several e-grocery companies. The Local Food Supply Chain (LFSC) concerns the local production and delivery to food consumers, in a more economically and environmentally efficient way, but it remains a less explored business. The paper discusses whether a new LFSC model for e-grocery is useful and proposes an innovative solution based on ICT and mobile applications.*

Keywords: E-grocery · Last mile · Supply-chain · City logistics

1 Introduction

E-commerce is drastically changing the way business is managed. In particular, B2C e-commerce represents a new channel that completely replaces physical shops, enabling consumers to purchase products and services online. While e-commerce revolutionized the retail business of travel, clothes, and consumer electronics as the big online sellers, e-grocery is still at an early stage. This does not refer to a temporal dimension, in fact according to [1], the grocery industry is considered pioneer in home delivery service, but e-grocery has not been still able to find the model of success that ensures profitability to their businesses. This paper deals with the e-grocery distribution in urban areas and proposes a model specialized for the Local Food Supply Chain (LFSC) and the Smart Cities environment. The project, named Simulation and Optimisation of Urban Logistics (SOUL), develops in collaboration with Telecom Italia, a prototype for urban B2B freight distribution fleet routing management system in integration with business modeling and near field communications technology for LFSC. In details, SOUL has a twofold purpose. First, reduce with the use of ICT based solutions, the issues that affect the e-grocery (e.g., the inefficiency of the picking and delivery operations), determining the failure of the majority of pioneering e-grocery retails. Second, to deal the e-grocery with an innovative

E. Alba et al. (Eds.): Smart-CT 2016, LNCS 9704, pp. 22–31, 2016.
DOI: 10.1007/978-3-319-39595-1_3

point of view, paying the attention on fresh food and LFSC, which are less considered in literature, as we will discuss. The combined usage of a Decision Support System and mobile application let us provide a solution to increase the effectiveness and the efficiency of the e-grocery operations. The paper is organized as follows. Section 2 examines the literature, providing some references about the industry state-of-the-art and an overview of LFSC. The proposed model is introduced and discussed in Sect. 3. Finally, Sect. 4 reports some results.

2   Literature Review

The literature of e-grocery retailing can be split into two different main streams. The first one includes the analysis of the retailer's point of view focused on the efficiently design and management of the e-grocery supply chain, taking into account the relevant factors that determinate the successful of the business model. The second stream concerns the potential benefits in terms of externalities reduction and the impact of e-grocery on the more comprehensive urban freight distribution. For a more general discussion about the different aspects of Smart Cities application, the reader can refer to [2]. Regarding the retailer's point of view, some papers investigate on the definition of efficient operational models, by proposing an analysis of different models with a comparison of existing e-grocery companies ([3,4]). A great attention is paid for individuating the main reasons of the failures that occurred, which are classified in economical and perishability related factors. First, when designing the business and operational models, the key issues discussed in the literature are picking and delivery operations. A crucial point is in fact that the overall efficiency of these operations is essential for e-grocer retailers, due to lower gross margins that affect the e-grocery than in other markets. The reason are mainly economical, in fact for traditional bricks-and-mortar, retailers that enter the Internet market as multi-channel grocery retailers, order picking and home deliveries represent additional costs (see Fig. 1). In traditional supermarkets, the customer picks the desired products and bears the transportation costs from the store to home. By contrast, in online grocery the retailer incurs the picking and last mile logistic costs. Generally, these additional costs are higher than the fees customers are willing to pay for delivery, which is between euros 4 and euros 7 per transaction,

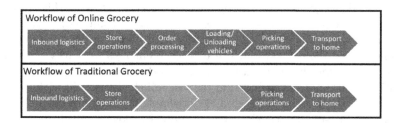

Fig. 1. Comparison of traditional and online grocery shopping activities.

depending on the market [5]. This means that only efficient picking and delivery processes would make the e-grocer business profitable as well as strike the right balance between cost and service [6]. Other issues, strictly related to the design of successful fulfillment and delivery options, affect the economical efficiency of the e-grocery supply chain, as the transportation costs related to the location of distribution centers, and the investment required (e.g., investment for highly automated centers). The second critical point for the failure of e-grocery solutions is the difficulty to guarantee the food temperature during the entire chain and the perishability of the food. In particular, according to the definition proposed by the International Air Transport Association, a shipment is perishable if its contents deteriorate over a given period if exposed to harsh environmental conditions, such as excessive temperature or humidity. This peculiarity increases the complexity related to the management of these parcels, about the need to guarantee their health, safety and economic value. The retailers must guarantee that frozen and perishable foods maintain their temperature all along the supply chain. While in attended home delivery service this can be easily achieved, in unattended delivery refrigerated containers are required. To solve this problem, different packaging solutions have been proposed. The reception box is a refrigerated and locked box installed in the customer's garage or yard. The delivery box is a secured box with a docking mechanism delivered to the customer and retired at the next delivery. Another type of complexity occurs when it is expected a transit to a distribution centre (DC). In fact, it is necessary particular attention for layout planning of DC, because the preservation of perishable goods required that there should be at least three different temperatures: room temperature, chilled and frozen [7]. The second literature stream is strictly related to the impact of e-grocery on the Last Mile distribution. It includes several studies ([8–10]), focused on the potential benefits, in terms of vehicles miles traveled and Green House Gas (GHG) emissions reductions, generated by the e-grocery home delivery compared to the case in which individuals use their own car for shopping trips. These papers estimate CO2 emissions reductions in the range between 18 % and 87 %, where the level depends on the home delivery model and the routing strategy used. Small reductions of GHG are observed when no scheduling rules are defined and customers to serve are selected randomly. On the contrary, larger reductions occur when the proximity assignment selection policy is used, i.e., the deliveries are first clustered in zones and then the trips associated to each zone are computed. [4] identify and analyzes the impacts of the last-mile delivery strategies adopted by e-grocery retailers. They show as Click & Collect service appears to be the most suitable, compared to HD service and hybrid HD and Click & Collect service, with almost a 9 % GHG emission reduction. From a holistic vision, the e-grocery emerges as a new challenging business channel for the food and beverage market. It combines the issues of distribution in urban areas included in the last mile logistics field with the problems arising in the manage of fresh and perishable foods. Moreover, it emerges a lack in the state-of-the-art of e-grocery applied to local food distribution. In particular, a framework of e-grocery LFSC combined with a business model has not been proposed yet. In fact, we can state that today e-grocery represents an additional channel for food distribution and it is used to create an online version of traditional grocery retailers (e.g., Walmart and Publix) who dominates the USA and European e-grocery-retailing. Moreover, consumer interest in local foods has increased sharply in recent years [11], also due to the policy programs promoted by the European Commission [12]. In this context a higher level of ICT could overcome the complexities that affect LFSC and help small local producers to be more competitive.

In the next section, we present a project named SOUL, which aims to response to this issue, with the integration of ICT and mobile application.

3   The E-grocery Distribution Model

As stated in Sect. 2, there is a lack of ICT application to the e-grocery LFSC. Therefore, the short food business would do well to improve the physical distribution process and re-engineer the logistics process by connecting the supply chain with ICT and real-time information. The ICT of the supply chain offers two main advantages: to provide final consumers with a valuable alternative to grocery stores and to support actors involved in the LFSC with an efficient distribution system. ICT helps to achieve these goals by solving problems related to the cost and the effectiveness of logistics operations, the management of B2B and B2C segments, the packaging of fresh products and the occurrence of unexpected events during the distribution (e.g., road congestion). In this context, ICT and Decision Support Systems (DSSs) have the potential to optimize the use of road capacity, save manpower, reduce the number of traffic accidents, and decrease the level of pollution [13], enhancing the quality and efficiency of the service. The proposed DSS for e-grocery is developed in the SOUL project field. SOUL is an attempt to consider multiple retailers that share the distribution of fresh food in urban areas. The DSS is embedded in a mobile application that allows retailers and consumers of fresh food to monitor the flow along the entire supply chain (e.g., order placement, inventory control, freight tracking, dispatching, delivering) and enables the exchange of real-time shipping and traffic-related information for the optimization of logistics operations and traffic congestion mitigation. We use in our DSS a vehicle-to-infrastructure (V2I) system, in which vehicles transmit their own data to a central server. The server aggregates data from external sources, including real-time data. Thus, it moves the computing power away from the vehicle and provides real-time information for third party applications, such as the fastest paths for vehicles and the detection of congestion in the urban area. This means that SOUL is able to retain information about users of the reference market, to elaborate traffic data from public and non-public sources, and to provide an intelligent core capable of processing and distributing this information for a better use of the transportation system. Moreover, SOUL ensures the exchange of information on the mobile network and the coordination of activities in a flexible and scalable manner. Figure 2 illustrates the main blocks of the SOUL architecture, responsible for the execution of the process described. More attention is paid to the analysis of the two key elements: Traffic Handler Service and Central Unit. On the contrary all blocks are briefly described in this section:

- Central Unit (CU): it is the operative core block that provides two main functions, traffic management and real-time control of fleets of vehicles.
- Traffic Handler Service (THS): it is a key block that aggregates traffic information in order to detect the congestion of urban streets and communicate the traffic events to the CU, which deals with them by updating in real time the routes of the vehicles.
- Data Broker Layer (DBL): it manages and facilitates the access to information through standard implementations and access policies. Using integration rules, it also supports the aggregation of data sources, preserving the meaning and the context of information. Finally, it guarantees data integrity and concurrent updating from different sources.
- Hosted Services: they provide a hosting system for applications and tools, and an interface to support interactions between services and users. For example, the Supply Chain Management Unit receives orders from users and sends them to the associated suppliers, manages information and tools for delivery planning and execution, allows electronic monetary transactions, updates inventory levels, and collects statistics about orders, deliveries and stocks to support distribution activities. Specific XML formats are defined to enable the exchange of information.
- Third Party Services: they do not need a hosting system and, on the one hand, can benefit from data aggregation and forecasting and, on the other hand, provide functions to services hosted in the architecture (e.g., cartography).
- Enabling Technologies: internal and external enabling technologies enhance the decision making process of ITS (e.g., map providers, localization system). In particular, high-speed local and/or geographic networks (e.g., LAN, internet) that enable the exchange of information between the various software and hardware modules.
- External sources: traffic data are available not only from the vehicles, but also from private or public networks of sensors (e.g., institutional and non-institutional portals). For the city of Turin, an important source is constituted by a broad traffic sensor network carried out by the Traffic Operation Centre 5 T and its public portal [14], which provide data about the road network in real time.
- Mobile devices: they access the services hosted in the SOUL architecture. Moreover, the smartphones of logistic providers represent possible sensors of traffic data as they are directly in contact with the situation in real time.

3.1   Central Unit

It is an intelligent real-time vehicle routing system able to build optimised routes for the distribution of fresh and perishable food, by taking into account changing traffic conditions ([15,16]). The goal of SOUL optimisation tools is to make the e-grocer business profitable reducing the costs and the criticisms of the home

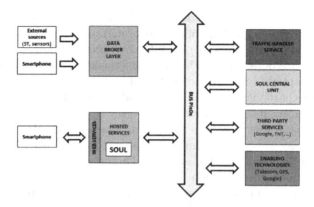

Fig. 2. Main blocks of the SOUL architecture.

delivery services, through its components: a routing optimiser and a post-optimiser. The first is based on a Tabu Search heuristic able to address the Vehicle Routing Problem with Time Windows (VRPTW) [17]. It computes the cheapest routes for a heterogeneous fleet of vehicles from a single depot to a set of geographically scattered points and considers the time windows within which the deliveries must be made and the capacity of vehicles. SOUL also provides solutions for the consolidation of foods from different retailers in distribution centres [18]. The outcomes of the routing optimiser are then stored in the DBL and retrieved by the application when the vehicles are ready. The post-optimiser manages a Dynamic Vehicle Routing Problem (DVRP) in which the source of dynamics is the online arrival of customer requests for goods during the operations. Once the SOUL CU has optimised the VRPTW, logistic operators or the retailer with equipped vehicles can use the navigator provided by the application. The navigator, based on Google Maps and navigation API defined in Android, uses the GPS navigation device to acquire position data and to locate the user on a road. The driver selects the vehicle from the application, which downloads the optimal route and draws it on the map. Upon selection of the vehicle, an association is made between the vehicle and the International Mobile Equipment Identity code of the on board mobile device guaranteeing the identification of the vehicle in the system for the entire duration of the deliveries. Moreover, dynamic and real-time navigation data are sent to the Traffic Handler Service, in order to aggregate them and to provide new estimates of the urban congestion by means of a crowd sensing aggregation module.

3.2   Traffic Handler Service

The Traffic Handler Service (THS) has two important functions. First, THS collects data from external sources and aggregates data to provide real-time traffic information. In particular, the sensory system of the traffic center (5T in the case study of Turin [19]) periodically monitors the rate of flow (cars/hour) and speed (km/hour) on the main roads and makes them available online. Then, THS retrieves the data from the public portal, collects them and performs statistical analyses (e.g., minimum, maximum, average), useful to report congestion on routing paths. We develop a simple detection tool based on the theory of traffic flow on freeways ([20,21]) and adapted to the characteristics of roads in cities. Periodically, THS checks conditions of roads under monitoring and, in case of congestion, communicates a new traffic event to the notification. On the contrary, when the congestion ends, THS eliminates the event from the system. The insertion of traffic events can be made in two other ways: (1) an administration screen allows placing traffic events directly from the map and (2) vehicles involved in congestion can report their position through the mobile application. The second function provided by the THS is the computation of the matrix of costs for the routing model corresponding to the distances and travel times between depots of logistic providers and destinations of delivery. Also, it computes alternative routes only for the vehicles affected by the congestion events.

3.3 Mobile Application

To represent the information to the user, SOUL uses a mobile application designed on the Android, written in Java, and uses db4o databases to store persistent data. It allows users to monitor the flow along the entire supply chain and enables different operations (e.g., order placement, inventory control, freight tracking, and receiving management). The mobile application connects users (consumers, supplier, retailers, and logistics providers) to the technology infrastructure of the DSS, allowing them access to services of the proposed architecture. [22] evaluated the DSS by a framework based on the System Dynamics methodology, which assesses the potential of and facilitates policies for benefits of SOUL. The outcomes of the evaluation model underline the importance of the adoption of the additional services (e.g., product tracing systems, electronic payment systems, time sensitive deliveries) in e-grocery. The advantages originating from the use of ICT in the e-grocery supply chain, in our opinion, should stimulate the use of SOUL-like systems, especially by retailers and consumers, and the diffusion of e-grocery services.

3.4 Perishable Goods

As discussed in Sect. 2, perishability of goods represents a crucial aspect related to the e-grocery LFSC and one of the levers of the SOUL project. In particular, for these goods SOUL tracks the position and monitors the temperature during the entire delivery from the depot to the final destination. This information is collected through mobile and remote sensors of the vehicles. This ensures the conditions and the reliability of perishable good, as well as signaling when environmental conditions are not satisfied.

4   Results

The analysis of SOUL was conducted by a simulation-optimization approach. In more details, we built realistic scenarios validating them in a focus group with practitioners and fresh food companies of the Turin area. Then, we used those data gathered during the URBan Electronic LOGistics (URBeLOG) Project field [23], to carry out a simulation where the optimization of the service was done by means of SOUL. In particular, we have considered two different scenarios. The first involves small-sized food companies, which are less capable to manage deliveries with an own fleet of vehicles, in an efficient way. On the contrary, the second involves medium-large sized retailers having a more consistent demand and vehicles with a capacity of about 50 % greater than the previous. The alternative in which each retailers performs the deliveries is compared with those where the consolidation of foods from different firms in distribution centres occurs. We performed our experiment campaign using data gathered from a database of 16000 customers, considering networks ranging from 3 to 45 customers. The results obtained throught the simulation are summarized in the Table 1, where are presented the amount of deliveries composing the demand for retailers, the percentages of improvement in terms of distances traveled, number of vehicles used, service times and cost savings, that the consolidation generates.

Table 1. Simulation results.

	Deliveries	Improvement [%]			
		Δ N. Vehicles	Δ Distance	Δ Time	Δ Cost
Scenario 1	30	- 50 %	- 47 %	- 40 %	- 47 %
	50	- 50 %	- 45 %	- 35 %	- 45 %
	100	- 25 %	- 32 %	- 23 %	- 32 %
	150	- 25 %	- 25 %	- 17 %	- 25 %
	200	- 25 %	- 28 %	- 19 %	- 28 %
	250	- 42 %	- 39 %	- 26 %	- 39 %
Scenario 2	300	- 33 %	- 30 %	- 19 %	- 30 %
	350	- 38 %	- 33 %	- 22 %	- 33 %
	400	- 31 %	- 28 %	- 28 %	- 28 %
	450	- 40 %	- 32 %	- 21 %	- 32 %

The results highlight that the consolidation of food operated by the logistics providers allow to obtain operative and economical efficiency, in both the scenarios, but mainly for the small-sized retailers. As showed by the cost savings reported in Table 1, an important benefit is the costs reduction, due to the outsourcing of the fleet management and the relative economical efforts. In general, the retailers obtain a better service time, essential in a time-sensitive context as transportation. For example, in the first scenario, considering a small network, the service time improves of about 40 %, due to the greater capacity of the logistics provider vehicles combined to the optimization of the routes. However, considering an equal capacity both for retailers and logistics provider, these benefits are confirmed, though to a lesser extent. In fact, serving a demand of 200 deliveries, the service time and the costs range from respectively the 19 % and the 28 % with different capacities, to the 5 % and the 7 % if the vehicles are identical. Notice that the adoption of logistics providers in the LFSC reduces the number of vehicles on the road, up to the 50 % as illustrated by the results, with a consequent positive impact on the environment. Finally, according to our results, the dynamics of user growth does not appear to be sensitive to the variation of the service fees, even when all the LFSC players are set to be extremely sensitive to pricing.

5 Conclusion

The simulation conducted in this paper underlines that e-grocery literature is affected by some lacks dealing with different aspects (e.g., the organisation of warehouses for multi-channel grocery retailers, the composition of vehicles and the support of decision maker). The SOUL project overcomes these gaps, introducing an ICT solution and integrating the e-grocery Supply Chain with a reference business model, to achieve the efficiency required in the urban context. However, the integration and the synchronization of the entire chain are also required to guarantee cost-effective robust solutions, which optimize logistics operations. The synchronization of handling operations and the fleet of vehicles has a key role in the SFSC, where the perishability of the products requires speedy and accurate operations. These new issues are presently tackled in a new project funded by the Horizon2020 programme called Synchro-modal Supply Chain Eco-Net [24].

Acknowledgments. Partial funding of this project was provided by Telecom Italia under the project SOUL. We also gratefully acknowledge the support of the Fonds de recherche du Quebec through their infrastructure grants.

References

1. Beatriz, G., Fernando, G.: Logistic model for the distribution of goods in the e-grocery industry: a new adaptation of the vehicle routing problem. In: HMS 2011 (2011)
2. Perboli, G., De Marco, A., Perfetti, F., Marone, M.: A new taxonomy of smart city projects. Transp. Res. Procedia **3**, 470–479 (2014)
3. Holmström, J., Tanskanen, K., Kämäräinen, V.: Redesigning the supply chain for internet shopping - bringing ECR to the households. In: 4th Logistics Research Network Conference Newcastle, pp. 261–267 (1999)

4. Bruno, D., Gonzalez-Feliu, J.: French e-grocery models: a comparison of deliveries performances. In: Colloquium on European Retail Research-CERR 2012 Book of Abstracts, pp. 230–253 (2012). mckinsey.com
5. Galante, N., López, E.G., Monroe, S.: The future of online grocery in europe. Perspect. Retail Consum. Goods **1**, 22–31 (2013). Spring 2013, mckinsey.com
6. Boyer, K., Hult, G., Frohlich, M.: An exploratory analysis of extended grocery supply chain operations and home delivery. Integr. Manuf. Syst. **14**(8), 652–663 (2003)
7. Kämäräinen, V., Smaros, J., Holmström, J., Jaakola, T.: Cost-effectiveness in the e-grocery business. Int. J. Retail Distrib. Manag. **29**(1), 41–48 (2001)
8. Cairns, S.: Promises and problems: using GIS to analyse shopping travel. J. Transp. Geogr. **6**(4), 273–284 (1998)
9. Siikavirta, H., Punakivi, M., Kärkkäinen, M.: Effects of e-commerce on greenhouse gas emission: a case study of grocery home delivery in Finland. J. Ind. Ecol. **6**(2), 83–97 (2003)
10. Wygonik, E., Goodchild, A.: Evaluating the efficacy of shared-use vehicles for reducing greenhouse gas emissions: a US case study of grocery delivery. J. Transp. Res. Forum **51**(2), 111–126 (2012)
11. Neff, R.A., Palmer, A.M., McKenzie, S.E., Lawrence, R.S.: Food systems and public health disparities. J. Hunger Environ. Nutr. **4**(3), 282–314 (2009)
12. Agriculture, rural development: Promotion of EU farm products. http://ec.europa.eu/agriculture/promotion/index_en.htm. Accessed on 29 Feb 2016
13. He, J., Zeng, Z., Li, Z.: Benefit evaluation framework of intelligent transportation systems. J. Transp. Syst. Eng. Inf. Technol. **10**(1), 81–87 (2010)
14. 5T SRL: Opendata. http://opendata.5t.torino.it. Accessed on 29 Feb 2016
15. Deflorio, F., Gonzales-Feliu, J., Perboli, G., Tadei, R.: The influence of time windows on the costs of urban freight distribution services in city logistics applications. Eur. J. Transp. Infrastruct. Res. **12**(3), 256–274 (2012)
16. Perboli, G., Pezzella, F., Tadei, R.: EVE-OPT: a hybrid algorithm for the capability vehicle routing problem. Math. Methods Oper. Res. **68**(2), 361–382 (2008)
17. Nguyen, P., Crainic, T., Toulouse, M.: A tabu search for time-dependent multi-zone multi-trip vehicle routing problem with time windows. Eur. J. Oper. Res. **231**(1), 43–56 (2013)
18. McKinnon, P., Cullinane, S., Whiteing, A., Browne, P.: Green Logistics: Improving the Environmental Sustainability of Logistics. Kogan Page, London (2010)
19. 5T SRL: Corporate web site. http://www.5t.torino.it/5t/en/. Accessed on 29 Feb 2016
20. Wardrop, J.: Some theoretical aspects of road traffic research. In: ICE Proceedings on Engineering Divisions, Vol. 1, pp. 325–362 (1952)
21. Pipes, L.A.: An operational analysis of traffic dynamics. J. Appl. Phys. **24**(3), 274–281 (1953)
22. Cagliano, A.C., Gobbato, L., Tadei, R., Perboli, G.: Its for e-grocery business: the simulation and optimization of urban logistics project. Transp. Res. Procedia **3**, 489–498 (2014)
23. URBeLOG: Project web site. http://www.urbelog.it/. Accessed on 04 Apr 2016
24. Sychro-Net: Project web site. http://www.synchronet.eu/. Accessed on 29 Feb 2016

Behavioral Factors in City Logistics from an Operations Research Perspective

Aljoscha Gruler[(✉)], Jesica de Armas, and Angel A. Juan

Department of Computer Science - IN3, Open University of Catalonia,
Av. Carl Friedrich Gauss 5, 08860 Castelldefels, Spain
{agruler,jde_armasa,ajuanp}@uoc.edu

Abstract. In the face of sharp urbanization around the world, metropolitan areas have started different initiatives and projects to make cities more efficient and sustainable. Hereby logistics and transportation activities have a major impact in the development of so called 'Smart Cities'. By addressing complex decision making problems through simulation and optimization, the Operations Research community has contributed to the development of sustainable city logistic systems. While technical and structural problems have been extensively discussed in the literature, many models neglect the importance of behavioral issues arising from risk aversion, stakeholder interaction and human factors that play an important role in the consolidation and optimization of logistical activities. This paper reviews existing work considering behavioral factors from an OR perspective. Simulation and optimization models to major problem settings in City Logistics are discussed and methodologies to conquer real-life urban L&T challenges are presented.

Keywords: Smart Cities · City Logistics · Operations Research · Behavioral research · Simulation-optimization

1   Introduction

Cities are the driving forces of economies around the world with 85 % of the Gross Domestic Product (GDP) of the European Union (EU) already produced in urban areas [25]. The importance of metropolitan areas is fostered by the fact that the world's urban population is expected to double from 2.6 billion in 2010 to 5.2 billion people until 2050 [20]. This urbanization trend has both positive and negative effects on a global level. On the one hand it leads to wealth, jobs, and an increase in cultural activities. On the other hand, increasing city populations augment carbon dioxide and greenhouse gas emissions, traffic jams and waste development [13,15].

Especially activities related to logistics and transportation (L&T) of urban freight has a major impact on urban society, environment, and economy [29,42]. In Europe alone traffic jams yield yearly costs of 100 Billion US\$, equal to 1 % of the EU's GDP [26]. Furthermore, transportation vehicles lead to excessive

© Springer International Publishing Switzerland 2016
E. Alba et al. (Eds.): Smart-CT 2016, LNCS 9704, pp. 32–41, 2016.
DOI: 10.1007/978-3-319-39595-1_4

noise levels in urban areas affecting as much as 41 million Europeans [26], while the sector accounts for 27 % in total greenhouse gas emissions in the USA [56]. In the development of sustainable urban areas (often addressed in 'Smart City' innovations and projects, see [6,27]), the planning of a sustainable and effective logistical environment is therefore of major importance.

In an approach to reduce the impact of urban freight transportation, the concept of *City Logistics* (CL) has emerged as new area of L&T planning [42]. Through the coordination and consolidation of logistic activities of different stakeholders, the aim is to develop integrated and sustainable urban logistics systems by reducing freight vehicles numbers, control their dimensions and characteristics, and optimize vehicle usage by reducing empty vehicle mileage [8]. Hereby Operations Research (OR) plays an important role by developing models to optimize and evaluate complex problem settings, e.g. the location of freight consolidation centers, routing of electric vehicles with limited driving ranges [33], or the scheduling of driver workplans.

Different simulation and optimization techniques to solve various real-life problem settings concerning technological-, process- and structural challenges have been presented by the OR community. However, behavioral issues such as lack of trust, natural risk aversion, or decision biases of people and companies typically lead to some kind of uncertainty in OR models, which has not yet been discussed to the same extend [10,28]. Within the OR community the people dimension in L&T is mainly addressed in the field of simulation to evaluate the behavior of different stakeholders (usually shippers, freight carriers, administrators and consumers) concerning different urban L&T measures [53]. In optimization issues of arising in the development of CL systems however, behavioral factors of individual decisions and stakeholder interaction has received less formal attention [5].

This paper contributes to this research line by reviewing how behavioral aspects of different CL stakeholders in main urban L&T problem settings such as the location of freight consolidation centers, development of routing plans, or workforce scheduling is addressed in existing operational research. The structure is hereby as follows: Sect. 2 highlights main concepts of CL and stresses the importance of considering human behavior to develop realistic and sustainable L&T systems; Sect. 3 reviews OR approaches addressing human factors in CL; Sect. 4 discusses possible future research work and concludes this paper.

2 Considering Behavioral Issues in City Logistics Concepts

2.1 City Logistics Concepts and Related Optimization Problems

CL is defined by Taniguchi et al. [51] as "totally optimizing urban logistics activities by considering the social, economic, and environmental impact of urban freight movement while providing an opportunity for the development of innovative solutions that allow to improve the quality of life in urban areas."

Crainic et al. [18] focus more on the optimization and utilization of transportation resources, by defining CL as "reducing and controlling the number, dimensions, and characteristics of freight vehicles operating within city limits, improving the efficiency of freight movements, and reducing the number of empty vehicle kilometers". The main goal is to make urban freight L&T more efficient while reducing the negative environmental impacts by viewing CL as integrated system instead of focusing on individual stakeholders. This process requires planning at a strategical, tactical, and operational level, in which behavior of macro- and micro stakeholders play a decisive role [5,8].

On a strategic level, especially the development of multi-tier transportation systems has been discussed [39]. The aim is to keep delivery-trucks away from city centers by consolidating logistics activities of different companies in so called Urban Consolidation Centers (UCCs). Instead of delivering products to the final customer, companies transport their freight to consolidation hubs which are usually located in direct proximity to the geographic areas of interest (e.g. the city center or a shopping mall). From the UCC, consolidated deliveries and other logistics services such as storing or packaging are then carried out [5,21].

Through tactical planning, efficient transportation plans concerning resource utilization and demand satisfaction are established. This leads to several OR problems, for example the well-known Vehicle Routing Problem (VRP) and its variants considering time windows, different load levels, and uncertainty. Also, the use of Electric Vehicles (EVs) in freight transportation brings new challenges to the OR community [12,33,34,36].

Operationally, human factors such as fatigue, education, or learning abilities have to be considered in the development of employee work schedules. Also the operational control and adjustment of transportation plans through the use of ICT, e.g. GPS to dynamically adjust routing plans and vehicle schedules, has been discussed in the literature [18].

2.2 The Importance of Behavioral Issues in City Logistics

The editorial for a special issue on behavioral operations of the Journal of Operations Management [19] defines behavioral operations "the study of potentially non-hyper-rational actors in operational contexts". Behavior of stakeholders is often ignored in mathematical modeling of complex decision problems. Indeed, most work in OR research considers them to be (i) a minor factor of the system, (ii) deterministic, (iii) independent, (iv) non-developing, (v) emotionless, and (vi) observable [10,47,55]. This is a drawback in the development of realistic problem-solving support tools, as they often proof to be difficult to implement in practice as they ignore important system characteristics related to behavioral influences [7].

In the context of CL, behavior plays an important role as the integration and cooperation among different stakeholders (public and private) and system planning does not only depend on technical and physical components, but also human and behavioral factors. Current research in supply chain management mostly neglects this fact and forgets about the "crucial importance of the behavioral and people dimension [48]", arising from risk-aversion of decision takers or the lack of trust and incentive misalignment between companies and their managers [7].

Urban freight transportation is the product of the interaction between different stakeholders, mainly from the commodity, transport and infrastructure sector. Even though most situations in L&T systems can be described and solved mathematically, the complete environment needs to be understood for the development of realistic and suitable optimization models. In CL the integration of logistical activities comes down to relationships between individuals, teams, and companies which in essence consist of people [2,49].

3   OR Problems Considering Behavioral Issues in City Logistics: A Review

OR models describing CL concepts can be generally categorized into: *simulation models* and *optimization models*. In the field of simulation, behavior of different stakeholders to different CL measures such as municipal subsidies of UCCs, road-pricing, or time windows in city centers has been addressed. Concerning optimization, different real-life algorithms to consider various combinatorial optimization problems (COPs) have been presented. These approaches (with special focus on publications considering human factors and stakcholder interactions) are reviewed in Sects. 3.1 and 3.2 respectively. Recently, some interesting methodologies combining simulation into optimization (mainly metaheuristic) based frameworks have been presented. As these techniques (e.g. simheuristics)

Table 1. Summary of reviewed papers

OR-Technique	Reviewed Papers	Behavioral Issues addressed
Simulation	[23]	Stakeholder interactions in UCCs
	[57]	Stakeholder interactions in joint delivery systems and car-park management
	[54]	Stakeholder behavior in e-commerce delivery
	[50,52]	Evaluation of CL measures from the point of view of different stakeholders
	[11,37]	Stakeholder behavior concerning local traffic regulations in multi-modal transportation
Optimization	[17,24,40,44,45]	VRPs with different constraints (e.g. time windows, load factors)
	[39,41]	Multi-criteria, multi-echelon LRPs
Sim-Opt	[30]	LRP with stochastic demands and travel times
	[32]	Different Safety-Stocks in the VRP with stochastic demands
	[31]	Scheduling problem with stochastic times

could be a promising tool to integrate behavioral issues such as different risk-attitudes of route dispatchers, they are outlined in Sect. 3.3. An overview over the discussed papers their relation to behavioral issues is given in Table 1.

3.1   Simulation Models

Simulation is often used to evaluate complex CL systems and predict the effects of measures such as the implementation of UCCs, road pricing, truck bans in city centers, time windows, load factor controls, or operational subsidies. Hereby, especially Agent-Based Modeling and Simulation (ABMS) allows the consideration of the behavior of different actors [38].

Stakeholder behavior in the opening of a UCC concerning different urban congestion levels, minimum vehicle loads, and time windows in city centers is discussed by Duin et al. [23]. Wangapisit et al. [57] use ABMS to fine tune the implementation of UCCs in congested cities considering stakeholder interaction and cooperation in joint delivery systems and car parking management. Teo et al. [54] evaluate CL measures in urban road networks in a e-commerce delivery system environment. Similar ABMS models to evaluate CL systems are presented by Tangawa et al. [50] and Tanguchi et al. [52]. The use of multi-modal transportation systems incorporating the use of EVs in consolidated logistics systems is modeled as result of interaction between different stakeholders and their reactions to local traffic regulations using ABMS by Boussier et al. [11]. Lebeau et al. [37] test the impact of using electric vehicles in UCCs using discrete event simulation.

While many simulation-based models have been applied to evaluate the behavior of stakeholders in the context of CL, the consideration of humans and companies as non-rational factors has not been done to the same extend. Badin et al. [4] use a representative EV simulator to test the impact of driver aggressiveness in the energy consumption of EVs by considering ordinary, economic, and aggressive drivers.

3.2   Optimization Models

Different complex COPs for optimizing CL processes with real-life constraints have been addressed by with OR solution methodologies, generally divided into exact- and approximate methods. While exact methods (e.g. Branch-and-Bound) are usually applied to smaller instances, approximate metaheuristics (e.g. GRASP, Tabu Search, Simulated Annealing, etc.) are able to solve large problem settings in short calculation times.

An overview over VRPs in the context of CL is given in Cattaruzza et al. [14]. Main VRP variants are hereby the VRP with access time windows in city centers, multi-modal heterogeneous vehicle fleets, routing problems with restricted zones for certain vehicle types, the 2-Echelon VRP or dynamic re-routing of vehicles according to real-time travel information [17,24,40,44].

Very current in the optimal integration of UCCs in CL systems is also the complex location-routing problem and its variants, in which facility locations and connected routing activities are planned together [22]. In this context, an exact

Branch &Cut algorithm to solve small and medium sized instances exactly of the capacitated 2-Echelon Loading Routing Problem (2E-LRP) is proposed by [16]. Metaheuristics such as Variable Neighborhood search (VNS), GRASP, and Iterated Local Search (ILS) to address different 2E-LRPs are presented by Nguyen et al. [41] and Schwengerer et al. [46].

Behavioral issues regarding problem owners have not been considered in much detail, and the interaction of stakeholders is also not considered in the works cited above. Awasthi et al. [3] employ a fuzzy model in the location planning of UCCs, in which different evaluation criteria such as accessibility, security, connectivity to multi-modal transport, costs, environmental impact, resource availability and the possibility for expansion are considered. Othman et al. [43] incorporate human factors into a workforce scheduling case, including aspects such as skills, training, workers personalities, breaks, fatigues, and recovery levels. Even though their problem setting is related to workforce scheduling in the context of production scheduling, their multi-objective mixed programming model could also be applied to workplan scheduling problems of drivers and UCC operative personal.

Other human factors such as the route-choice behavior of drivers are not yet considered in optimization approaches. They are more addressed in the field of behavioral research, done for example by Albert et al. [1], who use advanced traveler information systems to test the differences concerning geographic ability and sensation seeking of drivers experimentally. However, some promising research work considering uncertainty through human behavior and risk-aversion of decision-takers have been presented recently by combining simulation in optimization based frameworks, which is surveyed in the following sub-section.

3.3 Combining Simulation with Metaheuristics to Model Behavioral Issues

One of the main issues when modeling behavioral issues in the problem settings discussed above is the inclusion of uncertainty arising through stakeholder interactions and human factors. Simulation seems to be the method of choice in artificially reproducing complex systems to evaluate certain measures. But simulation itself is not an optimization tool. In this context, the combination of simulation with optimization is becoming very popular and seems a promising methodology to model different behavioral aspects in OR [9].

Juan et al. [35] discuss the concept of simheuristics to consider uncertainty in COPs. By implementing simulation techniques in metaheuristic optimization approaches, established COP plans (e.g. vehicle routing solutions) can be assessed by showing their behavior in stochastic scenarios. In this context, for example the VRP with stochastic demands has been discussed [32]. After finding promising VRP solutions with a metaheuristic, the authors evaluate the effect of different safety capacity factors (representing route planners willingness to take risks) by using Monte Carlo simulation. Herazo-Padilla et al. [30] apply a similar approach by combining Ant Colony Optimization with discrete-event simulation to consider stochastic demands and stochastic travel times (occurring for example through different driver behavior) in the LRP. Not directly related to CL problem settings, Juan et al. [31] discuss a simheuristic approach to the permutation flow shop problem with stochastic time, a well-known COP in which stochastic job termination times can be related to difference employee working speeds. A similar approach could be implemented in the context of CL.

4   Future Research Work and Conclusions

This paper has identified typical OR problems in the context of the development of City Logistics concepts and related behavioral issues. Especially simulation (through agent-based models) has contributed to research concerning the evaluation of stakeholder behavior and the interaction of different public and private actors concerning different urban L&T measures. In the context of optimization to establish efficient location-, routing-, and scheduling plans behavioral factors of individuals and their interactions are only scarcely considered. The reason for this seems to be the difficulty in including uncertainty (as one of the outcomes when considering behavior) in traditional optimization models. The combination of simulation and optimization seems to overcome this drawback, and has recently been successfully applied to logistical problem settings. As such, this could be a promising future research line to overcome existing drawbacks in modeling behavioral issues in OR.

Acknowledgments. This work has been partially supported by the Spanish Ministry of Economy and Competitiveness (TRA2013-48180-C3-P and TRA2015-71883-REDT), and FEDER. Likewise, we want to acknowledge the support received by the Department of Universities, Research & Information Society of the Catalan Government (2014-CTP-00001) and the doctoral grant of the UOC.

References

1. Albert, G., Toledo, T., Ben-Zion, U.: The role of personality factors in repeated route choice behavior: Behavioral economics perspective. Europ. Transp. **48**(48), 47–59 (2011)
2. Anand, N., Quak, H., van Duin, R., Tavasszy, L.: City logistics modeling efforts: Trends and gaps - a review. Procedia Soc. Behav. Sci. **39**, 101–115 (2012)
3. Awasthi, A., Chauhan, S.S., Goyal, S.K.: A multi-criteria decision making approach for location planning for urban distribution centers under uncertainty. Math. Comput. Model. **53**(1–2), 98–109 (2011)
4. Badin, F., Le Berr, F., Briki, H., Dabadie, J.-C., Petit, M., Magand, S., Condemine, E.: Evaluation of evs energy consumption influencing factors, driving conditions, auxiliaries use, driver's aggressiveness. In: World Electric Vehicle Symposium and Exhibition (EVS27), pp. 1–12 (2013)
5. Bektas, T., Crainic, T.G., Woensel, T.V.: From managing urban freight to smart city logistics networks, August 2015

6. Ben Letaifa, S.: Letaifa: How to strategize smart cities: Revealing the smart model. J. Bus. Res. **68**(7), 1414–1419 (2015)
7. Bendoly, E., Donohue, K., Schultz, K.: Behavior in operations management: assessing recent findings and revisiting old assumptions. J. Oper. Manage. **24**(6), 737–752 (2006)
8. Benjelloun, A., Crainic, T.: Trends, challenges, and perspectives in city logistics. In: Proceedings of the Transportation and Land Use Interaction Conference, no. 4, pp. 269–284 (2009)
9. Bianchi, L., Dorigo, M., Gambardella, L., Gutjahr, W.: A survey on metaheuristics for stochastic combinatorial optimization. Nat. Comput. **8**, 239–287 (2009)
10. Bourdreau, J.W., Hopp, W., McClain, J., Thomas, L.J.: On the interface between operations and human resources management. Manuf. Serv. Oper. Manage. **5**(2), 179–202 (2003)
11. Boussier, J., Cucu, T., Ion, L., Estrailler, P., Breuil, D.: Goods distribution with electric vans in cities: towards and agent-based simulation. World Electric Veh. J. **3**, 1–9 (2009)
12. Caceres-Cruz, J., Arias, P., Guimarans, D., Riera, D., Juan, A.A.: Rich vehicle routing problem. ACM Comput. Surv. **47**(2), 1–28 (2014)
13. Caragliu, A., Del Bo, C., Nijkamp, P.: Smart cities in Europe. J. Urban Technol. **18**(2), 65–82 (2011)
14. Cattaruzza, D., Absi, N., Feillet, D., González-Feliu, J.: Vehicle routing problems for city logistics. EURO J. Transp. Logistics **1**, 1–29 (2015)
15. Cocchia, A.: Smart and digital city: A systematic literature review.In: Dameri, R.P., Rosenthal-Sabroux, C. (eds.) Smart City - How to Create Public and Economic Value with High Technology in Urban Space, pp. 13–43. Springer International Publishing, Switzerland (2014)
16. Contardo, C., Crainic, T., Hemmelmayr, V.: Lower and upper bounds for the two-echelon capacitated location routing problem. Comput. Oper. Res. **39**, 3215–3228 (2012)
17. Crainic, T., Perboli, G., Mancini, S., Tadei, R.: Two-echelon vehicle routing problem: a satellite location analysis. Procedia Soc. Behav. Sci. **2**(3), 5944–5955 (2010)
18. Crainic, T., Ricciardi, N., Storchi, G.: Models for evaluating and planning city logistics systems. Transp. Sci. **43**(4), 432–454 (2009)
19. Croson, R., Schultz, K., Siemsen, E., Yeo, M.L.: Behavioral operations: The state of the field. J. Oper. Manage. **31**(1–2), 1–5 (2013)
20. Crossette, B., Kollodge, R., Puchalik, R., Chalijub, M.: The state of world population 2011, United Nations Population Fund, pp. 1–132 (2011)
21. Danielis, R., Rotataris, L., Marcucci, E.: Urban freight policies and distribution channels: a discussion based on evidence from italian cities. European Transport/Trasporti Europei **46**, 114–146 (2010)
22. Drexl, M., Schneider, M.: A survey of variants and extensions of the location-routing problem. Eur. J. Oper. Res. **241**(2), 283–308 (2015)
23. Duin, R., van Kolck, A., Anand, N., Tavasszy, L., Taniguchi, E.: Towards an agent-based modelling approach for the evaluation of dynamic usage of urban distribution centres. In: Proceedings of the Seventh International Conference on City Logistics (2011)
24. Ehmke, J., Meisel, S., Mattfeld, D.: Floating car based travel times for city logistics. Transp. Res. Part C Emerg. Technol. **21**(1), 338–352 (2012)
25. European Commission, Cities of tomorrow - Challanges, visions, ways forward. Publications Office of the European Union (2011)

26. Agency, E.E.: Eea draws the first map of europe's noise exposure (2009). http://www.eea.europa.eu/media/newsreleases/eea-draws-the-first-map-of-europe2019s-noise-exposure
27. Giffinger, R., Fertner, C., Kramar, H., Kalasek, R., Pilcher-Milanovic, N., Meijers, E.: Smart cities - ranking of european medium sized cities (2007). http://www.smart-cities.eu/download/smart_cities_final_report.pdf
28. Hämläinen, R.P., Luoma, J., Saarinen, E.: On the importance of behavioral operational research: The case of understanding and communicating about dynamic systems. Eur. J. Oper. Res. **228**(3), 623–634 (2013)
29. He, H., Cheng, H.: Analyzing key influence factors of city logistics development using the fuzzy decision making trial and evaluation laboratory (dematel) method. Afr. J. Bus. Manage. **6**(45), 281–293 (2012)
30. Herazo-Padilla, N., Montoya-Torres, J., Isaza, S., Alvarado, J.: Simulation-optimization approach for the stochastic location-routing problem. J. Simul. **9**(4), 296–311 (2015)
31. Juan, A.A., Barrios, B., Vallada, E., Riera, D., Jorba, J.: Sim-esp: A simheuristic algorithm for solving the permutation flow-shop problem with stochastic processing times. Simul. Model. Pract. Theory **46**, 101–117 (2014)
32. Juan, A.A., Faulin, J., Grasman, S., Riera, D., Marull, J., Mendez, C.: Using safety stocks and simulation to solve the vehicle routing problem with stochastic demands. Transp. Res. Part C Emerg. Technol. **19**(5), 751–765 (2011)
33. Juan, A.A., Goentzel, J., Bektaş, T.: Routing fleets with multiple driving ranges: Is it possible to use greener fleet configurations? Appl. Soft Comput. **21**, 84–94 (2014)
34. Juan, A.A., Mendez, C., Faulin, J., Armas, J., Grasman, S.: Electric vehicles in logistics and transportation: a survey on emerging environmental, strategic, and operational challenges. Energies **9**, 86 (2016)
35. Juan, A.A., Faulin, J., Grasman, S.E., Rabe, M., Figueira, G.: A review ofsimheuristics: Extending metaheuristics to deal with stochastic combinatorialoptimization problems. Oper. Res. Perspect. **2**, 62–72 (2015)
36. Kumar, S.N.: A survey on the vehicle routing problem and its variants. Intell. Inf. Manage. **04**(03), 66–74 (2012)
37. Lebeau, P., Macharis, C., Van Mierlo, J., Maes, G.: Implementing electric vehicles in urban distribution: A discrete event simulation. In: Electric Vehicle Symposium and Exhibition (EVS27), 2013 World (2013)
38. Macal, C.M., North, M.: Tutorial on agent-based modelling and simulation. J. Simul. **4**, 151–162 (2010)
39. Mancini, S.: Multi-echelon distribution systems in city logistics. European Transport - Trasporti Europei **54**, 1–24 (2013)
40. Muñuzuri, J., Grosso, R., Cortés, P., Guadix, J.: Estimating the extra costs imposed on delivery vehicles using access time windows in a city. Comput. Environ. Urban Syst. **41**, 262–275 (2013)
41. Nguyen, V.P., Prins, C., Prodhon, C.: Solving the two-echelon location routing problem by a grasp reinforced by a learning process and path relinking. Eur. J. Oper. Res. **216**, 113–126 (2012)
42. Nowicka, K.: Smart city logistics on cloud computing model. Procedia Soc. Behav. Sci. **151**, 266–281 (2014)
43. Othman, M., Gouw, G.J., Bhuiyan, N.: Workforce scheduling : A new model incorporating human factors **5**(2), 259–284 (2013)
44. Quak, H., de Koster, M.: Delivering goods in urban areas: how to deal with urban policy restrictions and the environment. Transp. Sci. **43**(2), 211–227 (2009)

45. Qureshi, A., Taniguchi, E., Yamada, T.: A microsimulation based analysis of exact solution of dynamic vehicle routing with soft time windows. Procedia Soc. Behav. Sci. **39**, 205–216 (2011)
46. Schwengerer, M., Pirkwieser, S., Raidl, G.R.: A variable neighborhood search approach for the two-echelon location-routing problem. In: Hao, J.-K., Middendorf, M. (eds.) EvoCOP 2012. LNCS, vol. 7245, pp. 13–24. Springer, Heidelberg (2012)
47. Sood, A., Sharma, V.: A study of behavioural perspective of operations. Procedia Soc. Behav. Sci. **189**, 229–233 (2015)
48. Storey, J., Emberson, C., Godsell, J., Harrison, A.: Supply chain management: theory, practice and future challenges. Inte. J. Oper. Prod. Manage. **26**(7), 754–774 (2006)
49. Sweeny, E.: The people dimension in logistics and supply chain management research and practice: its role and importance. In: Passaro, R., Thomas, A. (eds.) Supply Chain Management: Perspectives, Issues and Cases, pp. 73–82. McGraw-Hill, Milan (2013)
50. Tamagawa, D., Taniguchi, E., Yamada, T.: Evaluating city logistics measures using a multi-agent model. Procedia Soc. Behav. Sci. **2**(3), 6002–6012 (2010)
51. Taniguchi, E., Thompson, E., Yamada, T., van Duin, J., Logistics, C.: Network Modelling and Intelligent Transport Systems. Pergamon, Oxford (2001)
52. Taniguchi, E., Yamada, T., Okamoto, M.: Multi-agent modelling for evaluating dynamic vehicle routing and scheduling systems. J. Eastern Asia Soc. Transp. Stud. **7**, 933–948 (2007)
53. Taniguchi, E., Thompson, R.G., Yamada, T.: Emerging techniques for enhancing the practical application of city logistics models. Procedia Soc. Behav. Sci. **39**, 3–18 (2012)
54. Teo, J.S., Taniguchi, E., Qureshi, A.G.: Evaluating city logistics measure in e-commerce with multiagent systems. Procedia Soc. Behav. Sci. **39**, 349–359 (2012)
55. Tokar, T.: Behavioral research in logistics and supply chain management. Int. J. Bus. Manage. **21**(1), 89–103 (2010)
56. United States Environmental Protection Agency. Greenhouse gas emissions 1990–2013 (2013). http://www3.epa.gov/otaq/climate/documents/420f15032.pdf
57. Wangapisit, O., Taniguchi, E., Teo, J.S., Qureshi, A.G.: Multi-agent systems modelling for evaluating joint delivery systems. Procedia Soc. Behav. Sci. **125**, 472–483 (2014)

Comparing Wireless Traffic Tracking with Regular Traffic Control Systems for the Detection of Congestions in Streets

Antonio Fernández-Ares[✉], Maribel García Arenas, Antonio M. Mora,
Pedro A. Castillo, and J.J. Merelo

ETSIIT-CITIC, University of Granada, Granada, Spain
antares@ugr.es

Abstract. Detecting congestions on streets is one of the main issues in the area of smart cities. Regular monitoring methods can supply information about the number of vehicles in transit and thus the saturation of the streets, but they are usually expensive and intrusive with respect to the road. In recent years a new trend in traffic detection has arisen, considering the Wireless signals emitted by 'smart' on-board devices for counting and tracking vehicles. In this paper, two traffic monitoring methods are compared: detections using a regular Inductive Loop Detector on the road and an own Wireless Tracking System based on Bluetooth detection called *Mobywit*. The correlation between the day of the week and the hour with the traffic flow in a metropolitan busy street has been analysed. Assuming that our system is not able to defect all the vehicles, but just only subset of them, it is expected a causality between the results obtained using the two methods. This means, that the Bluetooth-based system can detect the same variations in the traffic flow that the regular loop detector, but having two main advantages: the tracking possibilities and a much lower cost.

Keywords: Smart cities · Traffic monitoring · Traffic tracking · Bluetooth detection

1 Introduction

The detection of traffic congestions in streets is an essential issue inside the philosophy of a Smart City. In it, a *smart traffic system* should be able of detect, predict and, ideally, manage, these traffic troubles. An optimal management system can provide a better performance in citizens' displacement time, the energy consumed by vehicles, and the resources or costs employed [1,13,15].

Regular Traffic Control Systems are based in several kinds of devices, such as pneumatic tubes, loop detectors, floating vehicles or automatic Optical Character Recognition [14]. Usually, those technologies are very expensive to be placed in every street and are quite intrusive. Thus, traffic monitoring technologies can

© Springer International Publishing Switzerland 2016
E. Alba et al. (Eds.): Smart-CT 2016, LNCS 9704, pp. 42–51, 2016.
DOI: 10.1007/978-3-319-39595-1_5

be classified as *intrusive*, when they are installed over or under the pavement, and *non-intrusive*, if they are not in contact with the road, so they cause a minimal effect on the traffic flow [8].

These regular technologies are normally expensive (above a thousand euros), they require altering the road, and they have a high cost of maintenance (several thousand of euros per year) [9,16]. However, they are the most precise way of measure the traffic density. That justifies their use used in important highways and roads with heavy traffic, where just deploying a few devices it can be possible to, virtually, monitor all the traffic.

In urban scenarios the problem is that the traffic flows move through several different points (streets), connected between them, so it is needed to gather a lot of information about most of these streets in order to study and model the traffic [12]. Major cities can afford installing traffic control systems only in main streets, but reaching most of the streets are normally beyond their possibilities.

Thus, it would be recommended to find a cheaper alternative, also less intrusive, to gather (and provide) information about the traffic. This could be implanted in every street, giving a fair level of accuracy, or at least, able to detect or 'recognise' the traffic fluctuations as a regular system does, i.e. being reliable.

In this line, this work applies a monitoring system called *Mobywit* [4] able to collect vehicle mobility data by means of a grid of low-cost devices (or nodes) connected to a central server. The nodes capture Bluetooth (BT) signals emitted by other devices, mainly hands-free systems and *smartphones* on board of vehicles. This type of traffic monitoring technology is becoming widely used in the private sector [3,5,17,18], as it is quite cheap (about a few hundred euros), it is non-intrusive with the road, it is easy to implement, and requires minimal maintenance. It has also become a very profiting research area [7,10,11].

Thus, this paper presents a study comparing a Regular Traffic Control System based in an Inductive Loop Detector and the *Mobywit* System. Specifically, it is analysed if a system based in Wireless Traffic Tracking (focused on Bluetooth) can provide the same information about the traffic flows and traffic congestion than a regular method. For each system, the influence of the weekday and the hour of the day in the congestion is studied. The goal is to determine if the same variations in the data collected by the regular method are reproduced in the data obtained using the Wireless Tracking System. And therefore a Wireless Tracking System can be used as an economic alternative to regular traffic measure methods.

In order to study the relationship between both systems, the Granger Causality Test [6] is used. The Granger test is a statistical hypothesis test for determining whether one time series X is useful to forecast another series Y. That means, it exists a causality between both time series.

The rest of the work is structured as follows: Sect. 2 presents the Wireless Tracking functioning applied to the traffic control and why it can be approximated the number of vehicles with the number of Bluetooth devices. Then, the problem studied is introduced in Sect. 3 that presents information about the data compared for each system. Section 4 shows the results of the studies of correlation of the information about the traffic flow and about indicatives of traffic saturation. Finally, Sect. 5 presents the conclusions reached in the work.

2   Wireless Tracking of Vehicles with Bluetooth

In this work the Wireless Tracking System is compared with a regular Inductive Loop Detector working as shown in Fig. 1. And Inductive Loop essentially is a square-form wire embedded into the road with an electric current. When a metal surface with certain minimum area passed or is stopped above the loop, a pulse is triggered and detected by a sensor. Two records are saved for a time interval, number of times that turns on flow field and how much time in total has been activated the field in that interval. With that information, it is estimated the number of vehicles that have passed by the road and their average speed.

In Wireless Tracking, a number of devices or nodes are placed near of the road as Fig. 2 shows. These devices are provided with antennas that are able to search for *Bluetooth beacons*. A Bluetooth beacon is a type of frame that Bluetooth devices drop for announcing a *"I am here"* message proclaiming their *MAC Address* and other information about his nature.

The *MAC Address*, also called physical address, is a unique identifier assigned to network interfaces for most IEEE 802 network technologies. *MAC Addresses* are most often assigned by the manufacturer of the network interface controller (NIC) and are stored in its hardware, such as the NIC's read-only memory or some other firmware mechanisms. Hence as it is assigned by the manufacturer, a *MAC Address* usually encodes the manufacturer's registered identification.

Obviously exists a huge variety of devices that use Bluetooth for their communications. So in can not be considered a priori that any detected Bluetooth device corresponds to a vehicle. In addiction, even with the energy management enhances of Bluetooth 4.0 LE, the devices that have some type of user interfaces (buttons, screens or dials) can disable the auto-sending of beacons for saving battery. This means that not all th devices are sending beacons all the time.

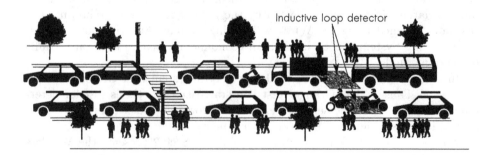

Fig. 1. Inductive loop detector for Traffic Control

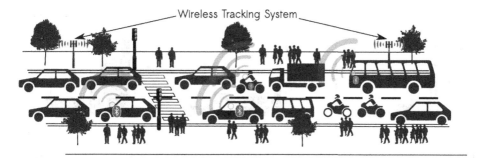

Fig. 2. Wireless Tracking of Vehicles

However a Bluetooth beacon contents information about the nature of the device, in a bit-code named Major and Minor Device Class[1]. This class and the manufacturer extracted from the *MAC Address* can provide information about the type of detected device.

So on the one hand, most advanced devices are not sending beacons all time, just those that do not have a friendly user interface. Furthermore disable the auto-sending of beacons correspond with the necessity of save battery, so most of the devices that not need save battery do not disable auto-sending of beacons.

Other hand, a Wireless Tracking system for traffic have some points of interest in vehicles. The vast majority of new cars on the road include a Bluetooth connection used as hands-free with a smartphone, to synchronise music player, in GPS, cellulars for emergency calls or even because they are smartcars. Fortunately a car is complex system, with a non-friendly user interface, in that not worth it give an option to disable auto-sending of Bluetooth beacons. Moreover a car have a huge and inexhaustible auto rechargeable battery when the engine it is in movement. So there are not a real necessity of save battery evading the auto-sending of beacons.

But all this is just a guess. It is needed to study in a functional Wireless Tracking System the nature of the detected devices. Figure 3 shows the manufacturer, major and minor class of the devices detected in the interval of time that was used in this paper by the *Mobywit* System.

The principal type of device detected by the System belong to hands-free devices. A similar number of cellulars and smartphones are detected. However, a surveys about the habits of the use of Bluetooth in smartphones made with more than 500 people showed that the 84.6 % of users only turn on Bluetooth when will be used, turning off it the rest of the time.

Loocking the manufacturer of the tracking devices can be seen that most of them are tracking devices that belong to hands-free manufacturer (PARROT, NOKIA, SAMSUNG, ERICSSON, HUAWEI, MOTOROLA, LG, ZTE and XIAOMI), GPS manufacturer (TOMTOM,GARMIN), music players manufacturer (PIONER, SAMSUNG, SONY),

---

[1] www.bluetooth.com/specifications/assigned-numbers/baseband.

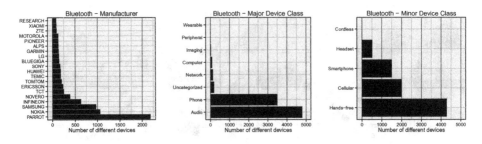

Fig. 3. Manufacturer, Major Device class and Minor device class of every different Bluetooth Device tracked.

manufacturers of NICs inside cars (NOVERO, TCT, TEMIC, BLUEGIGA, ALPS, RESEARCH) and smartphones (again NOKIA, SAMSUNG, ERICSSON, HUAWEI, MOTOROLA, LG, ZTE and XIAOMI).

It cannot be generalized, but a that the significant amount of device detected by a Bluetooth Tracking System belong to vehicles or devices travelling inside a vehicle.

Considered that Bluetooth devices inside vehicles or vehicles are the principal devices sending beacon, because need to save battery (the vehicle is providing it) and they usually do not have an easy way to disable the auto-sending of beacons.

3   Analysis of Traffic Flow in a Busy Street

Thanks to the collaboration with the Mobility Area of the Local Council of Granada City, it had the opportunity to compare the two systems in one of the most busy and conflicting streets of the city.

Figure 4 shows a map of the street. It is a main street that collects much of the traffic of the north area of city and allows the driving to move to other areas.

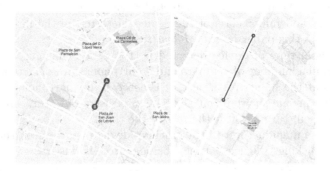

Fig. 4. Location and detailed location of the busy street Doctor Oloriz in Granada.

3.1   Data Sources

Historical Inductive Loop Detector. Unfortunately the council cannot yield recent data about the traffic because the Inductive Loop is not always working. Thus, historical data are provided from January to April 2015. Figure 5 plots the number of vehicles per hour detected for two Inductive loops placed near Point B of Fig. 4.

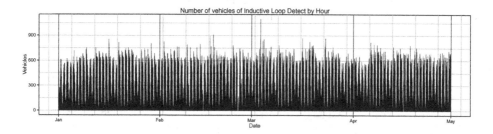

Fig. 5. Vehicles detected by Inductive Loop by hour in point B.

Bluetooth. The collaboration with the council allow to install two Mobywit device both A and B that have been tracking Bluetooth devices from 11 January 2016 to 29 February 2016. Figure 6 plots the number of devices detected by hour in that period.

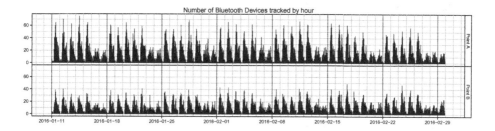

Fig. 6. Bluetooth devices tracked by Mobywit System per hour in points A & B.

4   Experiments and Results

Figures 5 and 6 show that Wireless Tracking System detects less devices (or vehicles) that the regular Inductive Loop Detector. It is necessary to study if there is a correlation between both system in the variation of traffic flow and in the indicators of a traffic congestion.

4.1 Traffic Flow

For a smart city, it is more important to know if there is a high or less utilization of the road than expected in the same period, than the real number of vehicles moving on that street [2].

There are not equal periods of data for the systems, so a correlation of the weekday and hour it is approximated. Figure 7 plots the variation and influence of the weekday and hour of the day in the number of vehicles detected for each system. Apparently the two systems behave similarly, but there are some statistical evidences reflecting they are related.

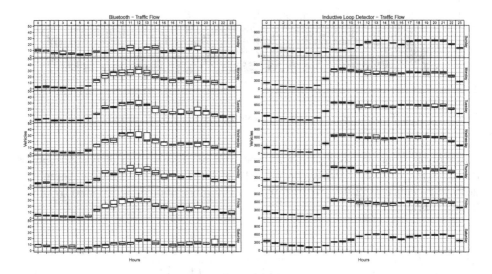

Fig. 7. Traffic Flow of Bluetooth and Inductive Loop Detector by weekday and hour.

Despite the similarity between the two measures, it is need some statistical evidence of the causality. A simple linear regression analysis yields a $R^2 = 0.6389$ that results insufficient to attain any conclusion. It is needed other test that uses the data as time series. Granger Causality introduced in on Sect. 1 is an optimal test to infer whether both series behave similarly.

The result of the Granger test yields a p-value equal to 0.0002355 that is less than the confidence threshold. This means a big statistical evidence which means that the variation of number of Bluetooth devices tracked by a Wireless Tracking System can be considered for measure the variation of the real traffic flow.

4.2 Indicatives of Saturation of the Street

Time of Use of the Inductive Loop Detector. With the use of Induction Loops Systems can be approximated the average speed of vehicles, using the total time the loop has been actived divided by the total number of vehicles and the length of the loop. This information is used for detecting congestion in traffic. If traffic is moving slower than usual, means that there are something hinder to the traffic go faster. However this speed is a punctual speed in the loop, not the cruising speed.

Time to Cross the Street. In a Wireless Tracking System with at least two nodes or devices. It can be calculated the real time needed for every single device to go from A to B. This time can be useful to compute the average time needed for example to cross a street or another.

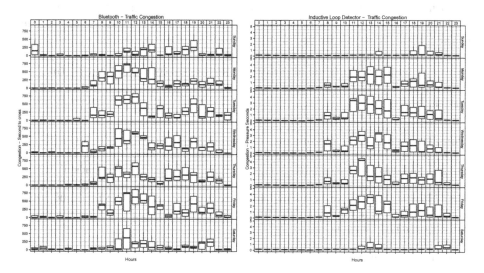

Fig. 8. Congestion indicative for Bluetooth and Inductive Loop Detector per weekday and hour.

As it has been done previously, a correlation between the weekday and the hour of the day has been calculated for both measures. Figure 8 plots the usual time needed to cross the street obtained with *Mobywit* system, and the time of activation of the loop for each vehicle (together with the length of the loop can be calculated the instant speed).

Again a linear regression drops $R^2 = 0.4662$ results poorly statistically significant. Granger Test of the two time series obtains a p-value of $0.5844 \cdot 10^{-11}$ that is almost zero. This means that there is a strong correlation between both time series measures.

5 Conclusions

This paper presents has been presented theoretical and empirical evidences of the tracking of Bluetooth devices mainly will detect vehicles (devices inside vehicles).

The detection of other type of devices detected is insignificant, because they are handy devices that have to save battery, and for that, usually auto-sending of beacons was disabled. Furthermore, if any device belongs to some other major and minor class, can be easily discounted by the node.

Has been statistically proved using the Granger Test, that there is a strong correlation between the number of tracking Bluetooth devices and the number of real vehicles (according to loop detections). The indicators of congestion in the streets, in both methods, are also strongly statistically correlated according to the Granger Test. This enables detecting the fluctuation and congestion of the real traffic using the Bluetooth devices tracked. But using a cheaper and less intrusive with the road system.

So finally, it can be concluded that using a Wireless Tracking System is a valid alternative for the control of the traffic flow and the detection of congestion on the street. That will be useful in smart cities, since it provide an economic system to control the traffic. With advantage of vehicle tracking so, that a system with more nodes can provide also information about the origin and destination of the traffic or the paths they follow. This topic will be explored as a future work in this line.

Acknowledgements. This work has been supported in part by project MOSOS (reference PRY142/14), which has been granted by Fundación Pública Andaluza Centro de Estudios Andaluces in the call 'IX Convocatoria de Proyectos de Investigación'. It also has been partially funded by national projects TIN2014-56494-C4-3-P and TEC2015-68752 (Spanish Ministry of Economy and Competitiveness), PROY-PP2015-06 (Plan Propio 2015 UGR), and project CEI2015-MP-V17 of the Microprojects program 2015 from CEI BioTIC Granada.

We also thank the DGT and local council of Granada city, and their staff and researchers for their dedication and professionalism.

References

1. Arnott, R., Palma, A.D., Lindsey, R.: Does providing information to drivers reduce traffic congestion? Transp. Res. Part A Gen. **25**(5), 309–318 (1991). http://www.sciencedirect.com/science/article/pii/019126079190146H
2. Batty, M., Axhausen, K.W., Giannotti, F., Pozdnoukhov, A., Bazzani, A., Wachowicz, M., Ouzounis, G., Portugali, Y.: Smart cities of the future. Eur. Phys. J. Special Topics **214**(1), 481–518 (2012). http://link.springer.com/article/10.1140/epjst/e2012-01703-3
3. Carnes, P.: TraffaxInc. http://www.TraffaxInc.com/
4. Castillo, P., Fernández-Ares, A., García-Fernández, P., García-Sánchez, P., Arenas, M., Mora, A., Rivas, V., Asensio, J., Romero, G., Merelo, J.: Studying individualized transit indicators using a new low-cost information system. In: Handbook of Research on Embedded Systems Design. Industry and Research Perspectives on Embedded System Design, pp. 388–407. IGI Global (2014). Advances in Systems Analysis, Software Engineering, and High Performance Computing
5. FMM: System and method for monitoring people and/or vehicles in urban environments (May 2011). EP Patent App. EP20,080,805,357, http://www.google.com/patents/EP2325823A1?cl=en

6. Granger, C.: Testing for causality: a personal viewpoint. J. Econ. Dyn. Control **2**, 329–352 (1980)
7. Kostakos, V.: Using bluetooth to capture passenger trips on public transport buses (2008). arXiv:0806.0874
8. Martin, P.T., Feng, Y., Wang, X., et al.: Detector technology evaluation. Technical report, Mountain-Plains Consortium (2003)
9. Menéndez, J.: Kilómetros a precio de Oro. DGT - Tráfico Noviembre-Diciembre, pp. 31–34 (2000)
10. Morrison, A., Bell, M., Chalmers, M.: Visualisation of spectator activity at stadium events. In: 2009 13th International Conference on Information Visualisation, pp. 219–226. IEEE (2009)
11. Nicolai, T., Kenn, H.: About the relationship between people and discoverable bluetooth devices in urban environments. In: Proceedings of the 4th international conference on mobile technology, applications, and systems and the 1st international symposium on Computer human interaction in mobile technology. pp. 72–78. ACM (2007)
12. Ramos, A., Ferreira, J., Barceló, J.: Intelligent urban traffic: a guide through micro modelling approaches. In: Proceedings of the IEEE International Conference on Systems, Man, and Cybernetics (SMC), pp. 2767–2772. IEEE, Anchorage, October 2011
13. Richard, A., Small, K.: The economics of traffic congestion. Am. Sci. **82**(5), 446–455 (1994). http://www.jstor.org/stable/29775281
14. Rodrigue, J.P., Comtois, C., Slack, B.: The Geography of Transport Systems. Routledge, New York (2013)
15. Rahane, S.K., Saharkar, U.R.: Traffic congestion - causes and solutions: a study of talegaon Dabhade city. J. Inf. Knowl. Res. Civil Eng. **3**(1), 160–163 (2014)
16. Skszek, S.L.: "state-of-the-art" report on non-traditional traffic counting methods. Technical report, Arizona Department of Transportation (2001)
17. TierpointLLC: Trafficnow. http://www.trafficnow.com/
18. Vilajosana, I.: BitCarrier. Go With the Flow. http://www.bitcarrier.com/

Cooperative Lane-Change and Longitudinal Behaviour Model Extension for TraffSim

Christian Backfrieder[1(✉)], Gerald Ostermayer[1], Manuel Lindorfer[1], and Christoph F. Mecklenbräuker[2]

[1] Research Group Networks and Mobility, UAS Upper Austria, Hagenberg, Austria
{christian.backfrieder,gerald.ostermayer}@fh-hagenberg.at
[2] Christian Doppler Lab Wireless Technology for Sustainable Mobility,
Vienna University of Technology, Vienna, Austria
cfm@nt.tuwien.ac.at

Abstract. Behaviors of drivers have an important influence on the throughput, safety and traffic flow of vehicular transportation systems. Especially in simulation scenarios, a smooth, realistic and fully reliable lane-change model is a precondition to achieve reasonable results. An extraordinary challenge is provided by situations with multiple congested lanes, including vehicles intending to change to the adjacent lane even if the target lane is occupied by vehicles stuck in a traffic jam. This paper addresses this special use case by introducing Cooperative Lane-Change and Longitudinal Behaviour Model Extension (CLLxt), which can be applied as an extension to models from literature. The result is a simple but well-functioning cooperative model, which covers both participants, the vehicle intending to change the lane and others which need to react to this intention by providing space. The utilization of CLLxt is demonstrated with an example in TraffSim.

Keywords: Lane-change model · Traffic simulation · Cooperative lane-change

1 Introduction

Behavioural models have a considerable influence on results of vehicular traffic simulation. Especially in cases where real time experiments are impossible to execute with reasonable effort, simulation of such situations are the only way to investigate different situations on the road. Numerous simulation frameworks of different types exist in literature [1–5], which make use of various models that encapsulate single tasks of the driver. The models can be separated into those which model the drivers behaviour, such as lane-change models and longitudinal models. Additionally, fuel consumption models or others which represent routing decisions can be applied. For microscopic simulations, where each vehicle is modelled as a separate entity with its special features (length and width, assigned fuel-consumption, longitudinal and lane-change models), driving tasks need to be executed fully automated on the one hand, and in a manner close to reality

© Springer International Publishing Switzerland 2016
E. Alba et al. (Eds.): Smart-CT 2016, LNCS 9704, pp. 52–62, 2016.
DOI: 10.1007/978-3-319-39595-1_6

on the other hand. Single-lane car-following models have been applied in the past which successfully define vehicle movement [6]. They can describe vehicle dynamics in different situations, instabilities or congestion situations. However, simulations with real road networks and realistic results can only be executed by using multilane roads. Therefore, a well-functioning lane-change and longitudinal model are of vital importance, as they basically control the steering and acceleration of all vehicles in the simulation.

The consideration of different traffic conditions and incomplete knowledge of other vehicles intentions makes the development of a lane-change model a complex concern. Further, safety plays an important role, as well as smoothness of lane-changes and realistic behaviour. Several microscopic models can be found in literature, which all are designed for specific use cases and have their pros and cons depending on the defined requirements, the environment, density of vehicles or characteristics of the road network [7]. An essential capability of such a model is also to be applicable in different situations. The original intention of changing a lane can be (1) to change to a neighbour lane to pass by a slow vehicle, (2) to change the lane due to the traffic laws (e.g. obligation to drive on the right in Europe), (3) to leave an ending lane (highway ramp, decrease of lane number, lane closure) or (4) to follow the desired route, which would not be possible on the current lane. The latter case constitutes the main focus of this paper. In particular, turn restrictions before intersections are considered. The intention of drivers to switch to the correct lane which allows them to follow their desired route must be executed before entering the intersection in order to enable automatic route guidance through the intersection. Especially in congested situations, individual lane-changes are often not possible without the cooperation of vehicles in the neighbouring lane. A reliable performance of the model is very important in simulations. Vehicles must use the correct lane when entering the intersection and this has to be guaranteed by the model. Otherwise, unexpected and indeterministic conditions could be the consequence.

The authors introduce an extension which is applied both to lane-change and longitudinal models. The main goal is to have a versatile and safe, but very simple mechanism that avoids entries of the intersection on the wrong lane and enables following the vehicles' routes correctly. The extension is evaluated and tested by example of the lane-change model MOBIL [8], implemented in the microscopic traffic simulator TraffSim [5].

The rest of this paper is organized as follows. The next section gives an overview of existing lane-change models. The extended model MOBIL [8] is elaborated in detail. Section 3 defines requirements which are defined for the proposed model. In Sect. 4, the cooperative extension is presented. Section 5 concludes the paper and gives an overview of planned future work.

2   Related Work

The importance of microscopic traffic simulation in general and the motion of vehicles in particular is increasing continuously. Accompanied by technological progress that keeps collection of continuous traffic data getting better, simulation models for vehicular traffic receive increasing attention since the 1980s [9]. The lane change models can initially be grouped into models for driving assistance (e.g. steering wheel adjustment to perform safe lane changes) [10–12], and models for simulation purposes. These deal with the driver's decision to perform the lane change, evaluation of the surrounding environment to determine whether or not a lane change is possible and different reasons for the lane change (necessity of giving way to a merging vehicle, change for overtaking, change for leaving a closed or blocked lane).

Lane-Change models for computer simulation can be classified into different categories [7]. Rule-based models, such as Gipps Model [13] or ARTEMiS Model [14]. However, those models do not consider congested situations and giving way to a merging vehicle. A different type are discrete-choice based lane-change models, like Toledo et al's Model [15] and incentive based models, such as MOBIL [8]. However, very few of the introduced models in literature consider cooperative behavior. To the authors knowledge, none of them considers special standstill situations, with multiple involved lanes and vehicles situated on the wrong lane.

The proposed extension addresses this particular question. It answers how a present combination of lane-change and longitudinal model can be extended to allow cooperative lane-changes before intersections.

3 Requirements Analysis

Basically, a lane-change model needs to consider the characteristics of the vehicles surrounding the subject vehicle, that are relative speed, positions and gaps between the potential new lead and lag vehicle. Further, it needs to function in different situations, such as congested traffic, freeflow traffic and with different speeds. An exhaustive, safe and simulation capable lane-change model needs not only to decide whether or not the current or a neighbor lane is optimal. Supplementary, it also has to deal with situations where the intended lane-change decision is impossible to execute without cooperation with other vehicles. This is essential especially in congested situations, where the target lane is occupied by other vehicles. Figure 1 shows such a situation, which is likely to happen before multi-lane intersections. In the left part, no problem will occur because the target lane for vehicle 4 is free and it can change without any problems. In contrast, Fig. 1b shows a problem situation where the vehicles 9 and 10 intend to move to the right lane that leads to exits B or C, but are blocked by vehicles 7, 11 and 13 which occupy this lane.

Vehicles 9 and 10 cannot stay on the current lane, because the upcoming intersection restricts turns to the left, which is not the intended direction. For this situation to solve, the lane-change model on its own cannot achieve satisfying results. Therefore, an interface to the longitudinal model needs to be defined, which can influence the acceleration and movement behavior to let the neighbor vehicle align and merge into the own lane. A realistic representation also requires consideration of multiple vehicles in front of the subject vehicle, on both the

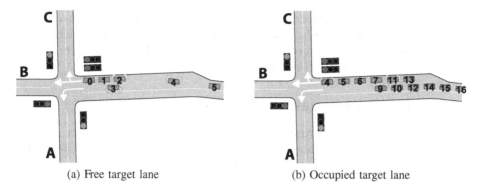

(a) Free target lane   (b) Occupied target lane

Fig. 1. Simple and problematic lane-change situations before intersection

right and left neighbor lanes. As soon as any of the front vehicles expresses its intent to change its lane to the subject lane, the model needs to take this into account when calculating its acceleration, speed and target lane. A deterministic strategy for providing space and letting the neighbor vehicle merge needs to be defined.

To conclude the requirements, the following aspects must be considered by a comprehensive behavioral model (including lane-change and longitudinal d movement):

1. Own interest
   (a) address lane-changes for reasons of speed advance (pass by slow vehicles)
   (b) follow own route (consider turn restrictions on lanes)
   (c) avoid standstill on obstacles or exits (accident, closed lane, road narrows)
2. Common interest
   (a) stick to traffic rules (obligation to drive on the leftmost/rightmost lane of the road)
   (b) lane-changes for providing space for other vehicles (highway-ramp)
   (c) brake for letting other vehicles change their lane

The presented model will focus particularly on the impacts of points 1.(b) and 2.(c) of the enumeration above. All other requirements are basically covered by lane-change models from literature.

4 Cooperative Lane-Change and Longitudinal Behavior Extension (CLLxt)

This section describes the extension to a given lane-change model, which then allows tactical lane-changes before intersections. It consists of two aspects which need to work together seamlessly, that are the perspective from the *invoking vehicle* **A** that needs to change its lane, and from one or more *supplying vehicle(s)* **B** providing space for vehicle **A**. The freeflow situation is not focus of this work, rather the situation before intersections as elucidated in Sect. 3. Further, route destinations are assumed to be assigned to each vehicle in the simulation. Also, basic knowledge of the road network is expected, which includes drivers awareness of turn restrictions or speed limits.

4.1   Perspective of the Invoking Vehicle

Determination of the Target Lane. First, the decision whether a lane-change is necessary to continue driving on the current route needs to be made. For performance reasons, the evaluation of the target lane is not accomplished continuously in each simulation time step, but starts not before a certain distance to the next intersection is undershot. This maximum distance d_{max} for considering lane-changes before an intersection is defined as

$$d_{max} = (t_{exit} + t_{change} * (N_{lanes} - 1)) * v_{limit}. \qquad (1)$$

This equation includes the following model parameters. The time threshold in seconds before arrival of the vehicle at the intersection is defined as t_{exit}. Further, t_{change} denotes the time that is needed for a vehicle to perform a lane-change. N_{lanes} is the number of lanes on the current road segment (hence $N_{lanes} - 1$ is the maximum number of lanes to change), and v_{limit} represents the speed limit.

As soon as a vehicle's computed distance to the next intersection is lower than d_{max}, the evaluation of the preferred lane in order to follow the route starts. Figure 2 shows a multilane intersection, with necessity of changing the lane for vehicle 1, which just at the moment reaches the range of influence of CLLxt by falling below d_{max}. For a better overview, only the relevant connecting lanes are included in the intersection.

The simulator needs to determine if the current lane is appropriate for driving along the defined route. If not, as is the case for vehicle 1 in Fig. 2, the simulation framework is assumed to deliver the desired direction of change. If the change can be achieved without any issues due to occupied lanes, the activity of CLLxt ends here. Otherwise (vehicles 9 and 10 in Figure 1b), the urgency of the change is calculated and potential neighbor vehicles' speed may be influenced if necessary.

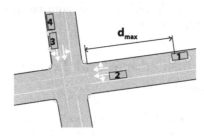

Fig. 2. Intersection with lane restrictions and required lane-change of *vehicle 1*

Urgency Function. Once a vehicle gets closer to the intersection at an inappropriate lane, the need of changing to a suitable lane becomes more and more vital. This urgency U is described by the urgency function in Eq. (2), depending on the current distance to the junction, denoted as d_{junc}. Additionally, a safety gap D is implemented, which specifies the minimal gap between vehicle and intersection border before the lane-change must be completed. Equation (3) defines the maximum needed distance d_{change} for reaching the target lane. It is also applicable for more than one lane-change by consideration of the difference in lanes between the current and target lane $n_{lanediff}$. The resulting urgency U in the interval $[0, 1]$ is used for slowing down and waiting for a chance to execute the lane-change.

$$U = \min\left[1, 1 - \frac{d_{junc} - D}{d_{change}}\right] \tag{2}$$

$$d_{change} = (t_{exit} + t_{change} * n_{lanediff}) * v_{limit} - D \tag{3}$$

Longitudinal Control. If the lane-change is not possible, the invoking vehicle needs to slow down until a safe change is feasible. In the worst case, this leads to a standstill, which can happen presumably before red traffic lights or in traffic jams.

However, the calculated urgency is used for this deceleration of the vehicle. An interface to the longitudinal model needs to be provided. We propose to simply adapt the maximum allowed speed on the current road segment, which is an input parameter for most longitudinal models [16–19] and therefore generally applicable. In TraffSim, the implemented longitudinal model IDM (Intelligent Driver Model) [19] is extended by this mechanism.

4.2 Perspective of the Supplying Vehicle(s)

In order to allow invoking vehicles to align in the lane, adaptation of the own longitudinal movement, i.e. braking may be needed to allow completion of the lane-change maneuver. Figure 3 depicts a situation, where invoking vehicles 9 and

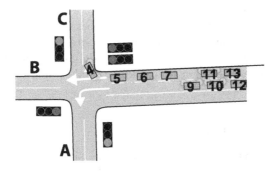

Fig. 3. Supplying vehicles *(11 and 13)* braking for invoking vehicles *(9 and 10)*

10 try to merge to the right lane to reach their destination exit C. The drivers of vehicle 11 and 13 recognize this intention through the direction indicator and reduce their speed to create a gap in front of them and let the invoking vehicles enter.

A politeness function is defined, which considers neighbor vehicles and adapts the calculated longitudinal acceleration appropriately. The following pseudocode describes the politeness function in detail, as extension to the longitudinal model. It can be parametrized by a defined amount of vehicle to look forward.

1: **function** UPDATEACCELERATION($acc_{current}, v_{current}, lookForward$)
2:     $acc_{min} \leftarrow$ Infinity
3:     **for** $i_{lf} = 1 : lookForward$ **do**
4:         $v_{neighbor} \leftarrow$ GETNEIGHBORVEHICLE($v_{current}, i_{lf}$)   ▷ check for potential neighbor vehicles
5:         **if** $v_{neighbor} \neq null$ **then**   ▷ calculate the longitudinal gap
6:             $gap_{long} \leftarrow v_{neighbor}$.position - $v_{current}$.position
7:             $acc_{new} \leftarrow$ CALCACCELERATION($v_{current}, v_{neighbor}, gap_{horz}$)
8:             **if** $gap_{long} > gap_{min}$ **then**   ▷ check for minimal gap
9:                 $acc_{min} \leftarrow acc_{new}$
10:            **end if**
11:        **end if**
12:    **end for**
13: **return** min[$acc_{current}, acc_{min}$]
14: **end function**

The method basically calculates an alternative to the standard acceleration value yielded by the applied longitudinal model. This alternative acc_{min} is determined by using the acceleration calculation function of the longitudinal model with a virtual front vehicle instead of the real front vehicle. The function GETNEIGHBORVEHICLE yields the virtual vehicle, which is the nth vehicle on the right or left lane next to the current lane, where n equals the parameter $lookForward$ (line 4). Figure 4 shows examples for the virtual front vehicle determination with different $lookForward$ distances. $\{L1..L3\}$ and $\{R1..R3\}$ mark the front vehicles of vehicle V on the left and right side, respectively (as returned by the GETNEIGHBORVEHICLE function), where the index number conforms to the $lookForward$ distance. F is the direct front vehicle. After a check of the gap between the supplying vehicle and potential candidate vehicle for lane-change (line 8), which must not undershot a minimal longitudinal distance, the minimum gained acceleration (longitudinal model value or politeness value) is returned.

4.3   Application Example

The proposed model is applied within the traffic simulator TraffSim [5], as an extension of the MOBIL lane-change model [8]. The implementation supports both the IDM longitudinal model [19] and an ACC (Adaptive Cruise Control) longitudinal model [20].

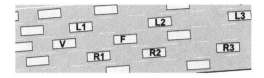

Fig. 4. Examples for neighbor vehicles with lookforward distance

Figure 5 shows the applied model in action within TraffSim, where the left part (Fig. 5a) shows the time of decision and the right part (Fig. 5b) illustrates the situation after completed lane change. The colors of the vehicles denote the current acceleration value, where green means positive acceleration, red describes negative acceleration (braking) and blue and black imply zero acceleration (steady drive and standstill, respectively).

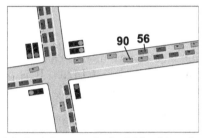

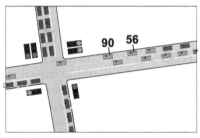

(a) Supplying vehicle 56 braking for gap creation

(b) Invoking vehicle 90 completely merged

Fig. 5. Snapshots of lane-change maneuver before intersection (Color figure online)

In order to provide better understanding of the influence of CLLxt, Fig. 6 shows history graphs of speed and acceleration over time for the affected vehicles 56 and 90, obtained from a TraffSim simulation. It's the very same situation as in Fig. 5. The blue solid line represents speed history, the red line shows the acceleration and time is plotted on the X-axis. The green dashed line $t1$ and the orange dotted line $t2$ mark significant timestamps. At time $t1$, the driver of the supplying vehicle (in this example number 56), recognizes the intended lane-change of the invoking vehicle (here vehicle 90). This behavior is reflected in the drop of acceleration, which becomes negative and the vehicle brakes. Thus, certainly also the speed drops and the gap between the vehicle 56 and its original front vehicle becomes larger. At time $t2$, the gap is large enough for the invoking vehicle 90 to merge. As a consequence, the acceleration and speed graphs in Fig. 6b rise and the lane-change can be completed. Figure 5a depicts the bird's view at exactly this point in time.

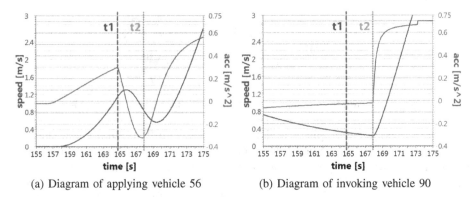

(a) Diagram of applying vehicle 56   (b) Diagram of invoking vehicle 90

Fig. 6. Speed and acceleration graphs for both supplying and invoking vehicles (Color figure online)

5   Conclusion and Outlook

This paper introduces an extension to existing lane-change models called Cooperative Lane-Change and Longitudinal Behavior Extension (CLLxt). It is particularly customized for application in situations where lane-change models from literature are stretched to their limits. CLLxt covers all situations which can lead to standstill of traffic flow and some vehicles are still driving on the wrong lane. This use case frequently happens before regulated multi-lane intersections, which involve multiple input lanes with turn restrictions. A change to the correct lane is then not possible due to lack of space on the target lane. CLLxt solves this by reacting to lane-change demand and creating gaps for merging. The authors present a very simple but well-functioning model for solving such situations by cooperative mechanisms. However, no bidirectional communication is assumed and thus a realistic vehicle movement is guaranteed. The utilization of the model is very simple, since it operates as extension to existing lane-change and longitudinal models. Additionally, the application of the extension is demonstrated by an example using the microscopic traffic simulator TraffSim [5], the longitudinal model IDM [19] and lane-change model MOBIL [8].

Future work will cover application of the presented model in large-scale microscopic traffic simulations. Additionally, an integration of human driver behavior into the model is planned, which covers reaction times, disturbance factors like cell phone or noise, external conditions such as rain or type of the driver (e.g. attentive, careful, aggressive).

Acknowledgments. This project has been co-financed by the European Union using financial means of the European Regional Development Fund (EFRE). Further information to IWB/EFRE is available at www.efre.gv.at.

Europäische Union Investitionen in Wachstum & Beschäftigung. Österreich.

References

1. Treiber, M., Kesting, A.: An open-source microscopic traffic simulator. IEEE Intell. Transp. Syst. Mag. **2**(3), 6–13 (2010)
2. Miller, J., Horowitz, E.: FreeSim - a free real-time freeway traffic simulator. In: IEEE Intelligent Transportation Systems Conference, ITSC 2007, pp. 18–23, September 2007
3. Behrisch, M., Bieker, L., Erdmann, J., Krajzewicz, D.: SUMO - simulation of urban mobility - an overview. In: SIMUL 2011, The Third International Conference on Advances in System Simulation, pp. 55–60, October 2011
4. Gora, P.: Traffic simulation framework. In: 2012 UKSim 14th International Conference on Computer Modelling and Simulation, pp. 345–349, March 2012
5. Backfrieder, C., Ostermayer, G., Mecklenbräuker, C.: Extended from EMS2013: TraffSim - a traffic simulator for investigations of congestion minimization through dynamic vehicle rerouting. Int. J. Simul. Syst. Sci. Technol. IJSSST V15 **15**, 8–13 (2015)
6. Helbing, D.: Traffic and related self-driven many-particle systems. Rev. Modern Phy. **73**(4), 1067–1141 (2001)
7. Rahman, M., Chowdhury, M., Xie, Y., He, Y.: Review of microscopic lane-changing models and future research opportunities. IEEE Trans. Intell. Transp. Syst. **14**(4), 1942–1956 (2013)
8. Kesting, A., Treiber, M., Helbing, D.: General lane-changing model MOBIL for car-following models. Transp. Res. Rec. J. Transp. Res. Board **1999**, 86–94 (2007)
9. Brackstone, M., McDonald, M., Wu, J.: Lane changing on the motorway: factors affecting its occurrence, and their implications. In: 9th International Conference on Road Transport Information and Control, 1998, (Conf. Publ. No. 454), pp. 160–164, April 1998
10. Rodemerk, C., Habenicht, S., Weitzel, A., Winner, H., Schmitt, T.: Development of a general criticality criterion for the risk estimation of driving situations and its application to a maneuver-based lane change assistance system. In: 2012 IEEE Intelligent Vehicles Symposium (IV), pp. 264–269, June 2012
11. Eidehall, A., Pohl, J., Gustafsson, F., Ekmark, J.: Toward autonomous collision avoidance by steering. IEEE Trans. Intell. Transp. Syst. **8**(1), 84–94 (2007)
12. Nagel, K., Wolf, D., Wagner, P., Simon, P.: Two-lane traffic rules for cellular automata: a systematic approach. Phy. Rev. E **58**(2), 1425–1437 (1998). arXiv:cond-mat/9712196
13. Gipps, P.: A model for the structure of lane-changing decisions. Transp. Res. Part B Methodol. **20**(5), 403–414 (1986)
14. Hidas, P.: Modelling vehicle interactions in microscopic simulation of merging and weaving. Transp. Res. Part C Emerg. Technol. **13**(1), 37–62 (2005)
15. Toledo, T., Koutsopoulos, H., Ben-Akiva, M.: Integrated driving behavior modeling. Transp. Res. Part C Emerg. Technol. **15**(2), 96–112 (2007)
16. Li, K., Ioannou, P.: Modeling of traffic flow of automated vehicles. IEEE Trans. Intell. Transp. Syst. **5**(2), 99–113 (2004)
17. Kumar, P., Merzouki, R., Conrard, B., Coelen, V., Bouamama, B.O.: Multilevel modeling of the traffic dynamic. IEEE Trans. Intell. Transp. Syst. **15**(3), 1066–1082 (2014)
18. Zhang, F., Li, J., Zhao, Q.: Single-lane traffic simulation with multi-agent system. In: 2005 IEEE Intelligent Transportation Systems, Proceedings, pp. 56–60, September 2005

19. Kesting, A., Treiber, M., Helbing, D.: Enhanced intelligent driver model to access the impact of driving strategies on traffic capacity. Philos. Trans. R. Soc. A Math. Phy. Eng. Sci. **368**(1928), 4585–4605 (2010). arXiv:0912.3613
20. Kesting, A., Treiber, M., Schönhof, M., Kranke, F., Helbing, D.: Jam-Avoiding Adaptive Cruise Control (ACC) and its Impact on Traffic Dynamics. In: Schadschneider, A., Pöschel, T., Kühne, R., Schreckenberg, M., Wolf, D.E. (eds.) Traffic and Granular FlowâĂŹ05, pp. 633–643. Springer, Heidelberg (2007). doi:10.1007/978-3-540-47641-2_62

CTPATH: A Real World System to Enable Green Transportation by Optimizing Environmentaly Friendly Routing Paths

Christian Cintrano, Daniel H. Stolfi, Jamal Toutouh, Francisco Chicano$^{(\boxtimes)}$, and Enrique Alba

Departamento de Lenguajes y Ciencias de la Computación, University of Málaga, Andalucía Tech, Málaga, Spain
{cintrano,dhstolfi,jamal,chicano,eat}@lcc.uma.es

Abstract. Road transportation is becoming a major concern in modern cities. The growth of the number of vehicles is provoking an important increment of pollution and greenhouse gas emissions generated by road traffic. In this paper, we present CTPATH, an innovative smart mobility software system that offers efficient paths to drivers in terms of travel time and greenhouse gas emissions. In order to obtain accurate results, CTPATH computes these paths taking into account the layout and habits in the city and real-time road traffic data. It offers customized paths to drivers (including personal profiles) in a distributed and intelligent way so as to consider the whole city situation.

Keywords: Smart mobility · Green transportation · Bi-objective shortest path

1 Introduction

Road traffic is becoming a major concern in modern cities, mainly because of the continuous increment of private and vehicle fleet operations. This generates serious problems related with road safety (e.g., increment the number of car accidents) and traffic efficiency (e.g., waste of time of the road users stuck in traffic jams), not to mention the continuous growth of pollution in modern cities. For this reason, new *smart mobility* solutions based on *Intelligent Transportation Systems* (ITS) are being developed to mitigate this type of problems [15].

Road traffic efficiency problems provoke longer road trips, economical costs in terms of fuel consumption, and higher pollution (greenhouse gas emissions). However, most of existing smart mobility solutions are focused on reducing the time and/or the distance of the journey without considering the generated pollution (e.g., iGO[1] and TomTom[2]). These solutions are based on the shortest path

---

This research was partially funded by the University of Málaga, Andalucía Tech, and the Spanish Ministry of Economy and Competitiveness and FEDER (grant TIN2014-57341-R).

[1] http://www.igonavigation.com.
[2] http://www.tomtom.com.

E. Alba et al. (Eds.): Smart-CT 2016, LNCS 9704, pp. 63–75, 2016.
DOI: 10.1007/978-3-319-39595-1_7

problem [4] and, thus, they only consider one criterion, such as time, distance, or any other.

However, the modern actors in a city (citizens, governments, and business organizations) demand a shift in the focus so as to consider reducing greenhouse gas emissions, because they are very sensitive about the environmental, healthy, ecological, and social effects of pollution. Thus, *green* road transportation has come as a discipline to limit and reduce the pollution generated during road trips, e.g., transportation by means of electric vehicles. An important approach to design green road transportation is to design environmental-aware logistic policies, i.e., to explicitly take into account the pollution when computing efficient paths for drivers.

In this paper, we propose CTPATH[3], which is an innovative software system (developed as both, a Web application and a smartphone app) that solves a bi-objective version of the shortest path problem to provide ecological and fast vehicle paths. One of its main features is that it considers real-time information about traffic conditions, including different types of vehicles, and driving profiles in order to allow a holistic and dynamic vision of road traffic in its computations that is unique in the present literature. In fact, it is also unique since it considers the whole chain of work from pure abstract and scientific problem solving up to a final user product for actual utilization in a real city. As a case of study, CPATH is being applied to the city of Málaga (Spain) where it successfully provides environmental friendly paths to road users.

This article is organized as follows: Sect. 2 formulates the bi-objective shortest path problem solved by CTPATH. Section 3 analyzes some previous related work. Section 4 presents the bi-objective optimization algorithm devised to provide the efficient paths computed by CTPATH. Section 5 describes the global architecture of the CTPATH system. Finally, Sect. 6 draws the main conclusions and the future research work.

2   Problem Formulation

The problem solved by CTPATH is a bi-objective shortest path problem [9], where the two objectives are travel time and CO_2 emissions. The main difference between this formulation and other bi-objective shortest path formulations is the way in which the objective functions are computed. While in previous bi-objective shortest path formulations the edges of the graph are labeled with two real values (one for each objective) that are fixed in the instance, in our formulation these values depend on three aspects that make the formulation more realistic: the traffic state, the vehicle used in the trip, and the driving profile of the driver. We will explain in this section how these real-world aspects are considered in the formulation at the same time that we detail how the objective value is computed.

Let $G = (V, E)$ be a directed graph that represents the road network of the city. An edge $e \in E$ is a street segment where no intersection occurs and the

---

[3] CTPATH Web Site - http://maxct.lcc.uma.es/ctpath.php.

vertices $u \in V$ are the intersections of streets. Each edge is labeled with two invariant quantities: the length of the edge $l(e)$ and the maximum velocity in the edge $m(e)$. In order to consider traffic state, we will also label each edge $e \in E$ with two additional values: the probability of traversing the edge without stopping due to traffic conditions $\rho(e)$, and the time to wait in the case of stopping due to traffic conditions $\tau(e)$. These values can change as the traffic conditions change in the city. Traffic lights, for example, affect both, $\rho(e)$ and $\tau(e)$. In particular, $\rho(e)$ increases with the fraction of time that the traffic light is in green and it decreases with the length of the street segment e.

In the shortest path problem an origin vertex $s \in V$ and a destination vertex $d \in V$ are given by the user. A candidate solution to the problem is a path in the graph starting at s and ending at d, that is, a solution for the (s,t) pair is a sequence of edges $\sigma = (e_1, e_2, \ldots, e_k)$ with $e_i = (u_i, w_i)$, such that $s = u_1$, $d = w_k$ and $u_{i+1} = w_i$ for $1 \leq i \leq k - 1$. Abusing of notation, we extend the definition of the labeling function ρ to paths in this way:

$$\rho(\sigma) = \prod_{e \in \sigma} \rho(e), \tag{1}$$

that is, the probability of traversing a path σ is the product of the probabilities of traversing each edge in the path. The previous expression assumes that the events of traversing different edges in a path are independent.

2.1 Speed Profile for a Path

Given a solution σ, we need a *speed profile* in order to compute the objective functions (time and CO$_2$ emission). A speed profile is a pair (v, t_{max}), where $t_{max} \in \mathbb{R}$ is the time required to traverse the path σ and $v : [0, t_{max}] \mapsto \mathbb{R}$ is a function that gives the speed of the car at each instant from the start of the trip $(t = 0)$ to the end $(t = t_{max})$. The speed profile depends on the driving profile of the driver and the traffic state.

In order to compute the speed profile, the path σ is first decomposed in several subpaths $\sigma_1, \sigma_2, \ldots, \sigma_p$ in such a way that the probability of traversing each subpath (except the last one) is below a threshold, that is, $\rho(\sigma_i) < \theta$ for $1 \leq i < p$. The subpaths σ_i cannot contain other subpaths with a traversing probability lower than θ, they are the longest subpaths with $\rho(\sigma_i) < \theta$ that give σ if they are concatenated. Intuitively, the subpaths σ_i are sequences of edges that we assume the car can traverse without stopping. Thus, we will called them *non-stop subatphs*. Let us denote with $N(\sigma)$ the sequence of non-stop subpaths of σ. Observe that $N(\sigma)$ depends only on the ρ labeling function.

In our formulation, we assume that the car is at rest at the beginning of each non-stop subpath. Then, it accelerates until it reaches a cruise speed, and, finally, it decelerates at the end of the non-stop subpath until it completely stops and waits for $\tau(e)$ time, where e is the last edge of the non-stop subpath. It repeats this process with the next non-stop subpath in the sequence until the destination is reached. We characterize the driving style of the driver using three values:

the acceleration α, the deceleration β, and a cruise speed factor γ, which determines how fast the driver cruise speed is compared to the maximum speed of an edge. This kind of speed profile is the one used in the SUMO traffic simulator [14]. While traversing a subpath, the driver could change the cruise speed to adapt it to the maximum velocity. During these changes we assume that an acceleration of α or a deceleration of β is used if possible. If there is no distance in an edge to use the characteristic acceleration or deceleration of the driver, we assume that the acceleration or deceleration is exceeded. Let us formalize all these ideas in the following. Let us assume that $S(l, \alpha, \beta, v_0, v_c, v_f)$ is a speed profile for an edge of length l starting at speed v_0, reaching a cruise speed of v_c and ending the edge at speed v_f. The acceleration should be α if possible and the deceleration should be β if possible. If $(v, t_{max}) = S(l, \alpha, \beta, v_0, v_c, v_f)$ we should have:

$$\int_0^{t_{max}} v(t)dt = l, \tag{2}$$

$$v(0) = v_0, \tag{3}$$

$$v(t_{max}) = v_f. \tag{4}$$

If possible, dv/dt should take three possible values at most: α, 0, and $-\beta$. When $dv/dt = 0$, then v should be v_c. However, these constraints could not be satisfied in very short edges (small l). In such cases we assume that dv/dt could take different values: appropriate values to satisfy (2), (3) and (4).

Let $(v, t_{max}) + (v', t'_{max})$ be the concatenation of two speed profiles to give another one. Intuitively, it corresponds to a speed profile where v is followed by v'. Formally, the concatenation $(v'', t''_{max}) = (v, t_{max}) + (v', t'_{max})$ is defined as:

$$t''_{max} = t_{max} + t'_{max}, \tag{5}$$

$$v''(t) = \begin{cases} v(t) & \text{if } t \in [0, t_{max}], \\ v'(t - t_{max}) & \text{if } t \in [t_{max}, t''_{max}]. \end{cases} \tag{6}$$

Observe that the concatenation is not commutative. We can now define the speed profile of a non-stop subpath as follows:

$$P_{ns}(\sigma = (e_1, e_2, \dots, e_k)) = S(l(e_1), \alpha, \beta, 0, \gamma \cdot m(e_1), \gamma \cdot m(e_1))$$

$$+ \sum_{i=2}^{k-1} S(l(e_i), \alpha, \beta, \gamma \cdot m(e_{i-1}), \gamma \cdot m(e_i), \gamma \cdot m(e_i))$$

$$+ S(l(e_k), \alpha, \beta, \gamma \cdot m(e_{k-1}), \gamma \cdot m(e_k), 0). \tag{7}$$

With the help of function P_{ns}, defined over non-stop subpaths, we can now define the speed profile for a complete path σ as follows:

$$P(\sigma) = \left(\sum_{i=1}^{p-1} (P_{ns}(\sigma_i) + (0, \tau(last(\sigma_i)))) \right) + P_{ns}(\sigma_p), \tag{8}$$

where $(\sigma_1, \sigma_2, \dots, \sigma_p) = N(\sigma)$, and $(0, t_{max})$ is a speed profile where the car is at rest during t_{max} time.

2.2 Objective Functions

Once we have computed the speed profile of a path σ we can easily define the objective functions. The first one is simply the time required to traverse the path, which is given by the speed profile. The second objective function is the amount of CO_2 emitted during the path. We use the HBEFA model [11] for the emission rate. This model estimates the CO_2 emission rate using the speed profile as follows:

$$h(v) = \max\left(0, c_0 + c_1 v \frac{dv}{dt} + c_2 v \left(\frac{dv}{dt}\right)^2 + c_3 v + c_4 v^2 + c_5 v^3\right), \qquad (9)$$

where the coefficients c_i with $0 \le i \le 5$ depend on the car. Observe that h is a functional (transforming a function into another one) and $h(v)$ is a function of time, as v is. We can compute the total CO_2 emitted during the trip through path σ integrating $h(v)$ between 0 (start time) and t_{max} (end time). Finally, the two objective functions to minimize are:

$$f_1(\sigma) = t_{max}, \qquad (10)$$

$$f_2(\sigma) = \int_0^{t_{max}} h(v) dt, \text{ where } (v, t_{max}) = P(\sigma). \qquad (11)$$

It is possible to define a new graph G' based on G where the nodes are augmented with probability values and transition speeds of the vehicles and the edges are weighted with 2-dimensional weights (one for each objective) such that the bi-objective optimization problem defined above is transformed into the bi-objective shortest path problem in G'. The transformation is possible thanks to the additivity of the two objectives.

3 Related Work

Some previous works on vehicle shortest paths have solved the single-objective shortest path problem to optimize aspects such as distance [2], costs [12], congestion of the traffic [3], etc. There are many variables that are interesting when improving road trips. Some of them are the congestion on the roads [13] and the emissions of polluting gases [1]. The latter is especially relevant nowadays. Among all types of pollutant gases, CO_2 is a good starting point for reducing the pollution and improving air quality in cities. However, existent algorithms do not usually take into account traffic or vehicle aspects [17] and they only shorten the travel time to get a reduction in carbon emissions. Instead of improving just one metric, we want to minimize both, travel time and CO_2 emissions. Thus, we need to solve a bi-objective shortest path problem (BSP), which was defined by Hansen [9] in 1980.

While the single-objective shortest path problem can be solved in $O(|E| + |V| \log |V|)$ time using Dijkstra's algorithm with Fibonacci heaps [18], the BSP is NP-hard [16]. In BSP the goal is to obtain a set of efficient solutions, that is, solutions that can be improved in one of the objectives only if they are worsened in the other (also called Pareto optimal solutions or non-dominated solutions).

Dijkstra's algorithm can be easily extended to solve the BSP [6], but it can take too much time to find a solution, due to the NP-hardness of the problem. One of the most recent advances in the exact solution of the BSP is the work by Duque et al. [5] where an exact algorithm, called *Pulse*, is proposed to solve the problem. The algorithm implements a depth-first search combined with several strategies to prune suboptimal paths. This algorithm is able to find the efficient set of solutions for cities with up to 2.8 millions of nodes in around 2 s.

Exact algorithms to find the complete set of efficient solutions for BSP have an exponential runtime in the worst case. This is not satisfactory for a real application providing paths to users. These applications should provide an answer in a fraction of a second. In addition, users are generally not interested in the complete set of efficient solutions, they only want a few options to select from. These two drawbacks of exact algorithms (runtime and amount of solutions) are avoided in this work by finding only *supported efficient solutions* of the Pareto front (see Sect. 4). We take the idea from the first phase of the Two Phase Method proposed by Ulungu and Teghem [19].

Most of the proposed solutions for BSP are maintained in the academic field [7,8] and usually they are not implemented on real-world applications. Commercial systems offer several routes according to different objectives (e.g., Michelin[4], TomTom, Waze[5]) but only tend to focus on one at a time. However, few systems like iGO, have an explicit goal of reducing ecological footprint. iGO takes into account the type of vehicle to calculate pollution emitted but this is not the only variable to take into account. It is important to consider the level of road congestion, as it is done in Google Maps[6], and which directly affects commuting times and therefore CO_2 emissions. Our proposal, CTPATH was designed with the idea of being exploited in practice by the citizens, and not only as a mere academic work.

4   Optimization Engine of CTPATH

This section describes the optimization algorithm used by CTPATH to provide different vehicle paths to the users. The main goal of CTPATH is computing vehicle paths that minimize both, the time to get the destination and the amount of CO_2 emitted during the trip (Eqs. (10) and (11)). The work of Duque et al. [5] has shown that the Pareto front for the BSP problem can be exactly computed in reasonable time for relatively large graphs. However, since BSP is NP-hard, we cannot certify to have the Pareto front in a short time, and a low response time is essential for our application. On the other hand, we don't need all the solutions in the Pareto front, showing the user a few solutions is enough for our purposes. For this reason, instead of solving the BSP problem, our approach is

---

[4] http://www.viamichelin.es/web/Itinerarios.

[5] https://www.waze.com.

[6] http://maps.google.com.

to find supported efficient solutions of the Pareto front, that can be obtained in polynomial time. A supported efficient solution is one that can be computed by solving a single-objective version of the problem where the objective is a weighted sum of the two original objectives:

$$f = wf_1 + (1 - w)f_2.$$
(12)

On one hand, this allows us to transform the BSP into a single-objective shortest path problem, which can be solved using Dijkstra's algorithm or other more intelligent techniques like A* algorithm [10]. On the other hand, we can obtain a limited number of solutions to show to the user: one for each value we assign to the weight w in (12).

In our case, we provide the user up to three different solutions. The first one is the *fastest solution*, which is obtained when $w = 1$ in (12). The second one is the *greenest solution*, obtained with $w = 0$ in (12). The greenest solution is the one that emits less CO_2 during the trip. Finally, we obtain a third solution between the fastest and the greenest. In order to do this we apply the idea used in the first phase of the Two Phase Method [19] to find a supported efficient solution in the rectangle determined by the fastest and the greenest solution in the objective space. Let x by the fastest solution and y the greenest solution, then the weight used to find the third (efficient) solution is:

$$w_s = \frac{f_2(x) - f_2(y)}{f_2(x) - f_2(y) + f_1(y) - f_1(x)}.$$
(13)

If the solution obtained with w_s has the same objective values as x or y, then no other supported efficient solution exists. In this case, only two different solutions are shown to the user. It could even happen that only one solution exist. In order to solve the single-objective shortest path problem, we use Dijkstra's algorithm.

5   The Developed CTPATH System

This section presents the CTPATH software, which has been developed to address the shortest path problem taking into account the travel time and CO_2 emissions. CTPATH has been applied to the city of Málaga in order to provide efficient and green routing paths.

5.1   CTPATH System Architecture

CTPATH is an intelligent and holistic route planner for urban environments. It is intelligent, because of the type of technology and the computer algorithms used, and it is holistic, because it analyzes not only the user or the city as other competitors do, but also the entire context of trips (and also in a dynamic fashion). In short, it aims to provide routes to drivers in the city. In spite of the fact that there already exists software that provides routes (e.g., Google Maps,

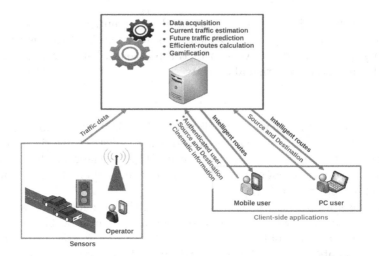

Fig. 1. Characteristics and components of CTPATH.

GPS navigators as TomTom or iGO), there are several key differences in our case as it evaluates the routes according to several opposed criteria.

The main functionality of CTPATH consists in providing routes to drivers in order to minimize travel times and greenhouse gas emissions. These routes are calculated by an intelligent central system and the final service which can be accessed by using mobile devices such as smartphones or tablets, as well as personal computers. Furthermore, the routes provided to users who have the application installed into their mobiles phones are personalized for them, as they are calculated according to their driving profile. Additionally, the central system is fed with data from the state of the city streets and driving behavior of its users, something that cannot be found in existing similar systems. Figure 1 shows the characteristics and components of CTPATH.

The system architecture consists of the components of the central server system (Fig. 2) and the components of the communication system (Fig. 3) described as follows.

- **Central Data Collector:** The central data collector receives data from the mobile app running in the users' devices and from the sensors distributed across the city. In this way, we have data from users and from the city itself where they move. All data received such as users' position, speed, and acceleration are stored in the local database.
- **Intelligent System of Estimation and Prediction:** This component accesses to the data stored in the database by the central data collector to process them in order to estimate: (i) the existing traffic in each street of the city; (ii) the driving time spent in each street; (iii) the future expected traffic (several minutes); and (iv) the driving profile of the registered users (how they accelerate, which is their cruise speed, etc.). These estimations are stored in the database as well, so that they can be used as source data for the route calculator.

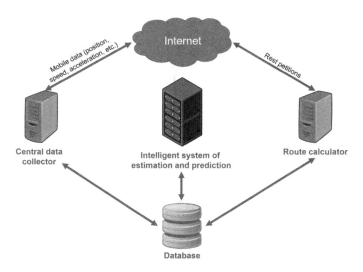

Fig. 2. Architecture of the central server system.

- **Route calculator:** The route calculator is accessed through a REST web service which allows the users to select the shortest/eco-friendliest route between source and destination. This web service is used by a single page web application included in the web server and the mobile applications. This component uses the traffic estimations and predictions as well as the user profile created by the intelligent system of estimation and prediction. Another important functionality of the route calculator is the management of the CTPATH users' accounts for personalizing the routes provided to them. Finally, the route calculator takes care of the user rankings according to the amount of CO_2 emitted per distance.
- **Communication system:** As can be seen in Fig. 3 data is collected via 3G sensors, Wi-Fi networks, and 3G infrastructure. Additionally, users can interact directly with the server in real time in order to send kinematic information (position, speed, acceleration, etc.) which will be used to infer the current traffic state as well as their driving profile. By doing this, users are behaving as mobile sensors, improving not only the granularity of the traffic information but also the estimation accuracy.

5.2   CTPATH Application

As aforementioned, the CTPATH system can be utilized via a web-based interface and a mobile based application (for smartphones and tablets). This section shows the interfaces of the two types of applications and summarizes a performance evaluation of the application.

Figure 4 shows the web based application layout, which is divided in three main areas:

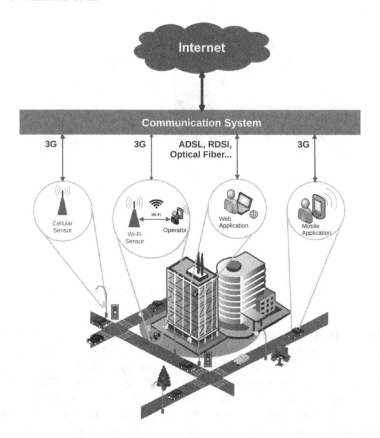

Fig. 3. Architecture of the communication system.

- *Road map:* It covers the entire web browser screen and shows the road map. After a given itinerary request, it illustrates in different colors the different routes computed by the system.
- *Itineraries details:* It is located in the top-left corner of the web browser, however it can be moved. It contains text information about the itineraries returned, including travel time, CO_2 emission, route indications, etc.
- *Trip options:* This area is located in the bottom-left corner of the web page and provides the application interface that allows users to introduce the options about the itinerary, e.g., the starting and ending points of the route, the departure time, and the vehicle type.

The mobile based application is shown in Fig. 5. As the screen size of mobile devices is limited, this application requires a higher number of different views to show the same information than the web based application. The *road map* and *trip options* are shown together (see Fig. 5a) and the *itinerary details* are presented separately (see Fig. 5b).

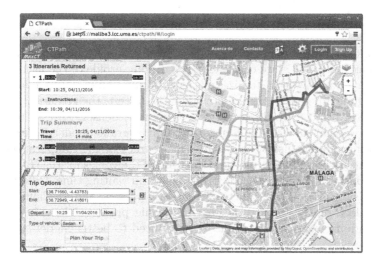

Fig. 4. The CTPATH web based application. (Color figure online)

a) *Road map* and *trip options*.   b) *Itinerary details*.

Fig. 5. The CTPATH mobile based application.

In order to evaluate the performance of the system, we have measured the response time of the system after submitting an itinerary request. As this time depends on the current network and server load, we have performed 30 requests of the same itinerary and computed their response times. The average response time measured was 32.267 milliseconds with a standard deviation of 10.546, which is a competitive response time to foster user interactions.

6   Conclusions and Future Work

In this work we have presented CTPATH, a route planner for vehicles that takes into account the traffic state of the city, the driving profile of the users and the car they drive to provide customized paths to go from an origin to a destination in a city. Three different paths are provided: the fastest, the greenest (minimum CO_2 emissions) and a third one between these two. Sensors spread in the city and mobile apps in the users collect data to build a traffic model of the city and driving profiles for the users, increasing the accuracy of the computations.

Future research will focus on the estimation of the values for the traffic model proposed considering the transition probability and waiting time. Different ways of doing this estimation from the traffic data are possible and we should analyze them to select the best one. The driving profile presented here is simplistic and some additional variables could be introduced to better model the driving behaviour.

References

1. Abdul-Hak, M., Bazzi, Y., Cordes, O., Alholou, N., Alamir, M.: Dynamic eco-routing methodology using petri net. In: SAE Technical Papers, vol. 2, April 2013
2. Cao, Z., Guo, H., Zhang, J., Niyato, D., Fastenrath, U.: Finding the shortest path in stochastic vehicle routing: a cardinality minimization approach. IEEE Trans. Intell. Transp. Syst. **PP**(99), 1–15 (2015)
3. Chen, H., Gao, Z., Yang, Y., Qiu, X.: An improved approach for route planning in urban traffic network. J. Comput. Inf. Syst. **9**(7), 2917–2924 (2013)
4. Dijkstra, E.W.: A note on two problems in connexion with graphs. Numer. Math. **1**(1), 269–271 (1959)
5. Duque, D., Lozano, L., Medaglia, A.L.: An exact method for the biobjective short-est path problem for large-scale road networks. Eur. J. Oper. Res. **242**(3), 788–797 (2015)
6. Ehrgott, M., Gandibleux, X.: Multi-objective combinatorial optimization. In: Al-Mezel, S.A.R., Al-Solamy, F.R.M., Ansari, Q.H. (eds.) Fixed Point Theory, Variational Analysis, and Optimization, pp. 307–341. CRC Press, Boca Raton (2014)
7. Erb, S., Kobitzsch, M., Sanders, P.: Parallel bi-objective shortest paths using weight-balanced b-trees with bulk updates. In: Gudmundsson, J., Katajainen, J. (eds.) SEA 2014. LNCS, vol. 8504, pp. 111–122. Springer, Heidelberg (2014)
8. Ghoseiri, K., Nadjari, B.: An ant colony optimization algorithm for the bi-objective shortest path problem. Appl. Soft Comput. **10**(4), 1237–1246 (2010)
9. Hansen, P.: Bicriterion path problems. In: Gal, T., Fandel, G. (eds.) Multiple Criteria Decision Making Theory and Application. LNEMS, vol. 177, pp. 109–127. Springer, Heidelberg (1980)
10. Hart, P.E., Nilsson, N.J., Raphael, B.: A formal basis for the heuristic determina-tion of minimum cost paths. IEEE Trans. Syst. Sci. Cybern. **4**(2), 100–107 (1968)
11. Hausberger, S., Rexeis, M., Zallinger, M., Luz, R.: Emission Factors from the Model PHEM for the HBEFA Version 3. Technical report I (2009)

12. Jamalluddin, M.H., Jaafar, M.A., Amran, M.I., Ainul, M.S., Hamid, A., Mansor, Z.M., Nopiah, Z.M.: Minimizing travel claims cost with minimal-spanning tree model. In: Proceeding of the 3rd International Conference on Mathematical Sciences, vol. 1602, pp. 541–545. AIP Publishing, June 2014

13. Jiang, B., Xu, X., Yang, C., Li, R., Terano, T.: Solving road-network congestion problems by a multi-objective optimization algorithm with brownian agent model. In: Corchado, J.M., Bajo, J., Kozlak, J., Pawlewski, P., Molina, J.M., Julian, V., Silveira, R.A., Unland, R., Giroux, S. (eds.) PAAMS 2013. CCIS, vol. 365, pp. 36–48. Springer, Heidelberg (2013)

14. Krajzewicz, D., Erdmann, J., Behrisch, M., Bieker, L.: Recent development and applications of SUMO - Simulation of Urban MObility. Int. J. Adv. Syst. Meas. 5(3&4), 128–138 (2012)

15. Picone, M., Busanelli, S., Amoretti, M., Zanichelli, F., Ferrari, G.: Advanced Technologies for Intelligent Transportation Systems, vol. 139. Springer, Heidelberg (2015)

16. Serafini, P.: Some considerations about computational complexity for multi objective combinatorial problems. In: Jahn, J., Krabs, W. (eds.) Recent Advances and Historical Development of Vector Optimization. LNEMS, vol. 294, pp. 222–232. Springer, Heidelberg (1987)

17. Tatomir, B., Rothkrantz, L.J.M., Suson, A.C.: Travel time prediction for dynamic routing using ant based control. In: Proceedings of the 2009 Winter Simulation Conference (WSC), pp. 1069–1078. IEEE, December 2009

18. Cormen, T.H., Leiserson, C.E., Rivest, R.L., Stein, C.: Intoduction to Algorithms, 3rd edn. MIT Press, Massachusetts (2009)

19. Ulungu, E., Teghem, J.: Application of the two phases method to solve the bi-objective knapsack problem. Technical report, FacultePolytechniquedeMons, Belgium (1994)

Electrifying Last-Mile Deliveries: A Carbon Footprint Comparison between Internal Combustion Engine and Electric Vehicles

Jesus Saenz-Esteruelas[1]([✉]), Miguel Figliozzi[2], Adrian Serrano[1], and Javier Faulin[1]

[1] Department of Statistics and OR, Public University of Navarra, Pamplona, Spain
{jesusmaria.saenz,adrian.serrano,javier.faulin}@unavarra.es
[2] Department of Civil and Environmental Engineering,
Portland State University, Portland, OR, USA
figliozzi@pdx.edu

Abstract. Last-mile management distribution is a growing challenge in big cities that affects to quality of life of many citizens. A way to mitigate greenhouse gas (GHG) emissions and congestion, as well as to promote and develop Smart Cities, is electrifying urban distribution by means of electric tricycles. This article evaluates the GHG of a tricycle logistics company (B-Line) in downtown Portland, OR. The goal is to analyze carbon footprint potential savings between electric tricycle last-mile distribution against a traditional diesel-powered van system. Real-world GPS and warehouse data were collected to assess B-Line operations. Results show a huge GHG emissions reduction, being tricycle logistic system twice more efficient that the traditional one.

Keywords: Smart city · Externality · Electric vehicle · Last-mile distribution

1 Introduction

Cities are evolving towards sustainability and efficiency; cities are moving to be smart. Globalization and the constant growth of world trade [1] have made transportation a key sector and a major contributor to progress and development. However, transportation activities frequently make indirect negative impacts on the environment such as air pollution and noise, usually named externalities. At the same time, people are concentrating around major urban areas. Actually, more than 50 % of world's population in 2014 lived in urban areas [2] what implies a high number of commercial deliveries in cities [3]. Consequently, commercial vehicles presence in urban areas has dramatically increased as some studies showed that vehicle miles of travel has rose 20 % from 1996 to 2006 [4].

Indirect effects of an economic activity are said to be externalities since those are out of the price system [5]. Research interest in externalities of freight transportation has continuously expanded because of the increasing impacts on economy, environment, climate, and society. Air pollution, noise, congestion, road damage and accidents are the usual externalities related to transport activities, nevertheless, due to the fact that

© Springer International Publishing Switzerland 2016
E. Alba et al. (Eds.): Smart-CT 2016, LNCS 9704, pp. 76–84, 2016.
DOI: 10.1007/978-3-319-39595-1_8

transportation activities account for a third of total greenhouse gas (GHG) emissions in the United States [6], air-pollution-related externalities are the most studied ones [7]. Air pollution is caused by emission of air pollutants such as particulate matter (PM), NOx and non-methane volatile organic compounds that affect people, vegetation, global climate and materials. Climate change or global warming impacts of road transport are, mainly, generated by emissions of greenhouse gases (GHG): carbon dioxide (CO_2), nitrous oxide (N_2O) and methane (CH_4). Nevertheless, CO_2 is the dominant anthropogenic GHG, and the remaining GHG can be expressed as CO_2 equivalent (CO2e) [8].

With regard to urban freight transportation, also known as last-mile distribution because it covers the movement of goods from a central hub in the city to a final destination [9]; several studies have shown that its contribution to total GHG emissions is extremely relevant. Actually, a fifth of CO_2 emissions come from urban freight vehicles [10]. Additionally, urban freight internal combustion engine vehicles (ICEV), commonly diesel-powered, are known to seriously affect public health. Diesel motor vehicles are a major source of air contaminants produced during the diesel combustion, like NOx which is responsible for acid rain.

In order to mitigate externalities, transportation policy makers are evaluating the possibility of electrifying urban delivery vehicles [11]. Advantages concerning Electric Vehicles (EV) in last-mile distribution have to do with their higher efficiency in the urban environment [12] and that is feasible the regular charging or battery swapping [13]. Thus, the switch from a fossil fuel combustion fleet to an electric-powered fleet seems like a suitable solution to reduce urban emissions. Moreover, actual cities go towards Smart Cities where a sustainable and efficient management of their resources must be considered [14]. Therefore, in the context of Smart Cities, EV development and adoption play a critical role. Even though there are several types of EV that could be used in urban freight transportation, electrically-assisted cargo tricycles are an ideal low-carbon alternative to transport light cargo in city centers. This situation is due, not only because their emissions-free nature, but also because their small size and easy access to congested city centers. Unlike conventional internal combustion vans, tricycles can legally use bike paths and be dropped on and off, on sidewalks or inside business [15]. Because the freight that is delivered by tricycle is often light and small, diesel vans are the natural competitor. Although electric tricycles do not produce tailpipe emissions, GHG emissions from electricity generation should be considered leading us to consider a Life Cycle Assessment (LCA) [16] ranging from extraction of resources to build up the vehicles, the operation phase, and disposal at the end.

Thus, this article aims to analyze the greenhouse gas (GHG) emissions potential savings of electric tricycles over their life time for last-mile delivery operations. B-Line [17], a tricycle logistics company in downtown Portland, OR, is used to record data related to route and warehouse and to test the methodology. The goal is to compare B-Line's carbon footprint against the footprint that B-Line would make using traditional diesel-powered vans.

The next section presents a brief literature review, and the following sections present the methodology used to compare different vehicle technologies, the case study, the results, and some concluding remarks.

2 Literature Review

Literature about EVs is spreading out during the last years due to a growing interest among researchers [18], mainly focused on Smart City contexts [19]. Most of them focus on challenges regarding batteries limitations [20] and their final adoption [21]. Hybrid vehicles are also studied in the literature as a mix alternative between ICEV and EVs [22]. Real cases analyses are also performed, for instance, how charging points distribution affect EVs [23]. However, from the best of the authors' knowledge, there are no published carbon footprint assessments of a tricycle logistics company in the existing literature. Urban distribution is often called last mile distribution because it occurs in the final echelon of the logistics chain, when goods go from an urban distribution center to final customers. Literature regarding last mile distribution using EV is mainly focused on European cities such as Brussels, London and Paris [24, 25].

In this paper, a Life Cycle Assessments (LCA) [16] will be carried out using real tricycles and diesel-powered vans in order to elicit their carbon footprint, which is the total set of greenhouse gas emissions caused directly and indirectly as a consequence of providing the transport service expressed as CO_2 equivalent (CO_2e), that is, translating all GHG into CO_2 using the Intergovernmental Panel Agency recommendations [26]. According to the GHG Protocol (an accounting tool to understand, quantify, and manage GHG emissions [27]), there exist 3 different scopes of GHG emissions depending on whether the emission sources are controlled by the company. Hence, Scope I is used to categorize all direct emissions, Scope II includes indirect emissions from consumption of purchased electricity, heat or steam; and Scope III consists of other indirect emissions, such as the extraction and production of purchased materials and fuels, transport-related activities in vehicles not owned or controlled by the company. While carbon footprint distinguishes between the 3 broad scopes, LCA considers the life cycle phases (ranging from extraction of resources to build up the vehicles, the operation phase, and disposal at the end) in such a way that it avoids shifting emissions from one phase to another.

Tricycles used in this paper have a maximum payload of 600 lbs. with curb weight of 500 lbs. Their maximum speed is around 10 mph being able to cover 30 miles and usual tricycle life expectancy estimation is around 5 years. On the other hand, alternative internal combustion engine vans can load 4,160 lbs. with a curb weight of 4,781 lbs. Their maximum speed is approximately 50 mph covering up to 465 miles when the tank is full and we will assume that van life expectancy is approximately 12 years [28]. Urban areas characteristics make tricycles as an ideal way to deliver light goods given the possibility of reducing and shortening the route by using pedestrian areas or riding up one-way streets on a sidewalk in the opposite directions as well as using sidewalks or business to park. Furthermore, taking into account that riders have to pedal, energy tricycle energy efficiency improves given the fact that on average fitted person could pedal a bicycle with the power output of 75 watts without suffering fatigue for 7 h [29]. Among cargo tricycle disadvantages, it is remarkable their limited payloads capacities which may make them reject orders that exceed the vehicle limit. In addition, the short travel range and the low speed in free-flow conditions are also highlighted.

3 Methodology

In order to compare carbon footprint of both logistic systems (electric tricycles and traditional vans such as the previously specified), the GHG Protocol methodology using the Scope III was followed; that is, including all life cycle emissions associated with the production, use and disposal of vehicles [30]. Splitting the logistic service into sources of emissions, we consider the following ones:

1. Vehicle. It covers the emissions made during the whole life of the van/tricycle, from raw material extraction (aluminum, plastic...), transport and disposal or recycling.
2. Well-to-tank. Emissions coming from energy production and distribution: electricity in tricycles and fuel in the van case.
3. Tank-to-wheel. Derived from the service provided itself. In that case emissions only came from diesel-powered vans.

Data necessary to carry out the analyses were collected from the Environmental Protection Agency [31] and, the eGRID database [32]. Finally, Life Cycle Assessment was performed using the Greenhouse gases, Regulated Emissions, and Energy use in Transportation (GREET [36]) a full life-cycle model that evaluates energy and emission impacts.

3.1 Vehicle

Applying the information about physical characteristics of the vehicles proposed, it is possible to estimate the carbon footprint of the vehicle life using GREET. In this phase we are considering the whole vehicle life cycle: extraction of raw materials (aluminum, iron, plastic...), transport to factories to product the materials needed, transportation to the plant where the materials are going to be assembled, final production of vehicles, transport and distribution of them to dealers, and lastly, disposal. By using the mass as the functional unit (in lbs.) vehicle life cycle GHG emissions are 2,677 lbs. of CO_2e for an electric tricycle and 32,073 lbs. of CO_2e for a diesel-powered van.

Note that the tricycles batteries were not considered in the previous calculation. Usually, electric tricycles use Lead-Acid (PbA) batteries, which last, on average, for 4 years. By using GWP values recommended by the International Panel on Climate Change it is estimated that battery life cycle GHG emissions are 3.94 lbs. CO2e per PbA battery lb.

3.2 Well-to-Tank

The fuel that a diesel-powered van consumes has been extracted as oil, transported, refined and transported again to stations. These upstream GHG emissions were estimated to be about 5.10 lbs. of CO_2e per gallon of conventional diesel using average values from GREET model.

The electricity that a tricycle consumes does not produce emissions when it is running. However, some emissions have been made to generate and distribute the electricity. Using the information of eGRID [33] with the U.S. average coal-based electricity generation as well as adding the estimated electricity that is lost due to transmission and distribution, we get 1,238.5 lbs. of CO2e/MWh.

3.3 Tank-to-Wheel

According to Environment Protection Agency [34] burning one gallon of diesel makes 22.47 lbs. of CO_2. By applying the GHG equivalent ratio, CO_2e emissions are estimated as 22.75 lbs. CO_2e/gallon. Electric consumption in tricycles is computed by measuring energy in batteries before and after a route is run. However, we should take into account the battery efficiency because it is a function of it state of charge [35]. This implies that from 0 % to 85 % of charge, batteries efficiency is almost 90 % meanwhile it decreases to 55 % when batteries are charged upper 85 %. Finally, CO2e emissions in both cases are converted in terms of distance travelled (lbs./mile).

4   Case Study

The methodology proposed was applied to a real case in order to compare carbon footprint between the two logistics configurations: electric tricycles and diesel-powered vans. The case study was held in Portland, OR; a bike-friendly city in U.S which its rather flat downtown area makes biking very convenient. Consequently, a company such as B-Line Sustainable Urban Delivery [17], a last-mile distribution service provider that operates in Portland downtown, has succeeded. B-Line transports a wide range of products (baked goods, office suppliers, bike components...) to businesses using electric tricycles. Moreover, B-Line also diversified its business by advertising and promoting companies and products through their eye-catching cargo box. B-Line logistics business model, which consisted of 8 partners and 80 final destinations, is organized as follows:

– Four partners, those that are far away from city center, deliver their products to B-Line distribution center and then B-Line transports them to final destinations.
– Four partners, those that are in the city center, wait for B-Line to picks-up products of their locations and distribute to final destination.

Data from B-Line operations were collected on May–June 2015 and it includes many days of detailed B-Line GPS routes and warehouse operations. B-Line fleet is compounded of 6 electric tricycles with 2 PbA batteries each in order to allow swaps. Using private information, fuel economy median is estimated at 48.50 W-h/mile. B-Line Carbon footprint can be calculated using the previous data.

Then, a hypothetical scenario is built considering that B-Line would provide the same service as it currently does using diesel vans as well as maintaining the previous partner structure. B-Line managers made hypothetical routes that diesel-powered vans would do in order to minimize the total distance traveled keeping customer service level. In this hypothetical scenario, neither time windows nor capacity constraints are assumed, because the van payload is much greater than the tricycle payload. However, service time per client using a van is likely to be greater than service time using a tricycle because tricycles can park on sidewalks while vans have to find parking slots. Hence, to cover the 80 final destinations and assuming 10 min service time each, at least two vans are required to maintain the tricycle service level. GHG emissions made by those partners that have to transport their product to B-Line's warehouse are also included in the computation as they are inside Scope III we have adopted. On average, the daily distance covered by B-Line's partners, from their depots to the B-Line distribution center is 25 miles.

Therefore, a comparison between the B-Line current carbon footprint, against the footprint of a traditional diesel van delivery company can be made.

5 Results

Current B-Line carbon footprint is assessed and compared against traditional diesel-powered van system carbon footprint. Figure 1 shows that CO_2e emissions as a result of tricycle delivery system fall from 23 to 12 tons of CO2e emissions per year, which implied a 50 % of reduction. Thus, B-Line is avoiding approximately 11 tons of CO_2e emissions per year. However daily distance traveled increase significantly resulting in an increment of 50 % of miles traveled, even though here we are not including the 25 miles that the four farther partners have to travel to transport their products to B-Line's depot. That is not trivial at all because those 25 miles per day account for 60 % of total GHG emissions tricycle system does. Nevertheless, we should take into account that diesel-powered vans travel in congested streets at slow speeds. Subsequently, the global impact is not a reduction in CO_2e emissions for the traditional diesel company.

Figure 2 distinguishes between partner activity impacts showing lbs. CO2e emissions per delivery using electric tricycles and vans. Thus, a huge reduction can be achieved without including partner's transport activities: 6 tricycles have 80 % less environmental impact in terms of CO2e emissions than 2 common diesel cargo vans. Actually, a delivery made by an electric tricycle emits just 0.2 lbs. of CO2e while the same trip made by a van would emit 5 times more: 1 lb.

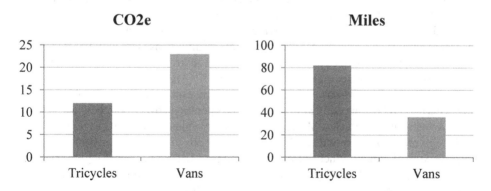

Fig. 1. Tons CO2e emissions/year [left] and miles travelled/day [right]

CO2e

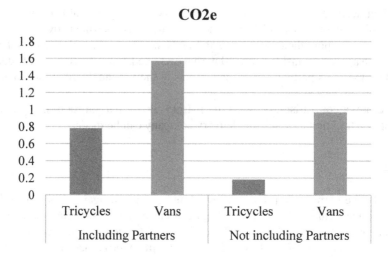

Fig. 2. Lbs. CO2e emissions/delivery

6 Conclusions and Ongoing Work

Last-mile management distribution is a growing challenge in big cities that affects life quality of citizens due to GHG emissions, noise or congestion. Therefore, sustainability and efficiency in that environment is threatened along with the concept of Smart City itself. Thus, electrification of last-mile deliveries, for instance using electric tricycles, would play an important role in reducing GHG emissions noise, congestion or service time. In this article, we have developed a methodology to evaluate carbon footprint of electric tricycle and common vans. This methodology was tested in the real case of B-Line [17], a logistic company that works in Portland, OR. B-Line currently operates an electric fleet of 6 cargo tricycles in last-mile urban distribution. Then, we compared its carbon footprint with the one that B-Line would make if they use traditional diesel-powered vans. Results show a huge saving of GHG emissions of electric tricycle with respect to a traditional fleet by halving them. This result is consistent with Browne et al. [36] that estimated a reduction of 54 % CO_2e emissions due to the use of an urban distribution center and electric vehicles in London.

Future research directions will face the economic aspect of electric vehicles adoption. This should be done taking into account the operation cost of both policies as well as the investment on vehicles. Moreover, a monetary valuation of GHG savings should be done in order to incorporate to the previous analysis to cover not only internal cost but also external. Finally, since this paper has compared a current electric logistic system against its hypothetical diesel-powered alternative; it would be interesting to do the same in an actual diesel-powered fleet against its electric alternative.

Acknowledgements. This work has been partially supported by the Spanish Ministry of Economy and Competitiveness (grants TRA2013-48180-C3-P and TRA2015-71883-REDT), and the   Ibero-American   Program   for   Science   and   Technology   for   Development

(CYTED2014-515RT0489). Likewise we want to acknowledge the support received by the CAN Foundation in Navarre, Spain (Grant CAN2014-3758).

References

1. World Trade Organization: World Trade Report 2014 (2015). https://www.wto.org/english/res_e/booksp_e/world_trade_report14_e.pdf. Accessed Feb 2016
2. United Nations: World Urbanization Prospects, United Nations (2014). http://esa.un.org/unpd/wup/Publications/Files/WUP2014-Report.pdf. Accessed Feb 2016
3. Lin, J., Chen, Q., Kawamura, K.: Environmental and energy benefits of freight delivery in consolidation in Urban Areas. National Center for Freight & Infrastructure Research & Education, Madison (2013)
4. National Cooperative Freight Research Program: Synthesis of Freight Research in Urban Distribution Planning, Report 23 (2013)
5. Laffont, J.: The New Palgrave Dictionary of Economics. Palgrave Macmillan, Basingstoke (2008)
6. Russo, F., Comi, A.: City characteristics and urban goods movements: a way to environmental transportation system in a sustainable city. Procedia Soc. Behav. Sci. **39**, 61–73 (2012)
7. Demir, E., Huang, Y., Scholts, S., Van Woensel, T.: A selected review on the negative externalities of the freight transportation: modeling and pricing. Transp. Res. Part E **77**, 95–114 (2015)
8. Bernard, S.M., Samet, J.M., Grambsch, A., Ebi, K., Romieu, I.: The potential impacts of climate variability and change on air pollution-related health effects in the United States. Environ. Health Perspect. **109**, 199–209 (2001)
9. Tan, K., Htet, K., Narayanan, A.: Mitigation of vehicle distribution in an EV sharing scheme for last mile transportation. Intell. Transp. Syst. **5**(16), 2631–2641 (2015)
10. Schoemaker, J., Allen, J., Huschebek, M., Monigl, J.: Quantification of urban freight transport effects I. BESTUFS Consortium (2006)
11. Lee, D.-Y., Thomas, V.M., Brown, M.A.: Electric urban delivery trucks: energy use, greenhouse gas emissions, and cost-effectiveness. Environ. Sci. Technol. **47**, 8022–8030 (2013)
12. U.S. DOE: FedEx Express Gasoline Hybrid Electric Delivery Truck Evaluation: 12-Month Report. National Renewable Energy Laboratory, Golden, CO (2011)
13. Martin, C.: Battery-Powered Trucks: Toys No More. Bloomerang Businesweek (2011)
14. Calvillo, C., Sánchez-Miralles, A., Villar, J.: Energy management and planning in smart cities. Renew. Sustain. Energy Rev. **55**, 273–287 (2016)
15. Tipagornwong, C., Figliozzi, M.: Analysis of competitiveness of freight tricycle delivery services in urban areas. Transp. Res. Rec. J. Transp. Res. Board **2410**, 76–84 (2014)
16. Asdrubali, F., Baldinelli, G., D'Alessandro, F., Scrucca, F.: Life cycle assessment of electricity production from renewable energies: review and results harmonization. Renew. Sustain. Energy Rev. **42**, 1113–1122 (2015)
17. B-Line: B-Line Sustainable Urban Delivery. http://b-linepdx.com/. Accessed Feb 2016
18. Juan, A., Mendez, C., Faulin, J., de Armas, J., Grasman, S.: Electric vehicles in logistics and transportation: a survey on emerging environmental, strategic and operational challenges. Energies **86**(9), 1–21 (2016)
19. Mathiesen, B., Lund, H., Connolly, D., Wenzel, H., Østergaard, P., Möller, B., Hvelplund, F.: Smart energy systems for coherent 100 % renewable energy and transport solutions. Appl. Energy **145**, 139–154 (2015)

20. Jhala, K., Natarajan, B., Pahwa, A., Erickson, L.: Coordinated electric vehicle charging solutions using renewable energy sources. In: Computational Intelligence Applications in Smart Grid (CIASG), pp. 1–6 (2014)
21. Sierzchula, W., Bakker, S., Maat, K., Wee, B.: The influence of financial incentives and other socio-economic factors on electric vehicle adoption. Energ. Policy **68**, 183–194 (2014)
22. Poullikkas, A.: Sustainable options for electric vehicle technologies. Renew. Sustain. Energy Rev. **41**, 1277–1287 (2015)
23. Salah, F., Ilg, J., Flath, C., Basse, H., Van Dinther, C.: Impact of electric vehicles on distribution substations: a Swiss case study. Appl. Energy **137**, 88–96 (2015)
24. Schliwa, G., Armitage, R., Aziz, S., Evans, J., Rhoades, J.: Sustainable city logistics - making cargo cycles viable for urban freight transport. Res. Transp. Bus. Manag. **15**, 50–57 (2015)
25. De Decker, K.: Cargo cyclist replace truck drivers on European city streets. http://www.lowtechmagazine.com/2012/09/jobs-of-the-future-cargo-cyclist.html. Accessed Feb 2016
26. Intergovernmental Panel on Climate Change: IPCC Third Asessment Report: Climate Change 2001 (2001)
27. GHG Protocol: Greenhouse Gas Protocol. http://www.ghgprotocol.org/about-ghgp. Accessed Feb 2016
28. Feng, W., Figliozzi, M.: Conventional vs electric commercial vehicle fleets: a case study of economic and technological factors affecting the competitiveness of electric commercial vehicles in the USA. Procedia Soc. Behav. Sci. **39**, 702–711 (2012)
29. Wilson, D., Papadopoulos, J., Whitt, F.R.: Bicycling Science. MIT Press, Cambridge (2004)
30. Saenz, J., Figliozzi, M., Faulin, J.: An assessment of the carbon footprint reductions of tricycle logistics services. Transportation Research Record (2016, forthcoming)
31. U.S. EPA: United States Environmental Protection Agency. http://www.epa.gov/. Accessed Feb 2016
32. U.S. EPA: eGRID Clean Energy. http://www.epa.gov/cleanenergy/energy-resources/egrid/. Accessed Feb 2016
33. US Environmental Protection Agency: How to use eGRID for Carbon Footprinting Electricity Purcharses in Greenhouse Gas emission inventories (2015). http://www.epa.gov/ttnchie1/conference/ei20/session3/adiem.pdf. Accessed Feb 2016
34. Environmental Protection Agency: Greenhouse Gas Emissios from a Typical Passenger Vehicle (2014). http://www.epa.gov/otaq/climate/documents/420f14040a.pdf. Accessed Feb 2016
35. Stevens, J.W., Corey, G.P.: A study of lead-acid battery efficiency near top-of-charge and the impact on PV system design. In: Conference Record of the Twenty Fifth IEEE Photovoltaic Specialists Conference, pp. 1485–1488 (1996)
36. Browne, M., Allen, J., Leonardi, J.: Evaluating the use of an urban consolidation center and electric vehicles in central London. IATSS Res. **35**, 1–6 (2011)

How to Incorporate Urban Complexity, Diversity and Intelligence into Smart Cities Initiatives

José-Miguel Fernández-Güell[✉], Silvia Guzmán-Araña, Marta Collado-Lara, and Victoria Fernández-Añez

Departamento de Urbanística y Ordenación del Territorio, Universidad Politécnica de Madrid,
Avenida Juan de Herrera 2, 28040 Madrid, Spain
`josemiguel.fernandez@upm.es`

Abstract. Under the term "Smart City", numerous technology-based initiatives are emerging to help cities face contemporary challenges while the concept itself is evolving towards a more holistic approach. Nevertheless, the capability of smart initiatives to provide an integrated vision of our cities is still very limited. Eventually, many of these initiatives fail to understand the complexity, diversity and intelligence that characterize contemporary cities. The purpose of this paper is to display an urban functional system, capable of interpreting the city in a more holistic way and of facilitating effective involvement of local stakeholders in the planning process of SCs initiatives.

Keywords: Smart City · Urban complexity · Urban diversity · Urban intelligence

1 Introduction

Besides the growing debate that Smart Cities (SC) initiatives are stirring up among their advocates and critics, the seemingly unapproachable complexity and intricate diversity of contemporary cities are hindering conceptual and technical progress in this kind of initiatives. Recent academic contributions recognize the need for developing more integrated and holistic approaches to SCs [1, 2]. In fact, the SC concept is evolving from the simple inclusion of technology in the city to the development of solutions to urban challenges in an interconnected and synergic manner; however, little real progress can be observed in this direction [3, 4].

Therefore, this paper proposes a novel approach that displays the systemic functioning of cities so that SC initiatives can be better assessed not only by technologists and urban planners, but also by a wide range of local stakeholders with no profound expertise in either technology or urban planning. In our view, the use of functional systems provides useful insights about how contemporary cities operate and evolve, and it facilitates the involvement of local stakeholders in the planning process of SCs.

© Springer International Publishing Switzerland 2016
E. Alba et al. (Eds.): Smart-CT 2016, LNCS 9704, pp. 85–94, 2016.
DOI: 10.1007/978-3-319-39595-1_9

2   Characteristics of Contemporary Cities

Complexity, diversity and intelligence are three key attributes that characterize most contemporary cities [5, 6]. A close look at those three characteristics may provide a clearer understanding of cities' nature to professionals not directly involved in city sciences.

The first common feature to all large and medium size cities is the high level of **complexity** of operational processes that take place within the city limits and on its hinterland. Indeed, it is widely accepted that cities are one of the greatest examples of complex systems because they generate an intricate and dynamic network of societal, economic, environmental and political relationships [7, 8]. That is why complexity has been a recurrent handicap for urban planners because it makes difficult urban analysis and policy making.

The second feature inherent to any big and medium size city is **diversity**. This important, but elusive feature is generated by the heterogeneity of local agents who intervene in the socioeconomic activities of a city [9, 10]. In brief, diversity is an important asset of cities as far as the different interests of urban stakeholders are harmonized in benefit of the whole community.

The third attribute of contemporary cities is **intelligence**. For some authors, urban intelligence means maximizing all the possible connections within the city to improve its operations [11], while for others, the term intelligent city is closely related to the concept of Smart City because it applies a wide range of technological devices [12]. In this paper, we understand the term intelligence as the capability of urban stakeholders to use effectively and efficiently new technologies for managing city operations and for making well informed policy decisions.

Confronted with these challenges, many cities have found in SCs initiatives a strategic option to pull out from present and future problems by heavily investing in technology-oriented solutions. Nevertheless, SCs are presently subject to a heated debate about its advantages and disadvantages. Advocates express the potential of SCs to solve urban challenges [13, 14], while there is growing group of critical voices who warn about their potential threats [12, 15, 16]. Despite their pros and cons, SCs could provide reasonable answers about how to approach urban complexity, diversity and intelligence.

3   How to Approach Urban Complexity

One way to deal with the complexity of contemporary urban territories is to conceptualize the city as an evolving functional ecosystem. Based on several contributions made in the field of systems theory [17–19], a general system may be defined as a large number of elements which interact among themselves and with the context in which they operate. More specifically, complex systems are characterized by being emergent since they have the ability to generate a new collective behavior through self-organization.

A city may be regarded as a complex ecosystem of connected elements or parts with common purposes, in which human activities, linked by communications, interact as the system evolves dynamically within a given socioeconomic and physical context [20, 21]. In other words, a city is built from multiple singular initiatives taken through time by a great number of players who are tightly interconnected among themselves. In this ecosystem, any spatial or structural alteration in one of its elements can modify the other parts of the system. Cities, understood as complex systems, are adaptive as they evolve and are not readily predictable because they do not necessarily act in a deterministic fashion.

Compared to other functional systems, cities have some distinctive features that should be taken into consideration [5, 22]. The change process in the city is not sequential (one thing directly affecting another), but rather simultaneous (many things happening at the same time). The city is a functional system with a heavy inertia, so there are limits to a city's ability to accelerate or slow down the pace of change. Cities are immersed in a space configured by infrastructures and natural features, all of which influences its functional dynamics. Finally, such a complex system is constantly reacting to external changes, so cities strive to adapt or dominate them, otherwise, they decline.

For the purpose of explaining the complex functioning of a contemporary city, a conceptual model has been developed recently [23] in which the urban ecosystem is synthesized and visualized as a set of different interrelated subsystems (see Fig. 1).

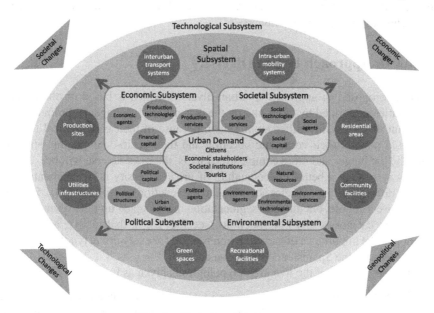

Fig. 1. City's functional system

First of all, urban demand (composed of citizens, economic agents, societal institutions and visitors) is placed in the center of the model. All of them pose a number of requirements on resources, services and infrastructures provided by the urban subsystems so that they can live and work in a city under good conditions. Secondly, acting as suppliers, the city's societal, economic, environmental and political subsystems strive to interpret and satisfy requirements from the different demand segments. Every subsystem is described by its resource capital, operating agents, services provided and technology used. Thirdly, those four subsystems request specific physical conditions to the spatial subsystem to operate properly. Thus, the spatial subsystem, regulated by urban planning, is responsible for providing basic infrastructures, transport systems and a wide range of community facilities and housing units. Fourthly, all the previous functional subsystems and demand segments are serviced by a technological subsystem made up of multiple platforms, which ideally should be of transversal nature, though they usually operate for a single sector. Finally, the overall urban system is subject to external change factors, such as demographic transformations, economic cycles, technological innovations or environmental impacts, which affect its functional balance. Indeed, in reality this flow does not happen in such a linear sequence since there are plenty of feedbacks among urban subsystems.

Though it can be perceived as reductionist, this systemic conceptualization of the city has a clear advantage: it displays a simplified, intelligible abstraction of the inherent complexity of our urban reality, which is easily understood by technicians, local stakeholders and citizens. It also analyzes the diverse relationships between urban components as well as it exposes the dominant or dependent positions of both stakeholders and functional subsystems. Thus, the systemic approach strives to reach a better understanding of the urbanization process as well as to establish a common ground for reconciling technologists and urban planners.

4   How to Approach Urban Diversity

This paper proposes an approach to urban diversity which is based on the different functionalities performed by cities and on the disparity of local agents. From the functional point of view, cities differ among them because of their geographical location, their spatial pattern, their economic vocation and their socio-demographic structure. Obviously, the bigger and more complex the city is, the most diverse will be.

One way to gain a better understanding of urban diversity is by segmenting and analyzing different city typologies according to the functions performed [24, 25]. In this paper, we use a simple, but didactic segmentation matrix made up of two sets of variables: ranking categories and key functions (see Fig. 2). In that matrix, a qualitative evaluation of the importance of each function is made for every urban typology that may be encountered in the Spanish and European context.

A brief description of the five urban typologies is given as follows:

- **Global City.** Its influence overpasses national borders. It is characterized by a high level of connectivity, strong technological capacity, wide offering of advanced and financial services, and relevant cultural projection. Multinational corporations are the major urban stakeholders. One of its main challenges is urban governance.
- **National Metropolis.** It extends its area of influence all over the national state and is strongly linked to other national capitals. They are usually strong decision and administrative centers just as well as important knowledge and transport centers. Some of them are also important industrial centers and tourism destinations. One of their main challenges is to reach a sustainable urban mobility.

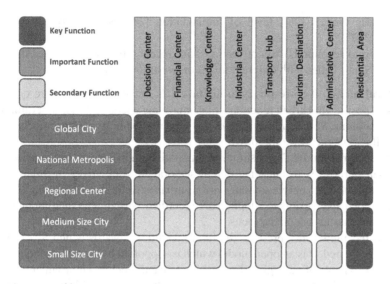

Fig. 2. Segmentation matrix of urban typologies

- **Regional Center.** Its influence is circumscribed to the regional scale and it serves as a link between national metropolis and intermediate cities. Regional centers tend to be a stronghold of administrative services and they also perform a wide array of urban functions. They are well connected at the national level.
- **Intermediate City.** It's a key element in structuring urban systems because they play the role of interlinking rural areas with large metropolis as well as balancing territorial development. Because of their limited size, most intermediate cities only specialize in few urban functions. Decisions are taken by local stakeholders.
- **Small City.** Its influence is usually limited to county borders. Small cities operate as transport centers at the sub-regional level and their economic base is dominated by primary sector activities. Though there are exceptions, in general terms small cities hardly have any specialized functions.

Obviously, this evaluation will vary from country to country, and from continent to continent, when taking into consideration climatic and socio-cultural differences. Nevertheless, this simple segmentation approach may provide plenty of clues for differentiating cities when planning and implementing Smart Cities initiatives. Moreover, intelligence could be considered as an additional transversal variable for further enrichment of the segmentation exercise.

5   How to Approach Urban Intelligence

Nowadays, Smart Cities are still a growing phenomenon which is conceptually ambiguous, so there are many "labels" or categories attempting to define the concept [26]. Some of this labels draw attention towards technological aspects [27], while others turn into business models [28], level of implantation [29], or maturity of operational processes [30].

Taking into account those contributions, in a recent article we discussed three basic models of Smart Cities with different levels of evolution [31]:

- **Sectoral model.** It corresponds to the first SCs initiatives which were oriented to satisfy specific vital urban functions, like improving energy efficiency or diminishing CO_2 emissions. Some authors refer to this model as ad-hoc projects or technological silos. It is governed by a top-down approach.
- **Multi-sectoral model.** It constitutes a qualitative improvement of the prior model. Its main purpose is to cluster different sectoral SCs initiatives in order to foster collaboration and synergies among various urban stakeholders. A common language is developed and barriers to adoption are identified. Sustainable funding models and governance issues become a focus.
- **Integrated model.** It represents the future direction towards which SCs initiatives should be geared. It is an open model which is supported by a citywide technological platform, capable of managing diverse city demands such as environmental sustainability, social inclusiveness, economic competitiveness and citizen participation. It is governed by a mix of top-down and bottom-up approach. In brief, this model constitutes an integrated system of systems and continuous improvements.

According to the integrated model of Smart Cities, urban intelligence is understood as a growing level of connection and integration of services to improve management and decision-making in urban contexts as well as an important tool to empower urban

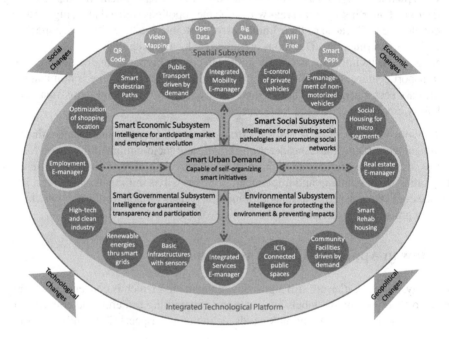

Fig. 3. Integrated model for Smart Cities initiatives

demand for getting involved in the development of their cities (see Fig. 3). Consequently, all smart devices will be integrated in a transversal platform which will provide smart services to all urban subsystems.

In this context, intelligence becomes a critical part of large and complex city subsystems, which deliver a wide range of products and services requested by a growing smart demand. Therefore, the degree of interoperability or connectivity among urban subsystems will be a key indicator of smart city maturity.

6 Implementing the Concepts into a Mass Tourism Destination

As stated before, not all contemporary cities are the same. This paper has opted for displaying just one city typology in order to show the potential of the proposed holistic approach. The selected typology has been a mass tourism destination analyzed in a previous foresight study [32]. Mass tourism destinations are well represented in Spain by cities such as Benidorm, Marbella or Salou.

If we were to plan a future mass tourism destination using the proposed systemic approach, a number of guidelines would be given as follows (see Fig. 4):

Urban Demand: It will be made up of visitors very heterogeneous, demanding and well-informed. City residents will be strongly involved in planning the destination.

Economic Subsystem: It will be driven by innovative tourist business models, adapted to the requests of incoming visitors. Tourism clusters will be developed including several destinations. Tourism services will improve their technological level. Local consumption behavior will be influenced by external demand patterns.

Social Subsystem: The social fabric of the city will be constantly threatened by the large volume of visitors. Destinations will have to manage seasonal immigration flows of low-skilled workers. Social services will have to be adapted to seasonal needs of visitors and workers.

Environmental Subsystem: Mass tourism destinations will have to enhance the value of natural and landscape ecosystems. Tourists' seasonality will be managed to minimize environmental impacts. Attention will be paid to prevent natural hazards.

Political Subsystem: Local governments will implement integrated strategic planning to guide their tourism model. Collaborative planning processes will be based upon citizens' consensus. Tourism demand will be assessed on real time.

Spatial Subsystem: There will be excellent transport connections with tourists' home markets. Within destinations, non-motorized transportation modes will be dominant. Destination's public spaces will be connected to external natural spaces. Tourism facilities will be widely diversified and highly specialized.

Technological Subsystem: Mass tourism destinations will become test-beds for urban technological innovations. New technologies will be tested and applied to urban infrastructures, tourist facilities, transport and public spaces. During holiday periods, tourists will be relaxed and willing to try and enjoy urban innovations.

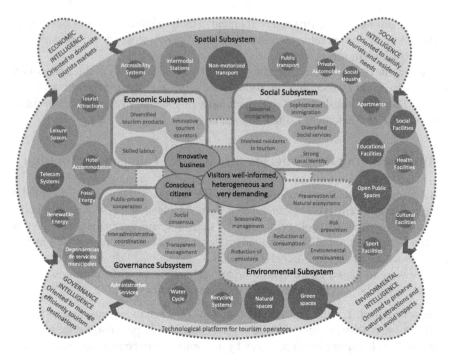

Fig. 4. Functional system of a future mass tourism destination

Some additional interpretations are needed to fully understand Fig. 4. First of all, urban demand is composed of various segments – citizens, business and visitors—with significant differences; however, they share a common interest, the development of the destination under strict sustainability criteria. Secondly, the economic, social, environmental and governance subsystems are well-linked among themselves so as to give timely and effective response to urban demand's requirements. Additionally, the environmental subsystem plays a key role. Thirdly, the spatial subsystem is made up of diverse elements, some of them displaying two concentric circles that show the changing seasonal demand for urban services. Fourthly, besides developing sectoral smart initiatives to solve ad-hoc needs, a citywide technological platform is needed to provide common intelligence to tourism operators, visitors and residents.

7   Conclusions

This paper has raised the issue of employing a systemic approach in the development of Smart City initiatives so as to deal with the attributes of complexity, diversity and intelligence, inherent to most contemporary cities.

A set of conclusions related to the systemic approach can be drawn from our paper. Understanding the city as a functional system will allow for an integrated and iconic representation of urban complexity which will be intelligible to most stakeholders. This approach will provide information about how particular subsystems deal with contextual issues and how they interact among themselves and develop over time. Increased knowledge about subsystems will improve their operational effectiveness by incorporating technology or other technical resources. Just as well, a systemic approach will facilitate the identification of urban stakeholders, their role and power relations within the community. Finally, under this approach, technology will appear in Smart Cities not like the dominant player, but as a set of tools that will improve malfunctions and will support, in an integrated fashion, the operations of the whole functional system in order to maximize efficiency.

In brief, the employment of a systemic approach will certainly reinforce urban analyses and will provide solid grounds for development strategies, especially when dealing with SCs initiatives. This approach will take into consideration the three key features of contemporary cities –complexity, diversity and intelligence—and will allow for the integration of the Smart City elements.

References

1. Perboli, G., De Marco, A., Perfetti, F., Marone, M.: A new taxonomy of smart city projects. Transp. Res. Procedia **3**, 470–478 (2014)
2. Chourabi, H., Nam, T., Walker, S., Gil-García, J., Mellouli, S., Nahon, K., Pardo, T.A., Scholl, H.: Understanding Smart Cities: an integrative framework. In: Proceedings of 45th Hawaii International International Conference on Systems Science, HICSS-45, 2012, Maui, 4–7 January 2012
3. Mattoni, B., Gugliermetti, F., Bisegna, F.: A multilevel method to assess and design the renovation and integration of Smart Cities. Sustain. Cities Soc. **15**, 105–119 (2015)
4. Lombardi, P., Giordano, S., Farouh, H., Yousef, W.: Modelling the smart city performance. Innov. Eur. J. Soc. Sci. Res. **25**(2), 137–149 (2012)
5. Fernández Güell, J.M.: Planificación estratégica de ciudades: nuevos instrumentos y procesos. Editorial Reverté, Barcelona (2006)
6. Camagni, R.: Incertidumbre, capital social y desarrollo local: enseñanzas para una gobernabilidad sostenible del territorio. Inv. Regionales **2**, 31–57 (2003)
7. Portugali, J., Meyer, H., Stolk, E., Tan, E.: Complexity Theories of Cities Have Come of Age: An Overview with Implications to Urban Planning and Design. Springer, New York (2012)
8. Allen, P.M.: Cities and regions as evolutionary complex systems. Geogr. Syst. **4**, 103–130 (1997)
9. Innes, J., Booher, D.: Consensus building and complex adaptive systems: a framework for evaluating collaborative planning. J. Am. Plan. Assoc. **65**(4), 412–423 (1999)
10. Jacobs, J.: The Death and Life of Great American Cities. Random House, New York (1961)
11. Borja, J.: Counterpoint: intelligent cities and innovative cities. Pap. E-J. Knowl. Soc. **5** (2007)
12. Hollands, R.: Will the real smart city stand up? Intelligent, progressive, or entrepreneurial? City **12**(3), 302–320 (2008)
13. Cisco: Smart + Connected Communities platform offers solutions in fields such as transportation, learning, safety and security, sports and entertainment, utilities, real estate, health and government (2013)
14. IBM: A Vision of Smarter Cities: How Cities Can Lead the Way into a Prosperous and Sustainable Future. IBM Institute for Business Value, New York (2009)
15. Greenfield, A.: Against the Smart City. Do Projects, New York (2013)

16. Townsend, A.: Smart Cities: Big Data, Civic Hackers and the Quest for New Utopia. W. W. Norton & Co., New York (2013)
17. Kauffman, S.: At Home in the Universe: The Search for the Laws of Self-organization and Complexity. Oxford University Press, New York (1995)
18. Forrester, J.W.: Urban Dynamics. MIT Press, Cambridge (1969)
19. Bertalanffy, L.: General Systems Theory: Foundations, Development and Applications. Braziller, New York (1968)
20. McLoughlin, J.B.: Urban and Regional Planning: A Systems Approach. Praeger, New York (1969)
21. Berry, B.J.: Cities as systems within systems of cities. Pap. Reg. Sci. **13**(1), 147–163 (1964)
22. Batty, M.: Cities and Complexity: Understanding Cities with Cellular Automata, Agent-Based Models, and Fractals. The MIT Press, Cambridge (2005)
23. Fernández Güell, J.M., Collado, M., Guzmán-Araña, S., Fernández-Añez, V.: Incorporating a systemic and foresight approach into smart city initiatives: the case of Spanish cities. J. Urban Technol. (2016, in press)
24. ESPON: ESPON Project 1.4.3 Study on Urban Functions. Final report. Luxembourg: ESPON, March 2007
25. Ministerio de Hacienda y Administraciones Públicas: Estudio sobre tipologías de ciudades españolas, sus necesidades y propuestas de intervención en el tramo de desarrollo urbano sostenible de la programación FEDER 2014–2020. Documento de discusión. Ministerio de Hacienda, Madrid (2014)
26. Caragliu, A., Del Bo, C., Nijkamp, P.: Smart Cities in Europe. J. Urban Technol. **18**(2), 65–82 (2011)
27. Anthopoulos, L.G., Vakali, A.: Urban planning and Smart Cities: interrelations and reciprocities. In: Álvarez, F. (ed.) FIA 2012. LNCS, vol. 7281, pp. 178–189. Springer, Heidelberg (2012)
28. Alcatel-Lucent: Getting smart about Smart Cities: Understanding the Market Opportunity in the Cities of Tomorrow (2012). http://www2.alcatel-lucent.com/knowledgecenter/public-files
29. European Parliament: Mapping Smart Cities in the EU. European Parliament, Directorate General for Internal Policies, Brussels (2014)
30. IDC Government Insights: Smart City Maturity Model Assessment and Action Path to Maturity. IDC (2013)
31. Fernández Güell, J.M.: Ciudades Inteligentes: La mitificación de las nuevas tecnologías como respuesta a los retos de las ciudades contemporáneas. Economía Industrial **395**, 17–28 (2015)
32. Fernández Güell, J.M., Collado, M.: Ciudades y ciudadanos en 2033: La transformación urbana de España. PricewaterhouseCoopers, Madrid (2014)

Mapping Smart Cities Situation +CITIES: The Spanish Case

Neus Baucells[1(✉)], Concepción Moreno[2], and Rosa M. Arce[1]

[1] Researcher at TRANSyT, Universidad Politécnica de Madrid, Madrid, Spain
{neus.baucells,rosa.arce.ruiz}@upm.es
[2] Researcher at Universidad Politécnica de Madrid, Madrid, Spain
morenoconcep@gmail.com

Abstract. Cities are currently undergoing a transformation into the Smart concept. The Smart concept emerged in the same way as Smartphones or Smart TVs. A number of initiatives are being developed in the framework of the Smart Cities projects; however, there is a lack of consistent indicators and methodologies for assessing, financing and prioritising these kind of initiatives. The main aim of the research is to develop an evaluation model for Spanish cities and show dynamically in a map the degree of Smart development and their territorial characteristics. The study was carried out in 62 cities of the Spanish Network of Smart Cities (RECI) in 2015. The map is a tool to overcome the deficiency of information and methodologies, easy-to-use to evaluate smart cities projects. Moreover, it is a way of manage knowledge and information advances about Smart City initiatives. The map offers a database query and dynamic display characterizing Spanish cities.

Keywords: Map · Tool · Evaluation · Progress · Indicator · Monitoring Center · Visualization · GIS · Query · Citizens · Smart · Cities

1 Introduction

The concentration of people, companies and institutions in cities promotes creativity, innovation, diversity and economic growth [12]. Moreover, the synergy between different sectors increases the economies of scale thus becoming a key in a country's sustainable development [3]. Although over 80 % of global GDP is generated in cities, nonetheless, cities also have the highest pollution levels worldwide [7, 8].

Urban development has brought about several imbalances in cities. Cities must embark on a process of transformation by developing strategies to meet the challenges of creeping urbanization, demographic change and the new demands caused by climate change and the depletion of natural resources. Having these challenges in mind, it is crucial to manage and plan the expansion of a city by supporting economic growth and competitiveness, as long as maintaining social cohesion and environmental sustainability [3, 4, 10]. This involves multiple actors, high levels of interdependence, and different fields of action, in addition to conflicting goals and social and political complexity; consequently a holistic and multidisciplinary approach is necessary [1, 9, 11].

Urban planning today is regarded as the integration of a plurality of interests and active public participation. Urban planning now takes a more participatory approach,

E. Alba et al. (Eds.): Smart-CT 2016, LNCS 9704, pp. 95–105, 2016.
DOI: 10.1007/978-3-319-39595-1_10

with new ways of representing data such as Geographic Information Systems (GIS) and new techniques for participation thanks to Information and Communications Technologies (ICT).

The concepts of Digital City or Connected City are closely linked to ICT in urban management and urban planning. A recently coined and related popular term is Smart City. The Smart City concept differs from the others by emphasizing environmental and social capital, and not only technology. It implies the use of ICT to provide sustainable economic development, tools for the judicious management of natural resources, and improvements to our quality of life, and offers an excellent opportunity to manage the urban future. ICT tools are essential for transforming traditional city into a Smart Cities [1, 13, 14, 16, 18].

Interest in Smart Cities has generated several theoretical discussions, but as yet insufficient progress has been made at implementing and evaluating related initiatives and projects. A Smart initiative must be evaluated through an integrated approach covering environmental, social and economic needs [2]. There are rankings of different city attributes such as quality of life and environment, and comparative studies between cities are emerging based on the Smart City concept [5, 11, 14, 15, 17, 19].

2 Objectives

There are numerous Smart City initiatives underway in the Spanish and European framework [6, 11, 14, 18]. However, indicators and standardized methodologies are required to evaluate, prioritize, implement and manage this type of projects. There is a lack of easy-to-use visual tools for interpreting vast amounts of information produced by these projects. The 2014 European report: "Mapping Smart Cities in the EU" clearly highlights the potential of mapping the situation of Smart Cities [14].

The +CITIES project is a research project coordinated by Rosa M. Arce from the *TRANSyT* (UPM) and funded by the Spanish Ministry of Economy and Competitiveness' State Plan for Scientific and Technical Research and Innovation *2013–2016*. This project goes one step further, by using maps as a dynamic tool to visualise the database and not only a way of representing data as static result. It solves the absence of visual tools and serves as a systematic evaluation method for assessing Smart City projects.

The +CITIES project is aimed at developing a comprehensive framework for assessing mobility and urban services projects to advance knowledge in this field and define methods for making informed decisions on smart investment strategies in a Smart Cities context. This system is of great interest to public and private bodies as a tool for prioritizing, developing and implementing strategies. Figure 1 shows the structure of the project development.

The project takes into account an expert opinion to complete the assignment. The vision of experts from a range of institutions and countries is essential to reinforce and validate the project. Consequently a survey was conducted involving experts in different fields related to cities.

The expected outcome of the +CITIES project is the improvement and development of more sustainable practices based on the application of ICT in transportation and urban services. This will lead to more effective management of energy consumption and improve mobility. It will also establish conditions to help business and economic activity in a context of maximum respect for the environment and a more efficient use of resources.

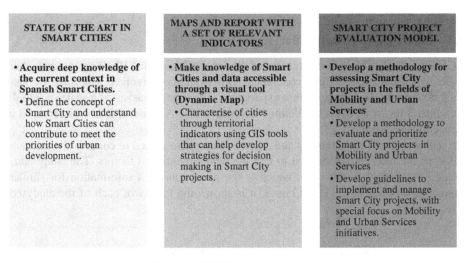

Fig. 1. +CITIES project structure

3 Methodology

A methodology for the evaluation of cities was developed according to the holistic concept of Smart Cities, and applied in 2015 to all cities in the Spanish Network of Intelligent Cities (RECI, www.reci.es). The aim was to contribute to the understanding of the processes of urban transformation designed to transform the conventional city into a Smart City (Fig. 2).

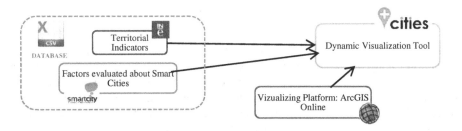

Fig. 2. General outline of the methodology

The purpose of this paper is to show the current information on Spanish Smart Cities on a dynamic platform. A query tool was developed by creating a dedicated database with a combined dataset, and merging it with a viewing platform. The data used for the tool are classified into two clusters: an assessment model for Smart City initiatives from a city inhabitant point of view found in a previous work [15]; and some territorial indicators such as demographic or economic data for the 62 cities from the RECI study.

3.1 Smart City Evaluation Factors

+CITIES analyse the current situation of the Smart Cities in the RECI up to September 2015, when the present study concluded. This evaluation involved assessing the factors, taking into account "citizen's experience" The rating consists of a scale of 0 to 4, in which a factor of over 2 is defined as Smart (SC). A score of 2 or less refers to a conventional city (C).

The website of city councils and other services were visited to compile the relevant information and services needed to rate the below mentioned factors. The study adds value to statistical information, which is the usual source of information for similar comparative studies [5, 11]. In Fig. 3, it is shown the factors of each of the analysed axes.

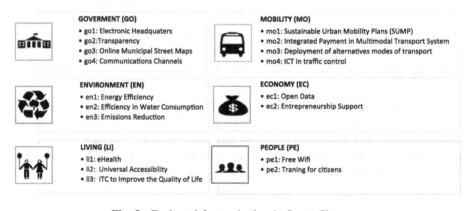

GOVERMENT (GO)
- go1: Electronic Headquaters
- go2:Transparency
- go3: Online Municipal Street Maps
- go4: Communications Channels

MOBILITY (MO)
- mo1: Sustainable Urban Mobility Plans (SUMP)
- mo2: Integrated Payment in Multimodal Transport System
- mo3: Deployment of alternatives modes of transport
- mo4: ICT in traffic control

ENVIRONMENT (EN)
- en1: Energy Efficiency
- en2: Efficiency in Water Consumption
- en3: Emissions Reduction

ECONOMY (EC)
- ec1: Open Data
- ec2: Entrepreneurship Support

LIVING (LI)
- li1: eHealth
- li2: Universal Accessibility
- li3: ITC to Improve the Quality of Life

PEOPLE (PE)
- pe1: Free Wifi
- pe2: Traning for citizens

Fig. 3. Evaluated factors in the six Smart City axes

A Smart degree of deployment is assigned for Governance, Mobility, Environment, Economy, Living and People issues for each city, which is the average value of the factors in each city axis. Finally, a development level was assigned to each Smart axis and the average of the six scores was calculated for the degree of Smart City development. The aim was to obtain an overview of how far the 62 cities tested have advanced in the process of transformation toward a Smart City.

The analysis involved an evaluation of 18 factors related to the six axes of a smart city: Government (Go), Mobility (Mo), Environment (En), Economy (Ec), Living (Li) and People (Pe) [11]. In Table 1 are included the factors and assessment criteria in the six pillars of the Smart City.

Table 1. Factors assessed in the six Smart City axes

Axis	Factors Evaluated		Smart City (SC) or Conventional City (C)
GOVERNANCE (GO)	(go1) Electronic Headquarters	SC: >2	With Electronic Headquarters
		C: =2	Electronic Headquarters in process and an easy-to-use source of information.
	(go2) Transparency	SC: >2	With a completed Transparency website
		C: =2	Transparency website in process or incomplete
	(go3) Online Municipal Street Maps	SC: >2	A Street map georeferenced with extra information for the citizen
		C: =2	Google maps or a basic map without extra information
	(go3) Communications Channels with the citizen	SC: >2	Municipal website, App with feedback
		C: =2	Traditional medias (email, telephone...)
MOBILITY (MO)	(mo1) Sustainable Mobility Urban Plans (SMUP)	SC: >2	With SMUP
		C: =2	Without SMUP
	(mo2) Payment Integrated in Multi-modal transport system	SC: >2	Smart Card, Smartphone
		C: =2	Impersonal ticket
	(mo3) Deployment of alternative modes	SC: >2	Integrated payment with Public Transport
		C: =2	Bicycle registration
	(mo4) ICT in traffic control	SC: >2	ITC integrated
		C: =2	Just basic control
ENVIRONMENT (EN)	(en1) Energy efficiency	SC: >2	With two or more initiatives to reduce energy consumption
		C: =2	With at least one initiative to reduce energy consumption
	(en2) Efficiency in water consumption	SC: >2	With two or more initiatives to reduce water consumption
		C: =2	With at least one initiative to reduce water consumption
	(en3) Monitoring and reducing atmospheric emissions	SC: >2	With two or more ICT initiatives to monitor emissions
		C: =2	With at least one plan to monitor emissions
ECONOMY (EC)	(ec1) Open Data	SC: >2	Open Data information in the website
		C: =2	No accessible Open Data
	(ec2) Entrepreneurship Support	SC: >2	An Action Center with innovative initiatives
		C: =2	Traditional information in a physical center (events, basic information to create a company...)
LIVING (LI)	(li1) eHealth	SC: >2	Telecare or telehealth with follow-up
		C: =2	Conventional health assistance and health tips in the website
	(li2) Accessibility	SC: >2	Measures with ICT technology: Accessible touristic route...
		C: =2	Conventional measures: Tactile Pavement
	(li3) ITC to Improve the Quality of Life	SC: >2	At least a municipal project with an ICT infrastructure
		C: =2	ICT application in some punctual municipal events
PEOPLE (PE)	(pe1) Free WiFi	SC: >2	WiFi in public space (parks, streets or squares) with the accessibility information in the website
		C: =2	Some WiFi points around the city, without information
	(pe2) Training	SC: >2	With training courses or initiatives about accessibility to Smart services and participative approach of the city
		C: =2	Without a training program offered in Smart Services

3.2   Territorial Indicators

The Territorial database indicators was classified into four groups (see Fig. 4). The information was extracted from several sources such as INE (National Statistics Institute), IGN (National Geographic Institute), local city council website, the LaCaixa yearbook, and the Ministry of Finance and Public Administration among others. The completed database using an extensive set of territorial indicators for the visualization tool was created and exported to a viewing platform.

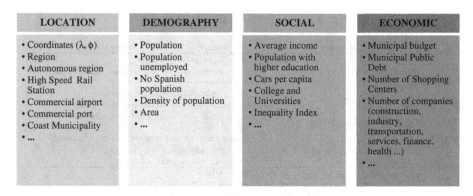

Fig. 4. Territorial indicators

3.3 Mapping Platform

A visualization tool was developed to represent and display the result, combining the RECI study database and the territorial indicators in a viewing platform. The platform used to visualize the results is ArcGIS Online by ESRI (*Environmental Systems Research Institute*), and is a complete, cloud-based mapping platform that makes and shares maps.

4 Results

The outcomes are presented as a set of graphics and 3 maps, which are the result of the tool. A sample of 62 Spanish cities with a population of over 50,000 inhabitants was analyzed. The sample represents 35 % of the Spanish population and 43 % of Spanish population living in municipalities with more than 50,000 inhabitants; it also includes all Spanish cities with more than half a million inhabitants.

Figure 5 shows, for each of the six axes, the percentage of cities in the Spanish Smart Cities Network with a Smart Factor classification above 2. The labels on each column indicate the number of cities classified as Smart. The six dash lines indicate the average mark of cities classified as Smart in each axis. A solid grey continues line shows the number of cities classified as Smart out of the total, the average of the six axes, and the percentage it represents.

It is worth pointing out the low presence of Smart Cities in Environmental (14 cities) and Economic (16 cities) aspects. In contrast, the best results are for the Mobility (71 %) and Living (77 %) axis.

If the results are analyzed in more detail, those obtained for the factors in each of the axes have wide differences between the several factors that can be observed. The worse valued factor is Training (18 %) and the best results are in eHealth (100 %).

From the 62 cities, 61 have at least one axis valued as *Smart* and the majority of RECI cities have at least three Smart axes (Fig. 6). The top-scoring cities with six axes Smart are Barcelona and Madrid (Table 2). The Top Ten rated cities in Smart Cities has a minimum of four Smart axes.

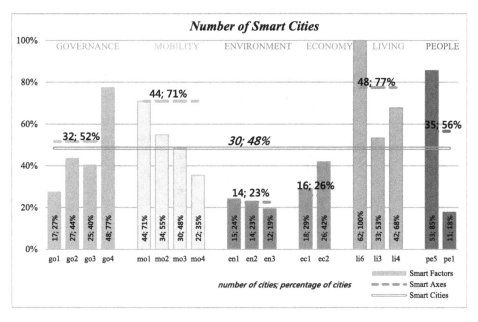

Fig. 5. Smart cities in each analysed factor

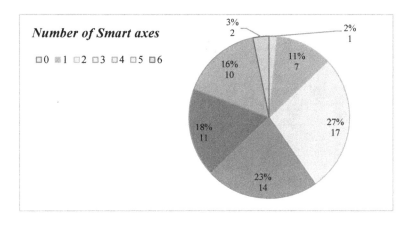

Fig. 6. Cities classification by the number of Smart axes

Figures 7, 8 and 9 are examples of the kind of data that can be represented on maps, such as the score for an evaluated factor–Transparency or Reduction of emissions in Fig. 7- or whether a city is classified as Smart in Mobility area (Fig. 8). In addition to the factors rated, the maps also show territorial factors such as the motorisation rate, population or the municipal budget per person in each city (Figs. 8 and 9).

Table 2. Top ten cities

Ranking Smart City	Municipality	Number of Smart axes	Population in 2014	Smart Score (0-4)
1	**Barcelona**	**6**	**1602386**	**3.29**
2	**Madrid**	**6**	**3165235**	**3.11**
3	Valencia	5	786424	2.68
4	Zaragoza	5	666058	2.67
5	A Coruña	5	244810	2.56
6	Sevilla	5	696676	2.55
7	Málaga	4	566913	2.54
8	Santander	5	175736	2.53
9	Gijón	4	275735	2.51
10	Pamplona	5	196166	2.47

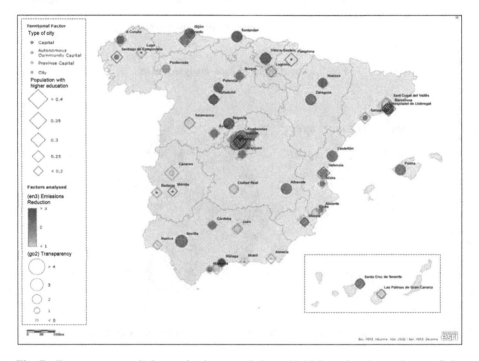

Fig. 7. Transparency, emissions reduction, population with higher education and type of city

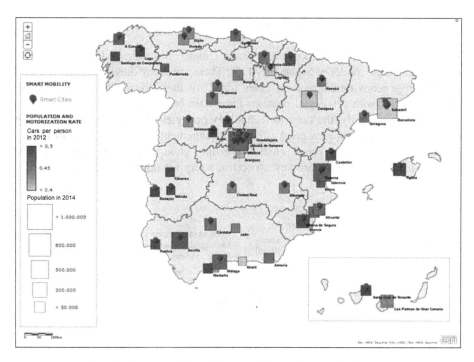

Fig. 8. Smart mobility cities, population and motorisation rate

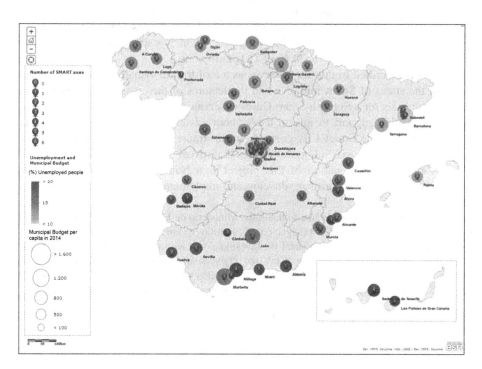

Fig. 9. Number of Smart axes, unemployed population and municipal budget

5   Discussion and Conclusions

The process towards what are known as Smart Cities is a reality, and, as can be seen, there is not a single model of Smart City [15]. There are many different kinds of smart cities: heterogeneous demographics, cities noted for their social or innovative commitment or cities with privileged contexts for certain businesses.

Cities evolve rapidly, the same as technology or society. The effect of cities on the lives of city dwellers requires good effective management of cities of each of the six axes described. Spanish smart cities have the good results for mobility and quality-of-life factors, which are key aspects in a city for inhabitants (Fig. 10).

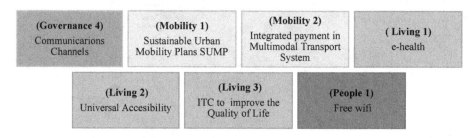

Fig. 10. Factors with a value higher than 2 in the 50 % of RECI cities

An example of Sustainable City due to the Smart City concept might be the Smart City Project in Málaga. This initiative was coordinated by Endesa "Smartcity Málaga" and has achieve an energy saving of more than 25 % in 5 years. This reduction means at the same time a decrease of 20 % of CO_2 emissions.

The map described in this study serves as a tool for the visualization and dynamic query of the status of Smart initiative and the features of the cities, and is intended to serve as the basis for a Spanish Smart Cities observatory. The purpose of this tool is to provide a graphic support to inform users about advances in the processes of urban transformation in the Smart City concept. In the future, this research should include more cities in the analysis and, more features that reveal their impact on the concept of Smart Cities. The culmination of this project is a National Monitoring Centre for Spanish Smart Cities to prioritize, develop and implement smart city strategies.

Acknowledgments. We would like to thank the Ministerio de Economía y Competitividad and the Secretaría de Estado de Investigación, Desarrollo e Innovación for funding the project + CITIES through the Plan Estatal de Investigación Científica, Técnica y de Innovación 2013-2016. We would also like to thank the Universidad Politécnica de Madrid for their encouragement and for promoting the Smart City philosophy in projects such as *Ciudad del Futuro* or *Campus del Futuro*. (www.upm.es/institucional/Investigadores/CiudadFuturo).

References

1. Abdoullaev, A.: A smart world: a development model for intelligent cities. In: The 11th IEEE International Conference on Computer and Information Technology, Paphos, Chipre (2011)
2. Abella, A.; Ruiz, J.L.: Medida del impacto dela Smart City: gestión de la experiencia ciudadana. Technical report, I Congreso de Ciudades Inteligentes, 24–25 marzo, Madrid, Spain (2015)
3. AMETIC. Smart Cities. 10 September 2015 (2012). http://ametic.es/es
4. ARUP: Smart Cities: Transforming the 21st century city via the creative use of technology (2010)
5. Berrone, P., Ricart, J.E.: Cities in Motion- Indice 2014. Centro de Globalización y Estrategia, IESE (2015)
6. Caragliu, A., Del Bo, C., Nijkamp, P.: Smart Cities in Europe. In: Proceedings of 3rd Central (2009)
7. Dobbs, R., Janna, R., Sven, S., James, M., Roxburgh, C., Restrepo, A.: Urban world: mapping the economic power of cities. J. Monetary Econ. **26**, 49 (2011)
8. European Commission: Smart Cities and Communities (2015). http://ec.europa.eu/eip/smartcities/. Accessed 28 Sept 2015
9. Fernández Güell, J.M., Collado Lara, M.: Ciudades y ciudadanos en 2033. La transformación urbana de España. Colección España 2033, Price Waterhouse Coopers (2014)
10. Fernández Güell, J.M.: Ciudades inteligentes: la mitificación de las nuevas tecnologías como respuesta a los retos de las ciudades contemporáneas. Economía Industrial. Ministerio de Industria Energía y Turismo 395, pp. 17–25 (2015)
11. Giffinger, R., Fertner, C., Kramar, H., Pichler-milanovic, N., Meijers, E.: Smart cities ranking of European medium-sized cities. Centre of Regional Science, Universidad Tecnológica de Viena (2007)
12. Harrison, C., Donnelly, I.A.: A theory of Smart Cities. In: Proceedings of the 55th Annual Meeting of the ISSS (2011)
13. Holzer, M., KIM, S.T.: Digital governance in municipalities worldwide. The Egovernance Institute. The National Center for Public Productivity of the State University of New Jersey-Newark and The Global e-Policy e-Governement Institute of Sungkyunkman University (2006)
14. Manville, C., Cochrane, G., Cave, J., Millard, J., Pederson, J., Thaarup, R., Liebe, A., Wissner, W.M., Massink, W.R., Kotterink, B.: Mapping Smart Cities in the EU, Department of Economic and Scientific Policy (2014)
15. Moreno Alonso, C.: Desarrollo de un modelo de evaluación de ciudades basado en el concepto de Ciudad Inteligente (Smart City). Ph.D. thesis, UPM, Madrid (2016)
16. Muñoz López, L., Antón Martínez, P., Fernández Ciez, S.: Estudio y Guía metodológica sobre ciudades Inteligentes. J. Deloitte, 13–30, November 2015
17. Neirotti, P.: Current trends in Smart City initiatives: some stylised facts (2012)
18. ONTSI, Observatorio Nacional de las Telecomunicaciones y de la Sociedad de la Información. Ministerio de Industria, Energía y Turismo.: Estudio y Guía Metodológica sobre Ciudades Inteligentes (2015)
19. Price Waterhouse Cooper: Cities of Opportunity 6 (2014)

Mixed Integer Linear Programming Formulation for the Taxi Sharing Problem

Houssem E. Ben-Smida[1], Saoussen Krichen[1], Francisco Chicano[2(✉)], and Enrique Alba[2]

[1] LARODEC, University of Tunisia, Tunis, Tunisia
he.bensmida@gmail.com, krichen_s@yahoo.fr
[2] Dept. de Lenguajes y Ciencias de la Computación,
University of Málaga, Málaga, Spain
{chicano,eat}@lcc.uma.es

Abstract. Given a group of people traveling from the same origin to multiple destinations, the Taxi Sharing Problem consists in assigning taxis to each person such that the total cost spent by the group of people is minimized. This problem arises in the context of Smart Mobility, where the resources of a city must be optimized to save costs and pollution while the mobility services are improved for the citizens. We propose a mixed integer linear programming formulation as an accurate way to solve the problem of taxi sharing. We empirically analyze our formulation solving different real-like instances of the problem with 9 to 69 people.

Keywords: Taxi Sharing Problem · Mixed Integer Linear Programming · Smart Mobility · Smart City

1 Introduction

The concept of *Smart City* implies the use of information and communication technology to improve the quality and performance of urban services in order to reduce costs, increase efficiency in the use of resources and allow the participation of more active citizens [4]. Transportation systems have a central role in a city. When applied to Transportation Systems, the use of information and communication technology leads to the concept of *Smart Mobility*. In this context, shared trips (known under the term *carpooling*) raised great interest among the public in recent years. Sharing vehicles with people on their way to nearby destinations generates benefits both economically and ecologically, at the individual and at the collective level [8].

This research was partially funded by the University of Málaga, Andalucía Tech, and the Spanish Ministry of Economy and Competitiveness and FEDER under grant TIN2014-57341-R. The authors are indebted with Renzo Massobrio, Gabriel Fagúndez and Sergio Nesmachnow for providing the datasets used in the experimentation.

E. Alba et al. (Eds.): Smart-CT 2016, LNCS 9704, pp. 106–117, 2016.
DOI: 10.1007/978-3-319-39595-1_11

The benefits of shared trips have resulted in various initiatives to address the public interest. Some examples are the exclusive lanes for shared trips present in many cities [9], campaigns to share the trips to and from the workplace [5], and a variety of online applications developed to find traveling companions. Some examples are BlaBlaClar[1] and Carma[2]. Taxis are a quick and reliable mean of transportation, especially in those cities where the public transportation system is very inefficient. However, taxis rarely travel with full capacity, thus its impact on traffic congestion and pollution in cities is usually important. Furthermore, fare rates can reach considerable values, which generally discourage the use of this model of transportation for the general public.

Currently there are some applications to find people to share a taxi, e.g., Carpling[3] and Sharetransport[4]. However, the majority of applications merely display the place where users can manually look for the shared trip. In the best case, they use very simple algorithms to propose traveling companions based on proximity, origin and destination. Using these algorithms we cannot certify that the minimum cost solution is taken. We are interested in this paper in finding optimal solutions to the taxi-sharing problem and compare them with solutions obtained using metaheuristic algorithms, in particular, Genetic Algorithms [6].

The organization of the rest of the paper is as follows. Section 2 presents the Taxi Sharing Problem and Sect. 3 proposes a Mixed Integer Linear Programming formulation to solve it using MILP solvers. The results of a preliminary experimental study are presented in Sect. 4. Section 5 presents the most important related work, and Sect. 6 concludes the paper.

2   Taxi Sharing Problem

Let us imagine that a group of people in the same place decides to travel to different destinations using taxis. The *Taxi Sharing Problem* is a combinatorial optimization problem which consists in determining the appropriate number of taxis, the assignment of people to taxis and the order in which the taxis must drop the people off, in order to minimize the total monetary cost of the group of people. Each taxi can be shared by a maximum number of people, depending on the capacity of the taxi (usually four people).

The cost of each trip depends on the distances traveled by each taxi and the specific fares of the city where each instance of the problem is defined. We also consider a minimum constant fare that does not depend on the distance traveled. In this version of the problem, we do not consider other possible costs related to events, special origins or destinations, or extra charges for luggage. However, the costs due to special origins or destinations could be easily included in our formulation without changing it. The costs associated with travel time are not covered (this would be equivalent to consider traffic flow scenarios). The problem, as it is defined here, was proposed in [18].

---

[1] https://www.blablacar.es.

[2] https://carmacarpool.com.

[3] https://www.carpling.com/info/taxi.

[4] http://www.sharetransport.sg.

In the following we will present the mathematical formulation of the problem. Let $P = \{p_1, p_2, ..., p_n\}$ be a set of n passengers that are in the same location d_0. Let us denote with d_i the location where passenger p_i wants to go. Let us assume that the maximum capacity of the available taxis is k (usually 4 people) and let us denote with b the minimum fare to pay in each trip regardless the distance traveled. The cost to travel from point d_i to d_j will be given by the matrix element c_{ij} of a cost matrix.

A solution to the problem is a set of m sequences of locations $\{s_1, s_2, \ldots, s_m\}$ such that every destination d_i with $i \geq 1$ appears exactly in one sequence (and no more than one), and the origin d_0 is the first location in all the sequences. Each sequence of locations represents a taxi ride, where the destinations in the sequence are visited in the order they appear. The length of each sequence s_l will be $k + 1$ at most, since k is the maximum capacity of the taxis and d_0 is the first location in all the sequences. The total cost of a solution is given by:

$$cost(\{s_1, s_2, \ldots, s_m\}) = \sum_{l=1}^{m} \left(b + \sum_{(d_i, d_j) \in s_l} c_{ij} \right), \tag{1}$$

where we use $(d_i, d_j) \in s_l$ to iterate over all the pairs of destinations that are adjacent in the sequence s_l.

The objective of the problem is to find a solution that minimizes the cost function defined in (1). This formulation does not provide a mechanism to distribute the cost associated with travel passengers who share a taxi and it is assumed that the decision is delegated to users. Some ideas to do this distribution of costs can be found in [18].

This formulation of the Taxi Sharing problem is NP-hard. We can prove this by transforming the Hamiltonian Path Problem into Taxi Sharing. The version of the Hamiltonian Path Problem we need is one in which the starting vertex $v \in V$ is given. Formally, this variant of the Hamiltonian Path Problem consists in finding a Hamiltonian path (visiting all the nodes exactly once) in a graph $G(V, E)$ starting in the vertex v. This variant is NP-hard, since we can use the same transformation from Vertex Cover to the Hamiltonian Path Problem provided in [10].

The transformation from Hamiltonian Path to Taxi Sharing is as follows. Given the graph $G = (V, E)$ where the Hamiltonian Path has to be found, we build a complete graph $G' = (V', E')$ where all the nodes in G are also in G': $V' = V$. The starting vertex $v \in V$ is d_0 in Taxi Sharing, the location where the passengers are picked up. G' is a complete graph, thus, $E' = V' \times V'$ and the weight of an edge $e \in E'$ is 1 if the edge is also in E and 2 if it is not in E. Finally, the minimum fare is the sum of all the weights in the complete graph and the capacity of the taxis is the same as the number of vertices in the graph minus one. These last requirements ensures that the optimal solution will have only one taxi. If the cost of the optimal solution is the minimum fare plus the number of vertices minus one, there is a Hamiltonian Path starting at vertex $v \in V$. Otherwise, no such path exists.

3   Mixed Integer Linear Programming Formulation

The Taxi Sharing Problem presented in the previous section can be transformed into a Capacitated Vehicle Routing Problem instance where the number of vehicles is unknown. This served as a motivation to adapt existing Vehicle Routing MILP formulations to solve Taxi Sharing. In particular, we base our formulation in that of Kulkarni [15]. Although this formulation has an error in it [1], it does not affect the Taxi Sharing problem presented here, since the error is related to the limit in the travel distance, which does not apply in Taxi Sharing.

In the CVRP the goal is to minimize the cost to serve a set of customers with goods stored in a depot. There is a fleet of vehicles that can serve the customers. Each vehicle has a maximum capacity that cannot be exceeded. All the vehicles have the same starting location, the depot, and they transport the goods to different destinations in order to satisfy the needs of customers. Each customer must be visited only once by one vehicle.

There is a similarity between CVRP and Taxi Sharing if we relate the customers with the passengers and the depot with the origin of all the passengers. The vehicles are the taxis and the maximum capacity is the number of people each taxi can take. The main differences are: (1) the taxis do not have to go back to the depot (as in CVRP), (2) there is a minimum fare that is not related to the distance traveled and, (3) there can be several passengers that want to go to the same location. We can transform a Taxi Sharing instance into a CVRP instance if we find a way to deal with these three differences.

In order to model the fact that taxis do not need to go back to the depot, we can do the cost of return equals zero. This way, although the solutions will be composed of closed paths, there is no cost related to the final segment (that goes back to the origin). The minimum fare can be added to the cost of the first segment of any path. In particular, it can be added to all the edges that leave the origin. Finally, all the passenger destinations can be considered as different. If some of them are the same in a particular instance of the problem, we add a zero cost edge between them. With these considerations, we can adapt the MILP formulation of CVRP to Taxi Sharing.

We assume c_{0i} is the cost from the origin to the location plus the minimum fare that the customers have to pay to the taxi. The values c_{i0} will be 0 as explained above. The Mixed Integer Linear Program formulation of the Taxi Sharing problem is:

$$\min \sum_{i=0}^{n} \sum_{j=0}^{n} c_{ij} x_{ij}, \tag{2}$$

subject to:

$$\sum_{i=0}^{n} x_{ij} = 1 \quad \text{for } 1 \leq j \leq n, \tag{3}$$

$$\sum_{j=0}^{n} x_{ij} = 1 \quad \text{for } 1 \leq i \leq n, \tag{4}$$

$$y_i - y_j + nx_{ij} \leq n - 1 \qquad \text{for } 1 \leq i \neq j \leq n, \tag{5}$$

$$u_i - u_j + kx_{ij} \leq k - 1 \qquad \text{for } 1 \leq i \neq j \leq n, \tag{6}$$

$$x_{ij} = 0 \text{ or } 1 \qquad \text{for } 0 \leq i \neq j \leq n, \tag{7}$$

$$u_i, y_i \in \mathbb{R} \qquad \text{for } 1 \leq i \leq n. \tag{8}$$

Constraints (3) and (4) ensure that each location is visited only once. Constraint (5) is designed to ensure that no subtours are formed and, thus, ensuring that all routes must visit the origin. The y_i variables are introduced to avoid subtours. They assign a value to each node where all the nodes in a tour have always increasing values. If $x_{ij} = 1$, that is, if node j is visited after node i, then $y_j \geq y_i + 1$. This way, subtours cannot exist unless they pass through the depot where the corresponding constraint is not applied. Constraint (6) ensures that the taxi capacity is not exceeded. The u_i variables follow the same idea as the y_i ones, but using the capacity instead of the length of the tour. If $x_{ij} = 1$, then $u_j \geq u_i + 1$. This way, the u_i are increasing in a tour, and the difference between the minimum and the maximum value of u_i in a tour can never exceed k, which means that no more than k destinations are visited. Constraints (7) and (8) define the domains of the variables.

4   Experimental Results

In this section, we show the results of a preliminary experimental study in which we compare the performance of CPLEX solving the MILP formulation presented in Sect. 3 with the parallel micro evolutionary algorithm (pμEA) proposed by Massobrio et al. [18]. Our approach provides an optimal solution, since we use a Mixed Integer Linear Programming solver to solve the problem, while (pμEA) is a metaheuristic algorithm that provides suboptimal solutions. Thus, it is clear that our approach will provide better quality solutions to the problem. The research questions we want to answer with this first experimental study are:

- RQ1: How much cost is it saved by using the MILP approach?
- RQ2: How long does it take to find the optimal solution using the MILP formulation?
- RQ3: When is it better to use a MILP solver instead of pμEA to solve the problem?

In order to answer these questions, we will run the MILP solver using a set of 24 instances and we will compare the cost of the obtained solutions and time required to solve the instances with that of pμEA.

4.1   Instances

In order to evaluate our approach and compare it with pμEA, we use the same set of real-like instances used in [18]. These instance were provided by the authors of [18], but they were originally generated with the help of Taxi Query Generator (TQG). This tool uses information from basic taxi trajectories obtained using

GPS devices installed in one week to 10,357 taxis in the city of Beijing, China. The data used to generate the instances are a subset of those used by Ma et al. [17].

TQG produces a list of origins and destinations for individual trips. To adapt those data to this problem, Massobrio et al. grouped the destinations having the same origin. They built instances with different sizes: *small*, with 10 to 25 passengers, *medium*, with 25 to 40 passengers, *large* with 40 to 55 passengers, and *very large*, with 55 to 70 passengers. This way, they created a benchmark of 24 realistic instances of the Taxi Sharing Problem.

4.2 Algorithms

In order to solve the Taxi Sharing Problem using the MILP formulation described in Sect. 3, we use IBM Ilog CPLEX 12.6.2 for Windows. The experiments were performed in a machine with Intel Core i5-4210U processor at 1.7 GHz, 8 GB of RAM, and Windows 10 operating system. Regarding the parallel micro evolutionary algorithm, several configurations of the algorithms were tested in [18]. For the comparison we use the configuration that reported the best results in [18]. This configuration uses 24 subpopulations (and CPU cores) with 15 solutions each, and a greedy initialization strategy. These experiments were run in the FING cluster with Dell Power Edge servers assembled with Quad-core Xeon E5430 processors at 2.66 GHz, 8 GB of RAM and Gigabit Ethernet.

4.3 Results

Tables 1, 2, 3 and 4 show the solution quality (cost) and the runtime required by our approach and pμEA to solve the 24 real-like instances of the Taxi Sharing Problem. In the case of pμEA, we report the average and the standard deviation of the cost in 20 independent runs of the algorithm.

We can observe in all the cases that the cost obtained by the MILP solver is significantly lower than the cost obtained by pμEA. We knew that the cost should be lower, since the MILP finds the optimal solution (except for small floating point errors). However, the results of the experiments show that the difference between the cost obtained with pμEA and the MILP solver is large enough to justify the MILP approach. There is an important benefit. In some cases, the MILP solver reaches almost half of the cost of the pμEA solution

Table 1. Comparison between the MILP solver and pμEA with 24 subpopulations and greedy initialization strategy for the small instances of the Taxi Sharing Problem. For pμEA, the average cost and standard deviation of 20 independent runs is reported.

Passengers		9	12	17	21	23	24
pμEA	Cost	125.5 ± 0.0	168.8 ± 0.0	191.2 ± 0.5	215.6 ± 0.1	298.4 ± 0.3	252.2 ± 2.4
	Time (s)	0.0	0.0	0.0	0.0	0.3	2.1
MILP	Cost	86.5	126.8	124.1	137.5	162.4	157.2
	Time (s)	0.1	0.1	0.1	0.1	0.2	0.2

Table 2. Comparison between the MILP solver and pμEA with 24 subpopulations and greedy initialization strategy for the medium instances of the Taxi Sharing Problem. For pμEA, the average cost and standard deviation of 20 independent runs is reported.

Passengers		26	27	33	33	37	39
pμEA	Cost	344.5 ± 5.6	323.1 ± 3.4	801.2 ± 4.2	357.4 ± 3.4	443.7 ± 3.8	367.0 ± 5.0
	Time (s)	5.6	3.6	4.2	3.4	3.8	6.1
MILP	Cost	245.0	212.3	486.2	233.7	301.5	274.2
	Time (s)	1.0	1.2	2.1	3.2	5.1	6.1

Table 3. Comparison between the MILP solver and pμEA with 24 subpopulations and greedy initialization strategy for the large instances of the Taxi Sharing Problem. For pμEA, the average cost and standard deviation of 20 independent runs is reported.

Passengers		42	44	44	46	53	54
pμEA	Cost	429.9 ± 7.1	319.8 ± 7.5	425.0 ± 4.3	367.7 ± 3.2	446.3 ± 2.6	562.1 ± 4.3
	Time (s)	3.7	7.5	4.3	3.3	4.8	4.3
MILP	Cost	312.7	189.0	287.6	244.5	301.9	376.1
	Time (s)	7.2	7.8	12.1	15.3	19.0	45.0

Table 4. Comparison between the MILP solver and pμEA with 24 subpopulations and greedy initialization strategy for the very large instances of the Taxi Sharing Problem. For pμEA, the average cost and standard deviation of 20 independent runs is reported.

Passengers		57	57	59	62	66	69
pμEA	Cost	637.7 ± 3.6	524.8 ± 4.5	498.4 ± 3.5	744.9 ± 6.1	560.6 ± 4.7	1424.6 ± 6.1
	Time (s)	3.6	7.7	3.5	8.0	4.7	6.1
MILP	Cost	462.4	327.5	332.0	503.2	398.4	N/A
	Time (s)	4927.0	6180.0	7353.0	69487.0	> 64000	> 64000

(see solution with $n = 23$ in Table 1). This observation is generalized, and it does not seem to change with the number of passengers of the instances.

Regarding the execution time of the MILP solver and pμEA, we have to be careful with the conclusions, since both algorithms are run in different machines, with different cores. Although an accurate comparison is not possible here, we can take some conclusions just seeing the order of magnitude of the runtime.

As we could expect both approaches require, in general, more time as the number of passengers grows. In the case of small and medium size instances, the MILP solver and pμEA require a few seconds (or fractions of seconds) to solve the instances. We can observe that the time in this case is in the same order of magnitude. The same is true for some of the large instances. However, in large and very large instances, the time required by the MILP solver grows up to impractical values. The execution time of pμEA in these instances is negligible compared to the one of the MILP solver.

4.4 Answering the Research Questions

We are now able to answer the three research questions. We can answer RQ1 on comparing the cost of the solutions obtained by pμEA and the MILP solver. We can observe that the difference in the cost is in all the cases significant in favor of the MILP solver. Regarding RQ2, the MILP solver takes a few seconds to solve small and medium instances, but requires from minutes to hours to solve large and very large instances.

Finally, RQ3 requires an analysis of the benefits and drawbacks of pμEA and the MILP solver. Considering the results of Sect. 4.3, we can conclude that the MILP solver is clearly the best option to solve small and medium instances. It obtains optimal solutions, with a significant quality improvement compared to the pμEA solutions, and in the same time. In the case of large instances, the MILP solver can still be useful in a real scenario, since the time required to exactly solve the instances is less than one minute, which is a reasonable time if we take into account the significant cost saving. Finally, for very large instances, the MILP solver requires too much time (hours of computation) while the pμEA only needs a few seconds. In this case, pμEA is the best option to solve the problem.

5 Related Work

The problem of taxi-sharing has several points in common with the problem of sharing a car (Car Pooling Problem, CPP). Hartman et al. [11] study the CPP as a graph theory problem, distinguishing two scenarios. In the first one, the set of drivers are known in advance. This scenario is equivalent to the assignment problem in bipartite graphs, for which there are polynomial time algorithms [12]. In large instances of the problem, however, the runtime of exact algorithms becomes prohibitive. For this reason, they propose a greedy algorithm to solve the problem. The solution obtained by the greedy algorithm attains an average of 96 % compared to the optimal solution. In the second scenario, there is no knowledge on who will act as driver or passenger. This variant of CPP is NP-hard, as it was proven in [14]. To solve it, two greedy algorithms are proposed and evaluated using data generated from simulations of movement in the region of Flanders, Belgium.

Yan and Chen [20] presented a formulation of a variant of CPP that uses information from past solutions: CPP with pre-matching information or CPPPMI. The information used in the CPPPMI includes the assignment of passengers to vehicles, selected routes and schedules for each car in previous assignments. The integration of previous data increases the stability in the allocation of passengers to vehicles over time, avoiding frequent changes of passengers. The problem is modeled as a special case of Multi-commodity Network Flow Problem, which is NP-hard [7]. The experimental evaluation was performed on a set of 30 test instances (between 600 and 1400 passengers), generated from information of the traffic in the city of Taiwan and setting preferences of each passenger randomly. The results show that the proposed algorithm converges to less than 3 % away from the optimal solution in all test instances.

A problem closely related to the CPP is known as Dial-a-Ride problem (DARP), where the main difference with the CPP is that the owners of the vehicles are not part of the group of passengers who wish to share the trip. Cordeau and Laporte [3] solve the static DARP for a set of vehicles that leave from the same deposit and must care orders from a customer group. In the variant studied, the goal it to minimize the operational cost of all vehicles, subject to the desired time windows for each passenger to leave his origin and reach his destination. A bound for the maximum time that a passenger can stay within a vehicle is given and considered a hard constraint. The problem is modeled through a graph and is solved using Tabu Search. The experimental evaluation was performed on a set of 20 test instances (between 24 and 144 orders) randomly generated using realistic information about the city of Montreal, Canada. They also used six real cases corresponding to a transport company services in Denmark. The results show that the implemented algorithm is able to find solutions less than 1.5 % of the optimal solution, in a runtime which varies (depending on the instance) between 2 and 90 min.

Chevrier et al. [2] presented a multi-objective formulation of DARP, which seeks to minimize the number of vehicles used, the travel duration and delays perceived by passengers. This problem is related to the multi-objective variant of the taxis ride sharing, which seeks to minimize the total cost of the group of passengers and perceived delay by each one. An experimental evaluation is performed which seeks to compare both computational performance and the quality of the solutions reached for each of the three Multi-Objective Evolutionary Algorithms implemented. The results of a set of 30 test instances between 100 and 1000 passengers randomly generated, suggest that the algorithm IBEA [21] is able to achieve better solutions than its two competitors, in less execution time.

Several studies have addressed the problem of taxis ride sharing, or Taxi Pooling Problem, from the point of view of both the taxi company that seeks to optimize its operating costs, and the passengers, who are looking to save by sharing their trips with other passengers.

Hosni et al. [13] propose a centralized system to receive customer orders and assign them to a set of taxis. The system comprises two mobile applications (one for passengers and another for taxi drivers) and a central server running the planning algorithm. The planning algorithm implemented oversimplifies the problem defining a predetermined region for each Taxi. It only assigns a taxi orders from the its region, reducing the search space. To solve the problem, an integer programming algorithm which considers the demand of taxis, preferences of drivers and customer orders is used. The experimental evaluation is realized through a single simulation using the open source traffic simulator SUMO (Simulation of Urban Mobility). The results show that the proposed model leads to a fair distribution of income among drivers and that the execution time of the algorithm can be integrated into an online application.

Lin et al. [16] studied the route optimization for taxis sharing, considering the interests for both drivers and passengers. The problem to solve is to minimize the operational cost of the vehicles (so to increase profits of drivers) and maximize passenger satisfaction (measured by travel time and waiting time). The problem is reduced to a single-objective formulation, having different weights for each objective that seeks to optimize. A simulated annealing algorithm is proposed to solve the problem after performing a preprocessing in order to reduce the search space, eliminating unfeasible solutions due to restrictions on time windows for each order. The experimental evaluation is performed on a screenplay with 9 geographical points acting as both sources and destinations in a total of 29 orders.

Ma et al. [17] studied TPP in their dynamic variant, which seeks to plan the orders of users in real time, as they are being generated. Given a fixed set of taxis and a flow of user requests, the problem is to define the taxi which serves each order, seeking to minimize the additional distance that should be traveled to address this new order. The proposed strategy is greedy, in the sense of seeking to minimize the additional distance traveled as arising each new order, which does not guarantee the minimization of the total distance traveled by all taxis in the overall planning. The experimental evaluation was performed using data taxis in the city of Beijing, China, composed by GPS trace over 33,000 taxis, collected over a period of 87 days. The results on a stage with 6 orders by taxi, show that the proposed algorithm can attend more than 25 % of orders thanks to the use of carpools, achieving the minimization of 13 % the distance traveled by all taxis.

Tao and Chen [19] presented two greedy heuristics to solve the TPP in its variant of a common origin to many destinations and in the reverse variant from many sources to the same destination. The algorithm groups the passengers according to the time windows of each one and considering the preferences indicated by each one about his travel companions. Each passenger can set the maximum number of people that he wants to share the trip, and if he agrees to share with a male or female. The algorithm forms groups of passengers assigned to each taxi, considering a fixed maximum capacity of four passengers per taxi. The experimental evaluation was performed through a real application of the algorithm in a system of shared taxi rides in the city of Taipei, Taiwan, made up of 10 taxis and 798 passengers. The reported results show a saving in the distance traveled thanks to sharing trips.

6   Conclusion

In this work we present a Mixed Integer Linear Programming formulation to solve the Taxi Sharing Problem. The experimental results show that for instances with 9 to 54 passengers, the MILP solver can find the optimal solution to the problem in a reasonable time (less than 1 min in all the cases). However, for very large instances the time required to find the optimal solutions is not reasonable (several hours). The parallel micro evolutionary algorithms previously proposed for this problem in the literature, is able to solve the problem in a few seconds regardless the size of the instance, but it only obtains far from optimal solutions.

The problem formulation of Taxi Sharing used here is very simple. A future line of research for this problem would be the consideration of traffic data in real time. It is also possible to enrich the formulation with real-world details, like different capacities of the taxis, or time constraints of the passengers.

References

1. Achuthan, N.R., Caccetta, L.: Integer linear programming formulation for a vehicle routing problem. Eu. J. Oper. Res. **52**, 86–89 (1991)
2. Chevrier, R., Liefooghe, A., Jourdan, L., Dhaenens, C.: Solving a dial-a-ride problem with a hybrid evolutionary multi-objective approach: application to demand responsive transport. Appl. Soft Comput. **12**(4), 1247–1258 (2012)
3. Cordeau, J.F., Laporte, G.: A tabu search heuristic for the static multi-vehicle dial-a-ride problem. Transp. Res. Part B Methodol. **37**(6), 579–594 (2003)
4. Deakin, M., Waer, H.A.: From intelligent to smart cities. Intell. Build. Int. **3**(3), 133–139 (2011)
5. DeLoach, S.B., Tiemann, T.K.: Not driving alone? American commuting in the twenty-first century. Transportation **39**(3), 521–537 (2011)
6. Eiben, A.E., Smith, J.E.: Introduction to Evolutionary Computing, 2nd edn. Springer, Heidelberg (2015)
7. Even, S., Itai, A., Shamir, A.: On the complexity of timetable and multicommodity flow problems. SIAM J. Comput. **5**(4), 691–703 (1976)
8. Fellows, N., Pitfield, D.: An economic and operational evaluation of urban carsharing. Transp. Res. Part D Transp. Environ. **5**(1), 1–10 (2000)
9. Fuhs, C., Obenberger, J.: Development of high-occupancy vehicle facilities: review of national trends. Transp. Res. Rec. J. Transp. Res. Board **1781**, 1–9 (2002)
10. Garey, M.R., Johnson, D.S.: Computers and Intractability: A Guide to the Theory of NP-Completeness. W. H Freeman and Company, New York (1979)
11. Hartman, I.B.A., Keren, D., Dbai, A.A., Cohen, E., Knapen, L., Janssens, D., et al.: Theory and practice in large carpooling problems. Procedia Comput. Sci. **32**, 339–347 (2014)
12. Hopcroft, J.E., Karp, R.M.: A n5/2 algorithm for maximum matchings in bipartite. In: 12th Annual Symposium on Switching and Automata Theory, pp. 122–125, October 1971
13. Hosni, H., Farhat, N., Nimer, R., Alawieh, N., Masri, C., Saroum, M., Artail, H., NaoumSawaya, J.: Solving a dial-a-ride problem with a hybrid evolutionary multi-objective approach: application to demand responsive transport. In: 20th International Conference on Software, Telecommunications and Computer Networks, pp. 1–7 (2012)
14. Knapen, L., Hartman, I.B.A., Keren, D., Cho, S., Bellemans, T., Janssens, D., Wets, G., et al.: Scalability issues in optimal assignment for carpooling. J. Comput. Syst. Sci. **81**(3), 568–584 (2015)
15. Kulkarni, R.V., Bhave, P.R.: Integer programming formulations of vehicle routing problems. Eur. J. Oper. Res. **20**, 58–67 (1985)
16. Lin, Y., Li, W., Qiu, F., Xu, H.: Research on optimization of vehicle routing problem for ride-sharing taxi. Procedia Soc. Behav. Sci. **43**, 494–502 (2012)
17. Ma, S., Zheng, Y., Wolfson, O.: T-share: a large-scale dynamic taxi ridesharing service. In: 2013 IEEE 29th International Conference on Data Engineering (ICDE), pp. 410–421, April 2013

18. Massobrio, R., Fagúndez, G., Nesmachnow, S.: A parallel micro evolutionary algorithm for taxi sharing optimization. In: VII ALIO/EURO Workshop on Applied Combinatorial Optimization, Montevideo, Uruguay (2014)

19. Tao, C., Chen, C.: Heuristic algorithms for the dynamic taxipooling problem based on intelligent transportation system technologies. In: Fourth International Conference on Fuzzy Systems and Knowledge Discovery, FSKD 2007, vol. 3, pp. 590–595 (2007)

20. Yan, S., Chen, C.Y.: A model and a solution algorithm for the car pooling problem with pre-matching information. Comput. Ind. Eng. **61**(3), 512–524 (2011)

21. Zitzler, E., Künzli, S.: Indicator-based selection in multiobjective search. In: Yao, X., et al. (eds.) PPSN 2004. LNCS, vol. 3242, pp. 832–842. Springer, Heidelberg (2004)

Night Time and Low Visibility Driving Assistance Based on the Application of Colour and Geometrical Features Extraction

Henry Cruz[(⊠)], Juan Meneses, Martina Eckert, and José F. Martínez

Research Center on Software Technologies and Multimedia Systems
for Sustainability, Technical University of Madrid, 28031 Madrid, Spain
{henry.cruz,juan.meneses,
martina.eckert,jf.martinez}@upm.es

Abstract. The present work shows an application to detect cars in night environments as a means to assist the car driving through HSV (Hue, Saturation, Value) colour extraction and geometric modelling. The developed algorithm has been implemented in smart devices through the platform Android. The detection and tracking of vehicles are implemented in low visibility environments such as night time, raining or snowing conditions; the different tests carried out confirm high performance rates of detection (p = 95.2 %). The information provided by the different sensors of the smart devices have been used to generate virtual information in a real driving environment (Augmented Reality) in order to complement the functionalities of the purposed solution. This information consists of visual, vibratory and auditory warnings that detect possible collisions and dangerous driving situations.

Keywords: Color extraction · Geometrical features · Smart devices · Augmented reality · Assisted driving

1 Introduction

According to the Global Status Report on Road Safety 2015 published by World Health Organization (WHO) [1] each year around 1.2 million people die by traffic injuries around the world and 1 million people lives are affected with permanent health issues due to this cause. The traffic crashes increases in low visibility conditions such as night time, raining and snowing. The proportion of tools that help to reduce the risks caused by these conditions are a current priority and the motivation of this work.

In addition, a study carried out in [2] the automation of the driving improves the capability of reaction in car incidents and generates security to the drivers. These statements are confirmed by the simulations carried out in [3] where it could be confirmed that the risk of collision decreases in an 80.7 % when the systems that provide early warning in an event of collision are present. The majority of the assistance in driving systems has been developed to be applied in daytime or in good lighting conditions [4] without considering other kind of conditions. The required information to assist the automatic driving is mainly obtained from the driving

© Springer International Publishing Switzerland 2016
E. Alba et al. (Eds.): Smart-CT 2016, LNCS 9704, pp. 118–127, 2016.
DOI: 10.1007/978-3-319-39595-1_12

environment through different kinds of sensors, which include the optical ones. The video cameras provide visual information of the driving environment and the algorithms extract information of interest that let identify traffic signals, pedestrians, pavements, traffic lights etc. Currently the smart devices provide other information different than visual that helps in the detection task and generates the timely warnings to avoid vehicle collisions and accidents.

This work shows a warning system to avoid vehicle collisions in low visibility environments, especially in night conditions, through the detection of vehicles by identifying the tail lights and using the sensors of the smart devices. The system guarantees an effective detection and the processing rates are very low as the tracking is continuous and the warnings are activated in real time. Also, the system is easily noticed as produces both visual and sounding warnings. The final result has been the generation of augmented reality through the introduction of virtual information in actual driving in night time environments. The development has been based on tools of free access and has led to create a specific APP that can be applied to Android devices.

The present article consists of the following sections. In the Sect. 2 related works to this work are commented. In the Sect. 3 the method and materials used in the development of the application are explained. In the Sect. 4 an extensive set of tests with their respective results are shown. In the Sect. 5 the main conclusions and future work are shown.

2   Related Works

The night vision systems have been used in the task of cars detection but they are unaffordable for many users due to their high cost [5] and are of limited efficiency as their use increases the risks of collision, especially when they are out of place or wrongly located [6]. In addition, the computational cost generated by this kind of sensors during the data processing is high. In [7] for example, neuromorphic vision sensors are used to classify and detect cars and trucks but the time of the processing of information can reach up to 200 meters making difficult the detection task in real time.

The approach of this implementation is based on the detection of cars acquiring the characteristics of their tail lights and the geometric relation between them. Some works showed in the state of the art use these characteristics to carry out detections in night time stages. In [8] a method for the detection of vehicles considering the variation of intensity levels of grey of the tail lights is presented, also an estimation of the distance from the monitor vehicle to the target vehicle considering the geometric relation established in [9] and a virtual horizon is presented. In [10] the detection of light of the tail lights using the space of colour L*a*b is done allowing the detection of vehicles in low visibility conditions. Also in [11] the distance between two tail lights as a source of information to the detection of cars in night time is considered; these detections do not take place in real time but through videos recorded previously. In the same way in [12] the tail light is segmented through a multilevel threshold histogram as a previous stage to the detection of vehicles and the estimation of distances. Following the same line in [13] a series of sensors to assist in the night time driving are implemented. The vehicle is detected through the identification of its tail lights. The monitoring and presentation of warnings take place in real time at the rate of 10 fps. In the same way in [14] the brightness of the tail lights is used to establish the geometric relations and temporary space in the detection and tracking of cars in night time, in this case the system is not implemented in real time. In [15] the implementation of the whole net of sensors and cameras to acquire information from both the external and internal, which refers to vehicle elements, driving scenarios are shown. These sensors are not embedded on an only platform.

Nowadays the miniaturization of the components has allowed that the smartphones mechanisms include sensors such as GPS, accelerometer, gyroscope, camera and others embedded on the same platform. These sensors provide useful data to establish position, location, acceleration and visual information. This data has been used in applications of driving assistance applications such as iCarBlackBox, Drivea, Augmented Driving, iOnRoad and Car Safe available in Android and IOS platforms. These applications have been developed to reach a good performance in controlled conditions but they make mistakes when lighting variations take place [16].

3 Materials and Methods

3.1 Materials

Multiple tools of software and hardware have been used in the detection and collision warning approach. Software tools have been chosen taking into consideration free access environments that guarantee functionality such as Open CV version 2.4.8 libraries on the operative system Android 4.4 Kit Kat. For the programming environment Eclipse, running on an Intel Core i5@3.1 GHz computed has been used. The tests have taken place in different smart devices, which characteristics are shown in Table 1.

Table 1. Technical characteristics of the smart devices.

Characteristic	Type 1	Type 2
Operating system	Android v2.1	Android v4.4
RAM	576 MB	2 GB
Processor	1 GHz	2.2 GHz
Display	3.7" (480 × 800 pel.)	4.95" (1080 × 1920 pel.)
Sensors	Accelerometer, GPS	Accelerometer, GPS
Camera	5 MP (2592 × 1944 pel.)	8 MP (3264 × 2448 pel.)

3.2 Method

In the developed application the accomplishment of the following requirements has been verified, they are: the execution of different kinds of Android terminals, the detection of different sorts of cars, the extraction of information of spatial location of the cars in the scene and the presentation of the parameters speed, precision, areas and calculation of the lighting centre of the vehicles' headlights. In addition, the system shows the visual and audible warnings screen, a friendly environment for the user and

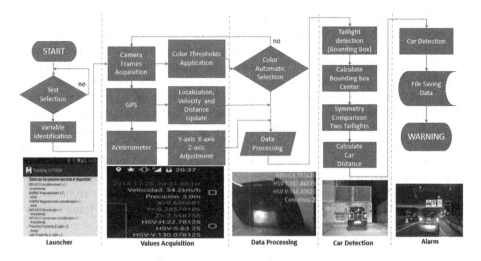

Fig. 1. General diagram of the driving assistance system.

avoids an adverse impact on the experience of processing data or when the system stops working momentary. Figure 1 shows the whole diagram of the system.

Summarising the system includes the following modules:

- **The Launcher and Test.** The launcher executes the application using the "Activity Splash Screen" function. The application menu is shown by the "Main Activity" function. On the other hand the calibration and operational tests of the accelerometer, GPS and the camera are executed. In this first part of the process an identification label is assigned to each of the functions of the sensors through a variable.

- **Acquisition of Values and Updates.** In this module the information of each of the variables is acquired. The GPS can serve as an example. In the GPS the coordinates acquire the location and the variables of speed and precision are updated, also the location changes taken place in the device are registered. In relation to the accelerometer a horizontal adjustment of the smart device is done allowing to obtain a spatial location of the smart device in a continuous form in relation to the 3 coordinate axis (x, y, z). On the other hand a register of the HSV values previously defined as thresholds according to a colorimeter study is done.

- **Data Processing.** In the data processing the function "Location DAO" is used to make a comparison. Here a comparison of the values of the thresholds corresponding to the outline bright and the colour of the tail lights in relation to the values obtained in whole image. The data inside the thresholds is automatically selected establishing regions of interest known as ROI's. The ROI's are labelled and the necessary variables for the detection of the corresponding outlines of those ROI's are initialized. In relation to the GPS an automatic register of the changes happening in the GPS signal is done continuously. In the same way continuous adjustments and registers of the spatial location of the smart device through the data collected by the accelerometer take place.

- **Car Detection.** Here the outlines of the ROI's are established. A bounding box is assigned to each ROI, a symmetry analysis between each of those ROI's is done and their values of areas, centres and dimensions are compered. Finally an analysis of the spatial location of the ROI's is done taking into consideration a framework. In other words it can be said that the ROI's are evaluated in relation to the virtual horizons. In this way a couple of ROI's that are symmetrically equal or almost equal and spatially aligned are obtained. These couple of ROI's correspond to the vehicle tail lights. In addition the values of the increase or decrease of the distance from the centre of the framework to the target vehicle are calculated through Euclidean distance and registered in other file. Also the increase or decrease of the obtained speed is registered by the smart device located inside of the car used in the test.

- **Warning.** Once the target vehicle is detected, its spatial location is recorded in a file, a new label is assigned and a continuous tracking of the different frames that are video frames takes place. The approaching or distancing of the target vehicle will generate different values of distance in relation to the vertical limits of the framework. The warning of the dangerous approaching is effectively generated when the decrease of distance values surpasses the established limits. This means that the target vehicle is approaching the framework and there is a risk of imminent collision. The warning is reinforced when it detects an increase of the speed obtained by the phone. In addition, audible and vibration warnings take place in order to make the system suitable to people with special needs. Figure 2 shows how the application works.

Fig. 2. The application shows information about the velocity, distance, spatial location, HSV colour components, detections and warnings in real time.

3.3   Colorimetric Study

The colorimetric study carried out in this work has allowed to define the values of HSV aligned to the tail lights bright and to the red light around that bright. The reason why this space of colour has been chosen is because of the high level of true positives (TP) and the low false positives (FP) obtained against to the models RGB and YCrCb from different tests developed. The lighting changes generate important problems of detection, especially in the RGB model due to a modification of any of the channels that affects in general, the global calculation and therefore the values of the thresholds should be valued continuously. On the other hand although the YCrCb model shows a better respond in processing time, the detection rates in relation to HSV are lower.

The model HSV allows the visual information to be more easily interpreted because separates the luminance from the chrominance. These sources of information refer to the colour tone (H) and saturation (S). The H values are acquired from the highlight of the reds that are presented in the tail light outlines. The S parameter is captured from the white colour of the intensity light. In the same way the two parameters, H and S, let adjust the component value (V) to the maximum tail light bright.

The intensity of the light emitted by the tail lights in cars are regulated under global standards that car manufacturers should follow. Therefore their values are kept constant and the thresholds that allow detecting these values should be of common use. The next step is to find the value of HSV in the tail lights outlines and in the bright. The HSV value rank considering 8 bits vary from 0 to 255, the decimal value obtained then is transformed into a binary value due to calculation reasons. For the conversion of RGB into HSV the maximum values of RGB have been considered in the way that $M = \max(R, G, B)$ and the minimum values $m = \min(R, G, B)$. From these two considerations S and V are given by:

$$S = \frac{M - m}{M}, \tag{1}$$

$$V = \frac{M}{255}. \tag{2}$$

Where V is the result of the max (R, G, B) that is the maximum value that the pixels could have up to 255. The component V is generated by the bulb of the tail lights. The component H, between the values 0 to 255 or 0–1, if the components have normalized. The values change in function of the angle θ that varies from 0 to 360°. This angle is formed between the two lines of the primary colours RGB. Due to conventional reasons the colour red has been chosen as one vertex, other vertex is formed by the white colour and finally the third vertex is formed by the green or blue. The value of H is expressed according to the relation shown in (3).

$$H_1 = arc\cos\frac{(R - G) + (R - B)}{2 * \sqrt{(R - G)^2 + (R - B)(G - B)}}. \tag{3}$$

Where $H = H_1$ if $B \leq G$ and $H = 360° - H_1$ if $B > G$. After the tests have been carried out, the average value of HSV obtained for the detection of tail lights bright is H = 42, S = 71, V = 255 and for the detection of the red colour of the outline is H = 62, S = 2, V = 55. These values have presented the highest rate of TP taking into account that multiple evaluations have been carried out at 15, 10 and 5 meters.

3.4 Geometrical Features in the Detection of Cars

The geometric features considerate for the detection of cars are the following: symmetries, distances, areas, geometric centres, shapes in a way that makes possible to identify a car in the scene.

The detection process starts with the matching between the thresholds of the values HSV found and the ones present in the scene, in this way is how the detection of the ROIs is done. Taking into consideration the characteristics of the ROIs such as the area measured in number of pixels, the centre, the maximum and minimum dimensions of height and width are calculated to locate the ROIs in the scene. Also a framework is implemented that represents the visual horizons as in Fig. 2 and descripted in the Sect. 3.1. The framework is related to a resize of the screen and allows efficiency in the processing due to the fact that carries out an initial rejection of the ROIs that are not inside of this. Also in order to ensure the detection of cars and to reduce the false positives, 4 regions of occurrence (R) are established. These regions are formed by dividing the framework in a way through which the vanishing point of the scene forms a series of triangles in perspective taking into account the lower vertex of the framework. It is necessary to indicate that this vanishing point is inside of the line of the virtual horizon. The R are weighed (W), so W will be higher where there is a higher likelihood of vehicles presence. This relation is presented as:

$$W_3 > W_1; W_3 > W_2; W_3 > W_4 \qquad (4)$$

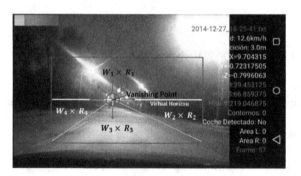

Fig. 3. Zone of detection probabilities based on regions and weights

The R vary according to the vanishing point spatial location in different places determined by the coordinates x, y. This proposal has resulted effective according to the evaluations carried out in different environmental conditions and are presented in the Sect. 4. The R_3 in general is the one with the highest occurrence of detections including when the vanishing point is moved near to the ends of the virtual horizon. The graphical description is shown in Fig. 3. On the other hand the virtual horizon and the upper and lower ends of the framework serve as a reference of the couple of bounding box that contains the tail lights to establish their alignment and effective detection as it is shown in the Sect. 3.

4 The Experimental Tests and Evaluations

The experimental tests have been carried out, firstly, in a laboratory to extract the values of HSV, establish outlines and estimate distances. Afterwards different tests have been carried out in real conditions taking into consideration the detection of vehicles in urban and interurban routes at night time when raining slightly and heavily and when snowing as it is shown in Fig. 4.

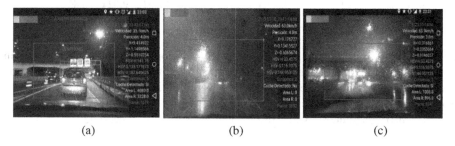

(a)   (b)   (c)

Fig. 4. Tests carried out under different climatic conditions: (a) detection when raining slightly (b) detection when raining heavily (c) detection when snowing.

The confusion matrix is used for the validation of the precision of the detection and therefore for each of the tests the values of the TP are acquired when a vehicle is predicted and the prediction is right; the values of the FP are acquired when the system registers a detection when actually there is not one; the values of true negatives (TN) are acquired when a vehicle is not predicted and the prediction is right and the values of false negatives (FN) are acquired when the system does not register a detection but the detection exists. This appreciation can be quite subjective, however, taking into consideration that the evaluations have been carried out in a laboratory by observing each pre-recorded video frame of a total of 500 and externally, it can be said that the evaluations are more reliable. In the external validations have been used more than one evaluator and two cars in a coordinated way. From the obtained data, the calculation of: false positive rate $FPR = \frac{FP}{FP+TN}$, the Dice index $DI = 2.0\left(\frac{pxr}{p+r}\right)$ that allows to calculate the precision grade of the detections, Jaccard Index ($JI = \frac{TP}{TP+FP+FN}$) that valuate the right detections against the mistakes, Manhattan ($Mh = \frac{TP+TN}{TP+FP+FP+FN}$) carries out a global evaluation of the detections, the values of the precision of the system ($p = \frac{TP}{TP+FP}$) and recall ($r = \frac{TP}{TP+FN}$) has been done. Where the closer the value is to 1, the higher the refinement grade is. The evaluation results are presented in the Table 2.

The results show that the overall detection index (DI) is 94. 81 % in night time driving conditions. On the other hand the ID is 82.44 % in low visibility driving conditions when snowing. Taking into account the adverse and the low visibility conditions that the experimental environment shows, generally it is observed that the

Table 2. The results of detections in different weather conditions.

Weather conditions	Average velocity (Km/h)	TPR/r	FPR	P	JI	DI	Mh
Night (good conditions)	73	0.9441	0.0457	**0.9520**	0.9014	**0.9481**	0.9489
Night + Light rain	57	0.9347	0.0477	0.9204	0.8648	**0.9275**	0.9458
Night + Hard rain	25	0.8474	0.0893	0.8576	0.7428	**0.8524**	0.8862
Night + Snow	24	0.8244	0.1071	0.8244	0.7012	**0.8244**	0.8669

proposed solution is effective as it is completely developed to be used in real time in contrast to [7, 13]. In addition, the result of precision of a 95.20 % is included in the ranks reached by [14] with the difference that the presented system is implemented on a platform with a limited resolution capacity considering that a better resolution of the optical sensor guarantees better results and it is totally accessible, compact and handheld.

5   Conclusions and Future Work

The present work shows a developed application in the operating system Android, which purpose is to provide a tool that helps the driving especially in night time scenarios when the visibility is limited. The system accomplishes with all of the stages for the technological implementation. It begins with an analysis of the requirements, it goes through the functional design of experimental tests and it reaches the validation of the obtained results. Here also it is shown how the integration of the obtained information by the different sensors of the smart device, the application of specific thresholds in HSV, the use of geometric relations of different kind allow the precise detection of the cars tail lights. Also it is important to mention that the strategy to eliminate the false positives through the extraction and weigh of the zones of occurrence has resulted effective. The precision of the detection of cars is of a 95.20 %. This percentage shows high chances to generate warnings related to possible collisions. Finally the virtual information of speed, distance and warnings generated to be applied in real driving conditions known as augmented reality makes of this application a highly practical and useful tool. The promising results obtained let make future developments associated with the traffic sign recognition and take automated driving decisions in low visibility conditions.

Acknowledgment. This work was supported by Spanish National Plan for Scientific Technical Research and Innovation, project number TEC2013-48453-C2-2-R.

References

1. World Helath Organization (WHO). http://www.who.int/violence_injury_prevention/road_safety_status/2015/en/
2. Russ, A., Wagner, A.S., Liesner, L., Küçükay, F., Vink, P.: Flow experience influenced by car adjustments. Transp. Res. Traffic Psychol. Behav. **36**, 46–56 (2016)
3. Lee, J.D., McGehee, D.V., Brown, T.L., Reyes, M.L.: Collision warning timing, driver distraction, and driver response to imminent rear-end collisions in a high-fidelity driving simulator. Hum. Factors: J. Hum. Factors Ergon. Soc. **44**(2), 314–334 (2002)
4. Dhanasekaran, S., Ramachandran, K., Selvamuthukumar, M., Velam, N., Pal, S.: A survey on vehicle detection based on vision. Mod. Appl. Sci. **9**(12), 118 (2015)
5. Digregorio, B.: Safer driving in the dead of night. Spectr. IEEE **43**(3), 20–21 (2006)
6. Schenkman, B.N., Brunnström, K.: Camera position and presentation scale for infrared night vision systems in cars. Hum. Factors Man. **17**, 457–473 (2007)
7. Gritsch, G., Donath, N., Kohn, B., Litzenberger, M.: Night-time vehicle classification with an embedded, vision system. In: Proceedings of the 12th International IEEE Conference on Intelligent Transportation Systems, pp. 1–6 (2009)
8. Chen, Y.L., Chen, Y.H., Chen, C.J., Wu, B.F.: Nighttime vehicle detection for driver assistance and autonomous vehicles. In: Proceedings of 18th International Conference on Pattern Recognition, vol. 1, pp. 687–690 (2006)
9. Stein, G.P., Mano, O., Shashua, A.: Vision-based ACC with a single camera: bounds on range and range rate accuracy. Proc. IEEE Intell. Veh. Symp. **2003**, 120–125 (2003)
10. Cabani, I., Toulminet, G., Bensrhair, A.: Color-based detection of vehicle lights. In: Proceedings of IEEE Intelligent Vehicles Symposium, pp. 278–283. IEEE, June 2005
11. Chan, Y.M., Huang, S.S., Fu, L.C., Hsiao, P.Y.: Vehicle detection under various lighting conditions by incorporating particle filter. In: IEEE Intelligent Transportation Systems Conference ITSC 2007, pp. 534–539. IEEE, September 2007
12. Chen, Y.L., Wu, B.F., Lin, C.T., Fan, C.J., Hsieh, C.M.: Real-time vision-based vehicle detection and tracking on a moving vehicle for nighttime driver assistance. Int. J. Robot. Autom. **24**(2), 89–102 (2009)
13. Chen, Y.L., Chiang, H.H., Chiang, C.Y., Liu, C.M., Yuan, S.M., Wang, J.H.: A vision-based driver nighttime assistance and surveillance system based on intelligent image sensing techniques and a heterogamous dual-core embedded system architecture. Sensors **12**(3), 2373–2399 (2012)
14. Wang, J., Sun, X., Guo, J.: A region tracking-based vehicle detection algorithm in nighttime traffic scenes. Sensors **12**, 16474–16493 (2013)
15. Ohn-Bar, E., Tawari, A., Martin, S., Trivedi, M.M.: On surveillance for safety critical events: in-vehicle video networks for predictive driver assistance systems. Comput. Vis. Image Underst. **134**, 130–140 (2015)
16. Kaplan, S., Guvensan, M.A., Yavuz, A.G., Karalurt, Y.: Driver behavior analysis for safe driving: a survey. IEEE Trans. Intell. Transp. Syst. **16**, 3017–3032 (2015)

Operationalising the Concept of the Smart City as a Local Innovation Platform: The City of Things Lab in Antwerp, Belgium

Nils Walravens[✉]

iMinds-SMIT, Vrije Universiteit Brussel, Pleinlaan 9, 1050 Brussels, Belgium
nils.walravens@vub.ac.be

Abstract. This paper gives an overview of two divergent approaches to what the Smart City can be, based on evolutions in the market today. A very top-down view on the Smart City sees corporate interest as a main concern, while purely bottom-up initiatives face challenges of scale, incentive and sustainability. This paper then proposes a point of view that bridges these two and makes an appeal for the city as a local innovation platform that balances different interests. Rather than remaining theoretical, we introduce the City of Things Lab that explicitly puts this approach into practice.

Keywords: Living labs · Smart city · Local innovation · Platforms

1 Introduction

While the concept of the Smart City has been developing for some time, the year 2008 signified a turning point in the field for three reasons. For the first time (1) there were more mobile than fixed broadband subscriptions active, (2) more "things" than people were connected to the internet, and (3) more than half of the world's population lived in cities [2, 9, 23]. The first point shows the growing importance of mobile connectivity. As prices for smartphones decrease and their capabilities to run more advanced and appealing software increase, consumers are depending on these devices more and more when travelling in their own cities or other areas, using more services that can increase their productivity, efficiency, communication skills or create experiences that enhance their quality of life.

The second turning point shows how context-awareness and network connectivity is increasingly added to physical objects around us. Sensors are gaining importance in this respect, while the prices for simple and complex sensors are decreasing dramatically [23], making more and innovative applications and services based on (real-time) sensor data a reality, an idea captured in the Internet of Things concept (IoT). Rather than relying on static or out-of-date data, sensor networks allow us to gather accurate statistics on a whole range of variables that can impact urban quality of life, and as a consequence, act on these variables. As more technologies gain the potential to interconnect, we however also need to be increasingly aware of the digital footprints and data trails we leave behind when using them.

© Springer International Publishing Switzerland 2016
E. Alba et al. (Eds.): Smart-CT 2016, LNCS 9704, pp. 128–136, 2016.
DOI: 10.1007/978-3-319-39595-1_13

The final point indicates that since 2008, more than half of the global population lives in cities. The UN estimates this number will only grow, to a predicted 70 % by 2050 [26]. As more citizens (and consumers) move to urban areas, actors from the ICT and mobile telecommunications naturally become increasingly interested in offering services that are tailored to life in the urban environment. Cities and local governments are at the same time exploring the role that new ICT services and products can play in increasing the quality of life of their citizens. In recent years, this quest is often captured in the "Smart City" concept. The concept has become key in bridging the research, projects and initiatives exploring the role of technology in urban life.

There is some hyperbole surrounding Smart Cities today. The Smart City concept has been criticized, a.o. for its self-congratulatory tendency, as well as its focus on I(C)T and the potential consequences towards reinforcing a digital divide [10, 14]. If insufficient attention is paid to this topic, the strong focus on information technologies in the Smart Cities discourse can dramatically impact the digital divide in the negative sense, creating even larger inequalities and social divisions in the city [10], a far cry from what would be labelled as 'smart'.

Considering these critiques and the three turning points introduced above, the need for new approaches to researching the Smart City topic is increasing and the still quite young field of so-called "Living Lab" research is beginning to provide answers [20]. By bringing together all relevant stakeholders and explicitly focusing on end users and the ways in which they adopt new technologies into their daily lives is providing new insights to the research community, as well as large and small companies developing or experimenting with new services and products. In order to properly respond to the trends above however, this paper proposes a more intensive approach to what a Living Lab can be, particularly in an urban context. We start with an overview of two very different approaches to the Smart City and aim to formulate a way to bridge these on an abstract level. In the subsequent sections, we introduce how the newly founded City of Things Lab in the city of Antwerp, Belgium wants to turn this vision into practice.

2 Different Approaches to the Smart City

The Smart City has been operationalized in many diverse ways, which can differ dramatically based on the perspective of the stakeholder describing the concept. This section briefly outlines two of those extreme approaches and a final one that aims to meet them in the middle.

2.1 The Top-Down Smart City

The first approach we assess here adheres to top-down dynamics, often closely related to the technologically deterministic idea of a "control room" for the city [12]. It aims at providing an ICT-based architecture to overview urban activities as well as the tools to (automatically) interact with infrastructures and adjust parameters to predefined optima [15]. Hall's definition of a Smart City above illustrates the strong emphasis on optimization through technology. Apart from gathering vast amounts of data, a large part of the processes that essentially constitute this approach consists of the calculations, visualizations and predictions based on the gathered metrics [3].

In its most extreme manifestation, a top-down approach translates to cities that are planned, designed and built from scratch with the optimization of urban processes through technology in mind. The examples of Songdo and Masdar can be seen as the pinnacle of this particular vision of the Smart City. But both have been heavily criticized for being sterile, overly planned, prohibitively expensive, anonymous, uniform and conformist [6, 21, 24] and the result is that these cities struggle to be completed within the predicted budgets and timeframes and/or do not attract enough economic activity (and thus jobs) so that people actually want to move there.

Of course in most cases, technology will need to be integrated into existing urban infrastructure. There are large potential benefits tied to having an integrated Smart City solution in a city: many different services and infrastructure systems can be managed from one central hub, keeping oversight on many divergent aspects of life in the city. The huge economic potential is - at least to the same degree as its potential for improving the urban sphere - the main driving force behind this approach and the main reason for its formation. Many major IT companies and municipalities around the world are looking for their slice of the Smart City pie (e.g. Cisco, IBM, Siemens) [25]. Market researchers and consultants of Pike Research have predicted that global investment in Smart City technology infrastructure will reach $108 billion by 2020 [19]. Cities at the same time are eager to adopt these technologies in some cases, as it can be a strong marketing tool on the one hand [15], but also promotes visions of increased efficiency, efficacy and reliability, which sound very appealing on the other. After all, which city would not want to be called "smart"?

Certain kinds of top-down visions have been heavily criticized with the main argument that they are dictated by commercial interests, and that they entail questions of control and privacy [14]. The "control room" Smart City approach, which aims at monitoring all aspects of urban life might soon result in an ubiquity of data collection, presenting a "set of potentials disturbingly consonant with the exercise of authoritarianism" [11]. Too much monitoring and too many integrated technologies and infrastructures can pose actual threats for freedom and privacy, whether controlled by private actors or ruling bodies.

The approach to the Smart City, as assessed above, then becomes an ambiguous one. On the one hand, top technology vendors have resources and knowledge at their disposal, on which the public sector needs to rely while facing urban challenges. Furthermore, the business potential in this context is too high for companies with ambitious commercial targets to resist. On the other hand, cities are about citizens, about the people who live and use them; in terms of for whom they are built, but also in regards of the potential for innovation and finding appropriate solutions to the challenges that are actually pertinent to these citizens. Therefore, this top-down vision is contrasted by the opposite: a purely bottom-up view on the Smart City, which is outlined in what follows.

2.2   The Bottom-Up Smart City

These architectural, topical, infrastructural or top-down viewpoints are juxtaposed against a more experimental, bottom-up understanding of what a Smart City could be. In this perspective, change and improvement comes only from the people "using" the city. It dismisses any form of top-down urbanization, in particular with the involvement of powerful private companies. The bottom-up Smart City is, foremost, about the Smart Citizen; those who live, work, and engage in all kind of activities in the city. Rather than working towards centralization, such a view on the Smart City takes a decidedly distributed approach, supporting and accepting some form of chaos [7].

Although these characteristics have positive impact on the local scale, they often conflict with objectives of decision-makers, urban-planners, and dynamics of the globalized economy. Chaotic bottom-up processes oppose the idea of a master plan, an 'ideal' state of place. Examples of these purely bottom-up approaches can be found in citizen initiatives and even (semi)-illegal interventions in the public space, such as so-called guerrilla bike lanes where citizens, unhappy with local biking infrastructure, gather via social media and paint bike lanes on the street without authorization [19]. These types of initiatives are also referred to as tactical urbanism [13]. Tactical urbanism tends to consist of "small scale interventions [that] are characterized by their community-focus and realistic goals" [1] and are often short-term or temporary, cheap and aimed at increasing quality of life in a certain way or addressing a specific neighbourhood concern. In such a perspective, what defines the Smart City is not the infrastructures or architecture it offers, but the ways in which its citizens interact with these systems as well as each other.

Bottom-up initiative can also come from large and small businesses or start-ups that aim to instigate innovation in a certain urban sector. One such well-publicised example is the mobile app Uber that offers an alternative private driver service that is completely organised within and via the app. In each city Uber has launched so far, protest has risen, in particular from the taxi services operating in these areas that saw it as a threat to their business. Nevertheless, Uber continues to operate and serves as an illustration of how a commercial entity can also be seen as a bottom-up approach to a Smarter City, even though it may clash with existing regulation or disrupt existing infrastructure (online housing sharing platform AirBnB could be another example).

Whereas the idea of a master plan, an ideal, measurable and controllable state often delivers deficient outcomes, relying solely on bottom-up processes also appears unlikely or even infeasible. Citizens are not detached from the wider urban context they live in, with other stakeholders playing - in some cases powerful - roles. Although the examples listed above can be appealing or charming and have in some cases impact and effect some change, they lack a vision on the issue at hand, are often (very) short term, can conflict with some long term goals set out by local policy and in some cases even be illegal. We like to argue for a "Smart Citizen" [27] that uses a variety of tools (that can be commercially developed) to interact with and move around the city, and for whom the emphasis lies on his/her citizenship, rather than technology as a primary factor. However, relying purely on bottom-up initiatives remains problematic with regards to scalability, regulation, interoperability, barriers and incentives to entry. Thinking about the city of the future then cannot only place any and all responsibility for its success with its citizens or entrepreneurs.

2.3   The Smart City as a Local Innovation Platform

While both views and approaches to the Smart City have their merits, we have also illustrated that they each exhibit substantial problems: "Change seldom arises from purely top-down or bottom-up systems and processes." [22] Therefore, we propose a more nuanced interpretation, one that combines top-down and bottom-up approaches, and establishes the Smart City as a platform that fosters collective (local) intelligence of all affected stakeholders. After all, cities essentially constitute shared responsibility and resources [3]. This means looking at the Smart City as a meeting place where the public sector, private interest and citizens can come together to generate new value, to collaborate and innovate together, an idea that has also been referred to as the triple helix (private sector, government and university actors) or quadruple helix (including citizens, the public or the user, depending on the formulation) [16, 28]. Smart Cities can only be successful if they act as local innovation platforms that bring together all involved stakeholders, however difficult this may be [22]. The "government as a platform" [18] is the intermediary, the enabler of interaction of multiple actors who have corresponding interests or needs. The delivery of public services in such a reciprocal relationship between all stakeholders, for instance, is very appealing and promising for developing truly Smart Cities [4].

In this light, the concept of open innovation is of course highly relevant [5]. It is about 'public-private-people partnerships', i.e. organized collaboration between all involved stakeholders (governments, businesses, academia, users/citizens etc.). It includes co-creation of services, products and much more, and the availability of open platforms that facilitate the necessary collaborative processes and interaction [8]. Open innovation is already being practiced, in the form of Living Lab projects that muster the stakeholders required to make an innovative initiative become a success [20]. Living Labs provide the platforms for open innovation, which facilitate productive collaboration and thereby ensure that development complies with real problems and needs.

We have illustrated that a purely bottom-up or top-down view on the Smart City will struggle to be effective and future-proof, and therefore suggest looking at the city as a platform. But also local innovation platforms are not without their potential difficulties. Organizing such an intense collaboration as required by this approach is not easy and it can run into issues of various natures: diverging visions, operational issues, financial inhibitors and so on. Alongside organizational difficulties, valorisation can be an issue of local innovation platforms as well. How one transcends the project context and can move a concept or idea into a real application or service that adds value to citizens is one of the major challenges.

2.4   Proposed Operationalization of a Smart City

These different approaches lead us the following operationalization of the Smart City concept. It should be clear we consider cases that are linked to the urban space and the interactions between the physical and the virtual, which are mediated by ICTs (be they social media, innovative wireless networks, mobile devices, cloud technology and so on) or developed using innovative methods (such as co-creation, living labs research, ppp-business models and so on), and that involve or engage citizens in innovative experiences with the goal of increasing their quality of life in meaningful ways. Smart Cities should capture creative and collaborative innovation through (direct) interactions between public bodies, businesses and citizens in:

- dealing with the next data flood, digital footprint and data trails (coming from use of linked open data, big data, IoT, sensor data etc.);
- identifying and tackling new relational complexities between actors;
- facing grand societal challenges in a local context (e.g. mobility, security, local and participatory governance etc.);
- offering new and engaging experiences to citizens.

These are the emphases we want to make in the on-going discussion and operationalization of the Smart City concept. We argue that collaboration is the key in making cities smarter. This refers not only to cooperation of citizens, companies or local governments amongst each other (i.e. horizontal collaboration). More difficult but also more important is vertical collaboration, working with all stakeholders on all levels; academia, public, private and citizens. It is working together in dealing with the vast amounts of information and data that modern cities increasingly produce that will allow them to tackle some of the major urban challenges of the future and today.

At the core of the Smart City then, we see the interdependence and interaction of three conditions as being the constituting characteristics of a future looking, "smart" city that is truly innovative: being collaborative, collective and contextual (Fig. 1).

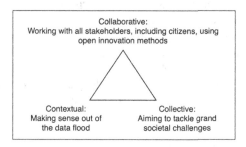

Fig. 1. The constituting characteristics of the smart city

As we have illustrated and argued above, a purely top-down view on the Smart City carries a danger of authoritarianism with it, while a bottom-up-only approach leans towards chaos and lack of long-term vision. We argue that rather than trying to find the perfect definition for what the Smart City is or should be, approaching the concept using the three characteristics presented above is one way of trying to keep a holistic perspective.

While appealing from a theoretical perspective, the true challenge lies in turning this operationalisation and idea into practice. Precisely this is the goal of the City of Things Lab, recently established in the City of Antwerp, Belgium.

3   Operationalising the City as a Local Innovation Platform: The City of Things Lab

We propose the challenge described above is best tackled through a living lab approach that pushes the concept to a new level by focusing on scale, sustainability and stakeholders. In recent years, a number of living labs have taken the form of 'smart city living labs', i.e. living labs in urban settings that are able to gather and process data about the city and citizens, and are increasingly able to combine linked (open) data (government, enterprise, etc.) and sensor data (environment, smartphones, transactions, etc.) with user feedback data and collective intelligence methods. The objective of such living labs is to provide companies, cities, and researchers with an accessible infrastructure for data-driven service innovation and business model experimentation that takes into account aspects of Big Data, the Internet of Things, service co-design, and business modeling.

What some of these labs have lacked so far however are (1) a truly large scale for experimentation involving a vast amount of citizens; (2) an approach that pays explicit attention to post-project sustainability and business models; (3) the direct participation of both the city and a commercial partner with this same focus on long-term collaboration, rather than project-based agreements; and (4) keeping very close links to the startups, SMEs and the local incubation scene.

It is in this context that iMinds has established the City of Things Lab in Antwerp. This initiative is part of a strategic cooperation agreement with iMinds, the largest Flemish ICT research institute, the City of Antwerp and the MVNO Mobile Vikings. Test users for any type of new mobile or location-based service or product can be selected from the Mobile Vikings community (over 200.000 members) and in the near future from the CityLife merchant community. From past projects with Mobile Vikings, it has been shown that response rates on user surveys surpass 17 %, which is exceptional in these types of living lab tests. Test panels and online focus groups can be selected based on the profile of the users and the objectives of the project. Users can easily be incentivized to participate to tests and experiments through so-called "Viking Points", the successful loyalty scheme that the MVNO already has in place. This potential panel of living lab participants is then supplemented by the panel iMinds already has access to in light of previous projects and living lab experiments.

The goal of this strategic cooperation is to make City of Things Europe's largest urban infrastructure for data-driven mobile service experimentation and innovation. This direct cooperation between academia, the city and a commercial player creates a triple win. It allows iMinds to expands its expertise related to living labs and scale up experiments to much higher numbers, allowing for innovative ways of testing as well. The combination with the community reward system and virtual currency that Mobile Vikings already has in place, not only allows for accessible incentives towards end users, but also facilitates experimental economics and real-life business model variation testing for example. For Mobile Vikings, the value of their participation is in learning more about their tight community of users and allows them to further capitalize on the innovative and young character this group. Participation also gives them more insight into the habits and interest of their customers, as well as in which types of innovative services they may be interested. Finally for the city of Antwerp, City of Things Lab can be a vehicle to more easily participate to European innovation projects and leapfrog when it comes to the innovative character of the city (which has been in something of laggard position in the last decade). Additionally, the city is keen to attract and support startups and SMEs in innovative areas and stimulate local economic activities related to technology and the urban sphere.

A first project that illustrates this triple win is related to the existing loyalty scheme of the City of Antwerp, called the "A-Card". This NFC enabled card currently allows citizens to physically check in at kiosks in the public city locations (e.g. pools, libraries, youth centres, museums and so on) to gather points that can be redeemed in those same locations (e.g. a free swim, a discount in the city shop etc.). The City has plans to expand the functionality of the card as well as the loyalty scheme and an experiment in the framework of City of Things will be the first step. iMinds will outfit the existing kiosks with iBeacons and develop a mobile application that automatically adds the A-points to the citizens online account (the A-profile) as soon as they walk in to the city location, with no other action required. In cooperation with Mobile Vikings, the city's loyalty scheme will be tied to that of the Vikings in an effort to make it more appealing to citizens and giving them more options to redeem their credit. By jointly running this project in a living lab setting, all partners get access to more relevant data and insight into the usefulness of such an approach and can better gauge the potential of such a city-related loyalty scheme.

By partnering academia and research, the public sector, a private company and the end user, City of Things' goal is to put the quadruple helix [16] into practice in a sustainable way and ensure that the city can play the role of a local innovation platform as described above.

4   Conclusion

This paper puts forward two divergent views to what the Smart City can be, based on evolutions in the market today. A very top-down view sees corporate interest as a main concern; while purely bottom-up initiative faces challenges of scale, incentive and sustainability. This paper then proposes a point of view that bridges these two and makes an appeal for the city as a local innovation platform that balances these different interests. Rather than performing this exercise from a theoretical perspective, we introduce the City of Things Lab that explicitly puts a quadruple helix approach into practice. The goal of the initiative is to push forward the scale and applicability of living lab research, while ensuring value and return for the involved stakeholders (the city, companies, startups, SMEs and citizens) in the longer term, by focusing explicitly on sustainability beyond the project context.

References

1. Berg, N.: The Official Guide to Tactical Urbanism - Nate Berg - The Atlantic Cities. The Atlantic Cities (2012)
2. Burger, A.: ITU Finds Two Times More Mobile Than Fixed Broadband Subscribers. ITU, 15 October 2012

3. Campkin, B., Ross, R. (eds.): Future & Smart Cities - Urban Pasmphleteer, vol. 1. UCL Urban Laboratory, London (2013)
4. Camponeschi, C.: The enabling city: place-based creative problem-solving and the power of everyday. Enabling City, Toronto (2011). http://enablingcity.com/
5. Chesbrough, H.: Open Innovation. Harvard Business Press, Boston (2003). 227p
6. Conway, R.: Are Smart Cities Just For Smart Arses? Sensemaking Blog, 25 November 2013
7. De la Peña, B.: The autocatalytic city. In: Books, T.E.D. (ed.) City 2.0: The Habitat of the Future and How to Get There (Ebook). TED Conferences (2013)
8. DG Communications Networks, Content and Technology. Open Innovation 2.0 Yearbook 2013. European Commission (2013)
9. Evans, D.: The Internet of Things. Cisco Blogs, 15 July 2011
10. Graham, S.: Bridging urban digital divides: urban polarisation and information and communication technologies. Urban Stud. 39(1), 33–56 (2002)
11. Greenfield, A.: The City is Here for You to Use. Wired, 5 February 2013
12. Hall, R.E.: The vision of a smart city. In: Proceedings of the 2nd International Life Extension Technology Workshop, Paris, France, 28 September 2000
13. Hamdi, N.: Small Change: About the Art of Practice and the Limits of Planning in Cities. Routledge, London (2004). 184p
14. Hollands, R.: Will the real smart city please stand up? City 12(3), 303–320 (2008)
15. IBM. How Smart Is Your City? IBM Institute for Business Value, Executive report (2009)
16. Leydesdorff, L., Deakin, M.: The triple-helix model of smart cities: a neo- evolutionary perspective. J. Urban Technol. 18(2), 53–63 (2011)
17. Muños, C.: Guerrila Bike Lanes Appear in NYC. Untapped Cities, 25 September 2013
18. O'Reilly, T.: Government as a platform. Innovations Technol. Gov. Globalization 6(1), 13–40 (2011)
19. Pike Research. Global Investment in Smart City Technology Infrastructure to Total $108 Billion by 2020. Navigant Research (2011)
20. Schuurman, D., Baccarne, B., De Marez, L., Mechant, P.: Smart ideas for smart cities: investigating crowdsourcing for generating and selecting ideas for ICT innovation in a city context. J. Theor. Appl. Electron. Commer. Res. 7(3), 49–62 (2012)
21. Sennet, R.: No One Likes a City That Is Too Smart, The Guardian, 4 December 2013
22. Shepard, M., Simeti, A.: What's so smart about the smart citizen? In: Hemment, D., Townsend, A. (eds.) Smart Citizens, vol. 4. FutureEverything Publications, Manchester (2013)
23. Silicon Labs. The Evolution of Wireless Sensor Networks. Silicon Labs. The Economist, 2013. Hotspots 2025: Benchmarking the Future Competitiveness of Cities. Research report (2013)
24. The Economist. Urban Dreamscapes: Starting from Scratch. The Economist, 7 September 2013
25. Townsend, A.: Smart Cities. Norton & Company, New York (2013)
26. UN HABITAT. State of the World's Cities 2010/2011. UN HABITAT (2010)
27. Vanolo, A.: Smartmentality: the smart city as disciplinary strategy. Urban Stud. 51(5), 883–898 (2013)
28. Yawson, R.M.: The ecological system of innovation: a new architectural framework for a functional evidence-based platform for science and innovation policy. In: The Future of Innovation Proceedings of the XXIV ISPIM 2009 Conference, Vienna, Austria, 21–24 June 2009

Smart Agents and Fog Computing for Smart City Applications

Andrea Giordano, Giandomenico Spezzano$^{(\boxtimes)}$, and Andrea Vinci

CNR – National Research Council of Italy, Institute for High Performance
Computing and Networking (ICAR), via P. Bucci 7-11d, 87036 Rende, CS, Italy
{giordano,spezzano,vinci}@icar.cnr.it

Abstract. New Internet of Things (IoT) applications that leverage ubiquitous connectivity, big data and analytics are enabling Smart City initiatives all over the world. These new applications introduce tremendous new capabilities such as the ability to monitor, manage and control devices remotely, and to create new insights and actionable information from massive streams of real-time data. Supporting this new approach requires the adoption of new paradigms. In this paper, agent tecnology is combined with the emergent concept of Fog computing to design control systems based on the decentralization of control functions over distributed autonomous and cooperative entities that are running at the edge of the network. We describe the Rainbow platform that is designed to bring computation as close as possible to the physical part. Multi-agent systems running on top of Rainbow create smart services using adaptive and decentralized algorithms which exploit the principles of collective intelligence.

Keywords: Smart City · Fog computing · Multi agent system · Internet of Things · Cyber-physical systems

1 Introduction

The Internet of Things (IoT) is a remarkable transformation of the way in which our world will soon interact [1]. Much like the World Wide Web connected computers to networks, and the next evolution connected people to the Internet and to other people, the IoT can interconnect devices, people, environments, virtual objects, machines and internet services with the goals of reducing the complexity of creating opportunities for a closer integration of the physical world with computer-based systems and developing efficient solutions for smart city services. Developing smart city services [2] such as transportation, parking, lighting, traffic, waste and safety requires the availability of a platform which permits speeding up and reducing the implementation costs of the services themselves, providing new capabilities for automation, analysis at multiple levels, greater scalability and virtualization. The IoT extends the current Internet-based technology by connecting different types of thing (objects or devices) with each

E. Alba et al. (Eds.): Smart-CT 2016, LNCS 9704, pp. 137–146, 2016.
DOI: 10.1007/978-3-319-39595-1_14

other and enabling them to communicate. However, while the things are connected with each other they are not necessarily able to cooperate with each other. Their ability to communicate with each other is determined by the similarity of the services that every object provides. Connected objects should also have the capability to learn about, think about, and understand both physical and social worlds by themselves [3]. Therefore, a new paradigm that enhances the current IoT with the ability to make decisions and support smart interaction between things must be developed. In the future IoT, interconnected things or objects will behave as autonomous agents, with minimum human intervention, and must have the ability to sense and analyse the environment where they are immersed and subsequently take intelligent decisions and actions to achieve their objectives.

We propose to use smart agents to mitigate the issues of lack of reasoning and intelligence in things in the IoT systems. The idea is that every thing should have embedded reasoning and intelligence capabilities. The intelligence in things can be achieved using software agents embedded in things. Their ability to reason about their environments can contribute to useful outcomes for humans, using collective intelligence techniques. Swarm intelligence [4] is the discipline that studies phenomena whereby a system composed of many locally acting individuals displays a meaningful global behaviour. Such swarm systems make use of self-organising, decentralised control mechanisms. Smart agents can exploit these techniques and their own capacity to sense their environmnet to cooperate, learn and adapt in order to reach a specific goal. This evolutionary perspective allows cities to develop new smart services exploiting a smart urban infrastructure which needs to be designed open, flexible, scalable and secure so as to execute smart agents that interact virtually among themselves from the external borders up to the cloud network. This vision is made possible using the concept of *fog computing*.

The term fog computing, also referred to as *edge computing*, essentially means that, rather than hosting and working from a centralized cloud, systems operate on network ends [5]. That concentration means that data can be processed locally in smart devices rather than being sent to the cloud for processing. This approach is particularly interesting in the context of IoT because it allows action in real time on the incoming data and working within the limits of available bandwidth. By using this kind of distributed strategy, we can lower costs and improve efficiencies.

In this paper we present Rainbow, an architecture that permits an easy development of smart city applications. The novelty of Rainbow is that it relies on the adoption of a distributed multi-agent layer on top of the physical part that is, in turn, wrapped in suitable *virtual objects* (VO), running at the edge of the network and assisted by cloud services. Rainbow aims to hide heterogeneity and to cope with complexity and real-time issues. Adaptive and decentralized algorithms have been explored as multi-agent systems for developing large-scale cyber-physical applications on top of the Rainbow architecture, such as those related to smart cities, acoustic maps, smart drainage systems and so on.

The paper is structured as follows: Sect. 2 describes the three-layer software architecture of the platform Rainbow. Section 3 presents the use of Rainbow platform for three smart city applications, showing: (i) a bio-inspired CPS (Cyber-Physical System), where smart agents are used to map noise pollution inside a city area, (ii) a fully decentralized approach for controlling an urban drainage network, and (iii) a real smart street application set up in the city of Cosenza (Italy). Finally, Sect. 4 concludes the paper.

2   Rainbow Architecture

Rainbow [6] is a three-layer architecture designed in order to bring the computation (i.e. the controlling part) as close as possible to the physical part. Since CPS provides for physical entities spread across a large (even geographic) area, the previous assumption implies the controlling part to be intrinsically distributed. Our proposal provides for the use of a *distributed agent-based* layer in order to address the aforementioned issues. The agent paradigm has several important characteristics, such as: (i) local views, with no agent having a full global view of the whole environment but behaving solely on the basis of local information and (ii) decentralization, i.e. no "master" agent controlling the others, but systems made up of interacting "peer" agents. Through these basic features, multi-agent systems make it possible to obtain complex *emergent* behaviours based on the interactions among agents each having a simple behaviour. Examples of emergent behaviour could refer to the properties of adaptivity, fault tolerance, self-reconfiguration, etcetera. In general, we could talk about *swarm-intelligence* when an "intelligent" behaviour emerges from interactions among simple entities. There is a plethora of bio-inspired swarm intelligence approaches in the literature that could be properly adopted in the context of CPS [4].

Rainbow architecture is shown in Fig. 1. As can be seen, the architecture could be divided into three layers. The bottom layer is the one that is devoted

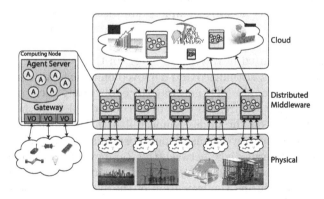

Fig. 1. Rainbow architecture.

to the physical part. It encloses sensors and actuators, together with their relative computational capabilities, which are directly immersed in the physical environment.

In the Intermediate layer, sensors and actuators of the physical layer are represented as VOs. VOs offer to agents a transparent and ubiquitous access to the physical part due to a well-established interface exposed as API. VO allows agents to connect directly to devices without caring about proprietary drivers or addressing some kind of fine-grained technological issues. Each VO comprises "functionalities" directly provided by the physical part. Essentially, a VO exposes an abstract representation (i.e. *machine readable-description*) of the features and capabilities of physical objects spread in the environment. Functionalities exposed by different types of VOs can be combined by agents in a more sophisticated way on the basis of event-driven rules which affect high-level applications and end-users. In summary, all the devices are properly wrapped in VOs which, in turn, are enclosed in distributed *gateway* containers. The computational nodes that host the gateways represent the middle layer of the Rainbow architecture. Each node also contains an agent server that permits agents to be executed properly. Gateways and agent servers are co-located in the same computing nodes in order to guarantee that agents exploit directly the physical part through VO abstraction. Instead of transferring data to a central processing unit, we actually transfer the process (i.e. fine-grain agent's execution) toward the data sources. As a consequence, less data needs to be transferred over a long distance (i.e. toward remote hosts) and local access and computation will be fostered in order to achieve good performance and scalability. Furthermore, since agents and VOs can be added or removed dynamically, if a system is well designed, it can be reconfigured dynamically and extended taking into account new physical objects and desired behaviour. More details on the Rainbow multi-agent system and VOs, along with a sketch of the API specification and some code examples can be found in [6].

The upper layer of Rainbow architecture concerns the cloud part. This layer addresses all the activities that cannot be properly executed in the middle layer, for instance, algorithms needing complete knowledge, tasks that require high computational resources or when an historical data storage is mandatory. On the contrary, all tasks where real time access to the physical part is required could be suitably executed in the middle layer. In the cloud part, a set of Rainbow nodes are properly virtualized and deployed on an existing cloud infrastructure. Such nodes lack of the VOs gateway since, obviously there are no physical entities connected. For this reason each node consists solely of the agent server. Communication between the nodes connected with the physical part and the nodes in the cloud occurs by means of message exchange. Agents located on the cloud nodes act as intermediary between the Rainbow MAS and cloud analytics services. The feature of adding new agents at runtime can be used to link new services in the cloud during the execution of the system (no reboot is needed). The Rainbow cloud part is PaaS (Platform as a Service), as it provides a software stack and a set of libraries for the application execution (Fig. 2).

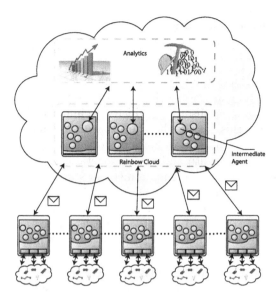

Fig. 2. Rainbow cloud layer.

The above described architecture is fully compliant with the paradigm of edge computing. A way to look at edge computing is to consider it as a virtualized platform that is typically located between end user devices and the cloud data centers hosted within the Internet. Thus edge computing can provide better quality of service in terms of delay, power consumption, reduced data traffic over the Internet etc. The main feature of edge computing is its ability to support applications that require low latency, location awareness and mobility. This ability is made possible by the fact that the edge computing systems are deployed very close to the end users in a widely distributed manner. Edge computing nodes hosted must possess sufficient computing power and storage capacity to handle the resource intensive user requests.

3 Using Rainbow for Smart City Applications

In the following, we detail three applications for Smart City, which exploit the features and capabilities provided by the Rainbow framework. Section 3.1 concerns the design of an application which aims at mapping the noise pollution on an urban area, and shows how Rainbow can be exploited to run swarm intelligence algorithms in order to realize CPS applications owning properties such as adaptivity, fault tolerance, self-reconfiguration. Section 3.2 provides both a sketch of a CPS for urban drainage networks, which is able to reduce their environmental impact when heavy rainfall event occur, and a set of preliminary simulation results underlining the benefits of the proposed system. The last application proposed concerns a smart street environment, physically set up in the city of Cosenza (Italy).

3.1   Noise Pollution Mapping

Many environments, such as airports, road works, factories, construction sites, and other environments producing loud noises, require effective noise pollution monitoring systems. Noise pollution is a common environmental problem that affects people's health by increasing the risk of hypertension, ischemic heart disease, hearing loss, and sleep disorders, which also influence human productivity and behavior [7]. For this reason the European Community passed the directive 2002/49/EC [8], which declares noise protection as one necessary objective to achieve a high level of health and environmental conservation. The directive imposes several actions to be made upon member states, including the mapping of noise in larger cities via noise maps. On the basis of these maps, the countries can formulate plans to counter the threat of noise pollution.

Noise maps are mostly based on numerical calculations providing good estimates of long-term averaged noise levels. However, such maps do not take into account the real-time variation of the noise levels. Using the rainbow platform we designed an agent-based, self-organizing system for the real-time construction of noise maps and identification of the sources of noise. Noise sensors are spread across the environment, linked to the computational nodes, and suitably wrapped inside the VOs. Each agent is directly associated with a VO representing a noise sensor. During the deployment phase, each agent is supplied by the knowledge of its neighbours (i.e. agent associated with a spatially near by sensor).

We use a simple self-organizing algorithm, proposed by [9], to let the sensor network self-organize in regions, with the partitioning based on similar sensing patterns (*noise levels*). Regions can grow or shrink according to the dynamic variation of noise levels. Organization in regions occurs by creating an overlay network made by agents connected by virtual weighted links. Agents belonging to the same region will have strong links, while agents belonging to different regions will have weak (or null) links. In the following the details of the algorithm are presented. Let s_i and s_j be two neighbour sensor agents. Let $n(s_i)$ and $n(s_j)$ the values of noise sensed by s_i and s_j, respectively. Let us assume that a distance function D can be defined for couples of v values. Region formation is then based on iteratively computing the value of a logical link $l(s_i, s_j)$ for each and every agent of the system as in following update_link procedure:

Update_link:
$$if(D(n(s_i), n(s_j))) < T\{$$
$$l(s_i, s_j) = min(l(s_i, s_j) + \Delta, 1)$$
$$\}else\{$$
$$l(s_i, s_j) = max(l(s_i, s_j) - \Delta, 0) \}$$

Where: T is a threshold that determines whether the measured values are close enough for $l(s_i, s_j)$ to be re-enforced or, otherwise, weakened; and Δ is a value affecting the reactivity of the algorithm in updating link. Based on the above algorithm, it is rather clear that if $D(n(s_i), n(s_j))$ is lower than threshold T, $l(s_i, s_j)$ will rapidly converge to 1. Otherwise it will move towards 0. Transitively, two nodes s_h and s_k are defined in the same region if and only if there is a chain of agents such that each pair of neighbours in the chain are in the same region.

In order to map the noise pollution properly, it is necessary that each and every agent within a region is locally provided with information related to the overall status of the region. To this end, it is possible to integrate forms of diffusive gossip-based aggregation [10] within the described general scheme. The algorithm requires that the agents periodically exchange information with their neighbors about some local value, locally aggregate the value according to some aggregation function (e.g., maximum, minimum, average, etc.), and further exchange in the subsequent step the aggregated value.

The proposed approach is planned to be implemented on top of smart street environment shown in Sect. 3.3.

3.2   Urban Drainage Networks

Recently, urban floods have become more frequent as a result of the increase of impervious areas and the occurrence of extreme weather conditions due to climate change. Furthermore, in conjunction with intense rainfall, obstructions and blockages due to infrequent maintenance of pipes and catch basins often challenge the hydraulic efficiency of an urban drainage system. In order to manage urban flooding, centralized stormwater measures, such as detention tanks and retention basins, have been introduced [11]. However, those solutions are not easily applicable because of a lack of space, especially in densely populated areas.

Our solution relies on a CPS which exploits the Rainbow architecture. A set of water level sensors and smart gates are spread in the drainage network, and directly linked on a set of interconnected computing nodes. The nodes network host a distribuited and decentralised cooperating agents application which aims at adjusting the gates in order to dynamically optimize the water load on all the conduits of the network. Such optimization makes the network able to exploit the full storage capacity of the pipeline by accumulating the excess stormwater volume that otherwise would overflow on the side-walks and street paving.

In our approach, we run the gossip-based algorithm [10] for computing the average of the water load as measured by all the agents of a generated network. When the algorithm converges, the estimated average value is exploited by each gate-agent for tuning its gate so as to bring water loads closer to that average. The relationship between the actuation upon the gate (i.e. its opening degree) and the actual change of water level is determined by the structure of the whole network and the dynamics of the water flowing through the system, so it is very hard or even impossible to deduce a tractable mathematical model for it. For this reason this task is accomplished exploiting a PID controller. This approach also allows the algorithm to adapt dynamically to unforeseen events occurring in the drainage network (e.g. damage, occlusions and so on).

Preliminary experiments were carried out using EPA SWMM software [12], which is widely used in the hydraulic scientific community, in order to simulate the behaviour of realistic urban drainage networks which include gates during severe rain events. SWMM software was customized, permitting it to communicate in real time with a separate multi-agent Java controller which implements our algorithm developed exploiting Rainbow Cyber-Physical middleware.

Our findings have shown that our algorithm used as a real time controller for an urban drainage system equipped with a series of moveable gates is actually able to control flooding by utilizing the storage capacity of the less overwhelmed conduits of the system during intense rainfall events. The results shown in Fig. 3 demonstrate that the proposed approach is able to decrease the flooding volume (the area between 1 and the dashed lines) in an urban drainage network significantly during a heavy rainfall event. Other results can be found in [13]

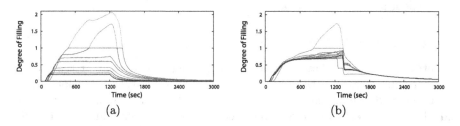

Fig. 3. Comparison of water loads (degree of filling) in different conduits, represented with different colors: base-line (a) vs. controlled (b) scenarios. The areas above 1 and under the dashed lines represents the flooding volume of each conduit.

3.3   Smart Street

In the context of the Res-Novae[1] project, a smart street environment has been designed and implemented in the city of Cosenza (Italy), exploiting the features of the Rainbow platform. This smart environment is called *Smart Street Cosenza*. The goal is to furnish the city with an IT infrastructure which provides services to the citizens, and which can be further extended over time, either covering new areas or providing new features and functionality. The target areas for a first deployment are shown in Fig. 4(a) and are located in the centre of the city. Specifically, the infrastructure covers: (A) a Bus Station, (B) a square, (C) the main commercial street of the city, (D) part of one of the main driveways and (E) the area around a commercial centre.

Over the chosen areas, a set of thirteen computational nodes (Fig. 4(b)) and seventy wireless sensors nodes (Fig. 4(c))are deployed. Each computational node consists of a Raspberry Pi mod.2 board, is mains powered, and hosts the Rainbow middleware. Each sensor node has a battery embedded and is powered by a solar panel. Sensor nodes can be of two types: *type A* nodes host noise, temperature, relative humidity and luminosity sensors, and *type B* nodes host air quality

---

[1] The RES-NOVAE - "Buildings, roads, networks, new virtuous targets for the Environment and Energy" project is funded by the Italian Government (PON 04a2_E).

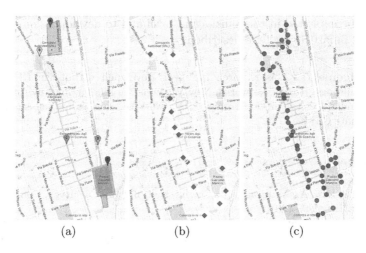

(a)   (b)   (c)

Fig. 4. Smart Street Cosenza. (a) Target areas; (b) Computational Nodes; (c) Sensors nodes. Green locations host one *type A* node and one *type B* node, blue locations hosts only a *type A* node.

sensors, measuring the concentration of CO, CO_2, NO and O_3. All the sensor and computation nodes are connected using a wi-fi network infrastructure, also deployed in the same areas.

Currently, the described CPS infrastructure hosts an application devoted to real-time monitoring the status of the areas involved. Raw measures are collected by the computational nodes, then filtered and aggregated and finally sent to a remote server that stores the data in a DBMS. A web portal is available showing geo-referenced sensor measures as well as aggregated information indexes such as Simmer Summer Index (SSI), Humidex and Air Quality Index (AQI). This information is available to the citizens, who can use it to figure out how much the different areas are comfortable and healthy, to the city administrator, who can monitor critical climatic or pollution events, and the research community, who can use it for further investigations and analysis. Both the cyber-physical infrastructure and the monitoring application are up and running since December 2015, with only a few sensors failures.

4   Conclusions

The paper presented the Rainbow platform and three smart city applications designed exploiting it, one of which is physically deployed and running in the city of Cosenza, Italy. Rainbow fosters the combination of multi-agent systems and fog computing, so as to allow the creation of distributed and swarm intelligence applications which can interact directly and in real time with the physical world. The case studies provided shows sketches of how to properly exploit this combination to develop applications for smart cities. Future work will be devoted to both enriching the Rainbow platform, providing social and analytics modules which can be exploited in the multi-agent level and to developing more services for the real Smart Street here described.

Acknowledgements. This research has been developed within the RES-NOVAE project, "Buildings, Roads, Networks, New Virtuous Targets for the Environment and Energy", funded by Italian Government. RES-NOVAE aims to implement new solutions for Smart Cities.

References

1. Atzori, L., Iera, A., Morabito, G.: The internet of things: a survey. Comput. Netw. **54**(15), 2787–2805 (2010)
2. Alba, E.: Intelligent systems for smart cities. In: Proceedings of the Companion Publication of the 2015 on Genetic and Evolutionary Computation Conference, pp. 707–722. ACM (2015)
3. Wu, Q., Ding, G., Xu, Y., Feng, S., Du, Z., Wang, J., Long, K.: Cognitive internet of things: a new paradigm beyond connection. IEEE Internet Things J. **1**(2), 129–143 (2014)
4. Bonabeau, E., Dorigo, M., Theraulaz, G.: Swarm intelligence: from natural to artificial systems. Oxford University Press, New York (1999)
5. Bonomi, F., Milito, R., Zhu, J., Addepalli, S.: Fog computing and its role in the internet of things. In: Proceedings of the 1st Edition of the MCC Workshop on Mobile Cloud Computing, pp. 13–16. ACM (2012)
6. Giordano, A., Spezzano, G., Vinci, A.: A smart platform for large-scale cyber-physical systems. In: Guerrieri, A., Loscri, V., Rovella, A., lo Fortino, G. (eds.) Management of Cyber Physical Objects in the Future Internet of Things, pp. 115–134. Springer, New York (2016)
7. Schweizer, I., Bärtl, R., Schulz, A., Probst, F., Mühläuser, M.: Noisemap-real-time participatory noise maps. In: Proceedings of 2nd International Workshop on Sensing Applications on Mobile Phones (PhoneSense 2011), pp. 1–5 (2011)
8. Directive, E.: The environmental noise directive (2002/49/eg). Official J. Eur. Communities (2002). http://eur-lex.europa.eu/legal-content/EN/TXT/?uri=celex%3A32002L0049
9. Bicocchi, N., Mamei, M., Zambonelli, F.: Self-organizing virtual macro sensors. TAAS **7**(1), 2 (2012)
10. Jelasity, M., Montresor, A., Babaoglu, Ö.: Gossip-based aggregation in large dynamic networks. ACM Trans. Comput. Syst. **23**(3), 219–252 (2005)
11. Piro, P., Carbone, M., Garofalo, G.: Distributed vs. concentrated storage options for controlling cso volumes and pollutant loads. Water Pract. Technol. **5**(3), wpt2010071 (2010)
12. Rossman, L.A., Supply, W.: Storm water management model, quality assurance report: dynamic wave flow routing. US Environmental Protection Agency, Office of Research and Development, National Research Management Research Laboratory (2006)
13. Giordano, A., Spezzano, G., Vinci, A., Garofalo, G., Piro, P.: A cyber-physical system for distributed real-time control of urban drainage networks in smart cities. In: Fortino, G., Di Fatta, G., Li, W., Ochoa, S., Cuzzocrea, A., Pathan, M. (eds.) IDCS 2014. LNCS, vol. 8729, pp. 87–98. Springer, Heidelberg (2014)

Smart Mobility by Optimizing the Traffic Lights: A New Tool for Traffic Control Centers

Yesnier Bravo[✉], Javier Ferrer, Gabriel Luque, and Enrique Alba

Universidad de Málaga, Málaga, Spain
{yesnier,ferrer,gabriel,eat}@lcc.uma.es

Abstract. Urban traffic planning is a fertile area of Smart Cities to improve efficiency, environmental care, and safety, since the traffic jams and congestion are one of the biggest sources of pollution and noise. Traffic lights play an important role in solving these problems since they control the flow of the vehicular network at the city. However, the increasing number of vehicles makes necessary to go from a local control at one single intersection to a holistic approach considering a large urban area, only possible using advanced computational resources and techniques. Here we propose HITUL, a system that supports the decisions of the traffic control managers in a large urban area. HITUL takes the real traffic conditions and compute optimal traffic lights plans using bio-inspired techniques and micro-simulations. We compare our system against plans provided by experts. Our solutions not only enable continuous traffic flows but reduce the pollution. A case study of Málaga city allows us to validate the approach and show its benefits for other cities as well.

Keywords: Traffic lights planning · Multi-objective optimization · Smart mobility

1 Introduction

Traffic lights are increasingly important elements for the efficiency, environmental care, and safety of our cities. These devices were initially positioned at road intersections, pedestrian crossings, and other locations to control conflicting flows of traffic and avoid possible accidents. At each intersection, all traffic lights are synchronized to carry out a sequence of valid phases periodically. Each phase consists of a combination of color's states and has a time span that vehicles are allowed to use a roadway. The assignment of the time span for each phase in the phase sequence of all intersections at an urban area is what we call a Traffic Lights Plan (TLP).

Finding the best TLP is crucial for reducing the number of stops for red lights thus minimizing the travel time of vehicles through the road network. Intuitive examples are the well-known green waves, which facilitate a continuous traffic flow in one main direction. Reducing the travel time of drivers prevents them from losing time and arriving late to their destination. As a side effect, this

© Springer International Publishing Switzerland 2016
E. Alba et al. (Eds.): Smart-CT 2016, LNCS 9704, pp. 147–156, 2016.
DOI: 10.1007/978-3-319-39595-1_15

also helps reducing the fuel consumption and CO_2 emissions while the vehicle is stopped for red lights.

Nowadays, the large number of vehicles and citizens moving around rises the inefficiency of current traffic control systems, designed to set local control policies but unable to optimize a global, real city scenario. In this article we present HITUL, a decision support system that helps traffic managers to generate optimal TLPs for actual cities, leading to above-mentioned potential benefits in terms of energy consumption, traffic flow management, pedestrian safety, and environmental issues. Unlike decentralized self-regulated lights, or traditional queue based systems, the use of metaheuristic algorithms [6,10] to find successful TLPs is still an open issue. The ability of metaheuristics and Nature inspired techniques [1,15] to solve very large problems with many restrictions and in competitive running times make them unique to build HITUL.

In addition, we use the well-known SUMO (Simulator of Urban Mobility) traffic simulator [4,14], which offers a detailed source of information about the vehicle's flow (velocity, fuel consumption, emissions, journey time, etc.), giving rise to configurations of realistic scenarios according to real patterns of mobility of the target city. This is a key difference from our systems to other solutions: not only the large dimension of the zones considered (previous works go for a street or a corner while we go for a city), but also the level of details and reality in our studies (e.g. real maps, driving regulations, car and driver individual analysis, times, pollution, etc.).

The remainder of this article is as follows. In Sect. 2 we mention some related works which have addressed this problem. Then, we introduce the HITUL system in Sect. 3. The Sect. 4 describes the practical case of Málaga city to validate our approach. Finally, Sect. 5 states conclusions and the future work.

2   Related Work

This problem has been tackled by both industry and academia, showing the importance and the impact of having an appropriate TLP to alleviating traffic jams which also allows to reduce hazardous substances emitted with car exhaust gas.

On the one hand, the industry has proposed several solutions (for example, SPROUT [17], Cross Zlin [7], or ATC [2]) but in general are focused on the real-time configuration of a single traffic light junction and they make use of some additional infrastructure which provides online information of the changing traffic situations. For example, the SPROUT System [17] proposes the utilization of ultrasonic detectors and optical beacons on the road to detect cars, thus determining the movement of cars on the road. Using this information, it predicts in real time when cars will arrive at streets corners, and estimates the number of times a car stops and the time of each stoppage, then it calculates and implements an appropriate traffic signal pattern.

On the other hand, in the academia this problem has been divided into two separate (but related) phases: the first one is about how real-time information of the current traffic can be gathered; while the second one focuses on the design of systems which provide optimized TLP using that previous information. In the first research domain, we can mention DATLCES [18], GLOSA [5] or POVA [19]. These works analyze the utilization of different technologies to gather the data (from classical detectors or cameras to recent communication systems such as RFID, VANET communications, ...). The second research domain focuses on the optimization of the TLPs using existing traffic information. The most common search engines used are queueing theory [18], fuzzy systems [12], and metaheuristics [9].

As it can be observed in the previous paragraph, this problem has been tackled in very different ways and with different objectives, but we have detected some topics which can be improved:

- Most current approaches are based on a limited number of traffic elements (roads, traffic lights, urban areas).
- Take a single goal (e.g., reduce the number of stops) and do not take into account other metrics such as emissions, travel time, ...
- Even when dealing with it, they will not quantify the benefits on emissions and other indicators.

Our proposed tool will solve these issues by addressing a large urban area (a complete city), with both mono- and multi-objective optimization, and using real and open data to provide solutions to real scenarios.

3   The HITUL System

HITUL is a support tool for decision-making regarding the planning of the city traffic light network, one of the ways to deal with congestion and traffic jams. Figure 1 illustrates this relationship between our proposed HITUL system and the external components or actors in the system.

In the context of a metropolitan area, the HITUL system takes advantage of open traffic data and information services to provide its functionality. These data sources are available to everyone without copyright restrictions or licensing fees. An example is OpenStreetMap [13], a free repository of geographic information supported by over 1.6 million users around the world, who collect data using manual survey. HITUL also uses information publicly provided by the city Traffic Control Center (TCC), such as the traffic intensity measured in specific locations of the road network.

In the following, the main functionalities implemented are listed. Next, the proposed design according to these software requirements is discussed, including the underlying functional architecture and the planning algorithm. Finally, the optimization strategy used to implement the system is described. Let us start with the main system functionalities.

3.1   Main Features

The HITUL system aims at supporting the decision-making of an officer at the TCC. Its main feature is the automatic generation of optimized TLPs (see

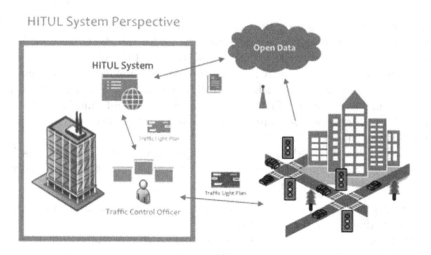

Fig. 1. Perspective of the HITUL system.

Sect. 3.3 for more details). But it also includes some additional characteristics in order to interact with the traffic center manager and make easy the utilization of our generated plans. The following list briefly outlines the major features that the system provides:

1. **Combine different objectives.** HITUL generates optimal plans based on a selection of different objectives at the same time: *waiting time*, *number of stops*, or *carbon footprint*. This functionality is intended to search for more stable TLPs according to multiple, possibly conflicting criteria, instead of satisfying one single requirement. Multi-criteria decision making is an important and hot issue in research not yet well exploited in final real applications.
2. **Consider different traffic profiles.** Adapt to the real behavior of the road traffic according to the time of the day, the day itself, and the moment of the year. Our system provides a list of available options: working day, rush hour working day, Saturday, Sunday, Saturday rush hour, and Sunday city return hours.
3. **Select an urban zone or optimize the whole city traffic.** This functionality allows to select a zone, a single district or the whole city, whose traffic lights are required to be optimized. The remainder city signals are configured according to a TLP provided by the traffic manager or by our system. This is a very practical feature for the traffic manager, since it helps them implementing temporal, localized traffic control policies.
4. **Comparisons between TLPs.** The system allows to compare obtained TLP among them, as well as compare a plan obtained by the system with another plan provided by an expert in a standard format. The plan selected to compare with is named *base plan*. As a result, the main differences will be drawn in a visual representation so that the officer can easily identify those traffic lights which differ more with respect to the base plan.

5. **Export/Import optimal TLPs.** The system supports the export of each TLP obtained using the XML standard format. At the same time, the system allows to load the base plan to compare with as far as it satisfies the afore-mentioned file format. This functionality enables the integration with other present and future TCC systems.

3.2   Architecture Overview

In this section we provide a technical overview of our proposed HITUL system. It is structured in three layers, each one grouping close related software compo-nents. First, a front-end server provides a single page application (SPA) exposing the traffic optimization dashboard, as well as the interfaces to take useful open data coming out from the software package.

Also, the system has a back-end numerical server running data processing and optimization tools in a Java EE platform that provides a high level of availability, reliability, and scalability. Implemented algorithms for computing optimized TLPs are based on bio-inspired techniques and some multi-objective versions based on crowding and using numerical archives for non-dominated solu-tions whose core intelligence is regulated mainly by the Non-Dominated Sorting Genetic Algorithm (NSGA-II) [8].

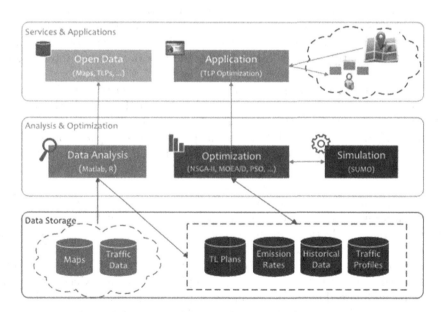

Fig. 2. Overview of the HITUL system Architecture.

Finally, the HITUL architecture involves a database server, comprising the data collections and the interfaces to manage them. We use a regular relational database since we have not relevant reasons to go for a non-relational data storage and access.

Figure 2 summarizes the main components at each layer as well as their interaction with other components in our software package. This flexible architecture will allow to develop future extensions of the HITUL service. A Client/Server utilization is amenable both for a truly remote internet access, or an in-house utilization, where users are in a room (floor, building) and the actual computational servers are in a cold room or computer facilities center, with data always flowing inside the premises, respecting the standard security measures of the TCC. This is highly dependent on the city, hence our decisions have been taken to help new scenarios of use in different cities.

3.3   Optimization Strategy

The objective of optimizing TLPs is to find cycle (timing) programs for all the traffic lights located in a given urban area with the aim of reducing the global journey time, emissions, and fuel consumption. Consequently, the solution is represented with a tuple of positive integer numbers $\mathbb{Z}^+$ within the time interval $[30, 120]^1$ meaning the phase duration of the different states in all the traffic lights of the studied area. We have also added an integer value associated to each intersection that is called offset within the time interval $[-30, 30]$. The offset of a signal is the delay of the beginning of the initial phase of the intersection. When offset is used it is possible to get green waves, which occurs when a series of traffic lights are coordinated to allow continuous traffic flow over several intersections in one main direction.

The proposed algorithm sets a value in the time interval $[30, 120]$ in each position of the vector solution that represents a phase and a value in the interval $[-30, 30]$ in the positions of the offset of each intersection. Let us say our largest instance has 3800 phases and 961 offsets, the problem search space would consist of $91^{3800} \times 61^{961}$ candidate solutions. Therefore, efficient automated approaches are required to tackle it. Evolutionary algorithms [3] have shown to be very effective in solving hard optimization tasks. For this reason, in the case of monoobjective optimization we used the so-called Genetic Algorithm (GA) [11]. Our implementation of the genetic algorithm in this paper typically uses a ranking method for parent selection and elitist replacement for the next population, that is, the best individual of the current population is included in the next one. The operators used are single point crossover and integer polynomial mutation. Note that the search algorithms used have been implemented using jMetal 5.0 [16], a Java framework aimed at the development, experimentation, and study of metaheuristics for solving optimization problems. The source code of the algorithms used in this tool are publicly available at GitHub[2].

---

[1] Recommended interval by the Mobility Delegation of the Málaga's City Council.
[2] https://github.com/jMetal/jMetal.

On the other hand, when more than one objective must be optimized at the same time and are considered as equally important, we used the Non-Dominated Sorting Genetic Algorithm (NSGA-II) [8]. NSGA-II is a genetic algorithm which is the reference algorithm in multi-objective optimization. Its main characteristic is the use of a ranking procedure and a density estimator known as crowding distance to sort the resulting population. The solution obtained by means of NSGA-II is not a single solution, but a number of them called *non-dominated solution set*. This is a set composed by solutions which are not worse than any other solution for all objectives. The representation of this set of solutions in the objective space is known as Pareto front.

As above noted, the evaluation of the generated TLP is performed by means of the well-known SUMO [14] traffic simulator, which offers a continuous source of information about the vehicle's flow (velocity, fuel consumption, emissions, journey time, etc.), giving rise to configurations of realistic scenarios according to real patterns of mobility. The output of a SUMO simulation is registered in a journey information file that contains data about each vehicle's departure time, the time the vehicle waited to set off (offset), the time the vehicle arrived, the duration of its journey, and the number of steps in which the vehicle speed was below 0.1 m/s (temporal stops in driving). Other output files gather information about emission traces in vehicles (CO_2, NO_x, PM, etc.) and hydrocarbon consumption. This information is used to evaluate the quality of alternative traffic light cycle programs.

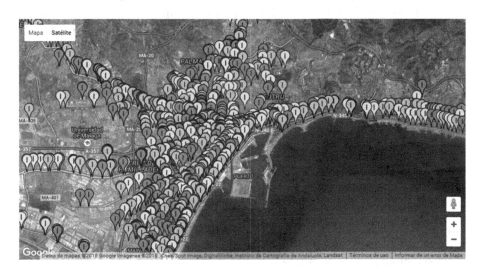

Fig. 3. Differences between base plan and the optimized traffic lights in whole Málaga city map (with 961 intersections). Red color indicates a big difference, yellow a medium one, and green a small one. (Color figure online)

4   Practical Use and Benefits: Case Study of Málaga

Since we are interested in developing an optimization tool capable of dealing with close-to-reality and generic urban areas, we have generated an instance by extracting actual information from real maps of Málaga, obtained from the Mobility Delegation of the City Council. To illustrate this case of study, we created 11 digital maps representing ten different districts and the whole city. In Fig. 3 is shown the traffic lights of a selected area of Málaga city. In the whole city, there are 961 intersections, composed by multiple traffic lights (from 4 to 16) each. Therefore, the optimization of the phases time span of each intersection is a great challenge for the optimization solver, and even more challenging for the team in charge of the Mobility in the city.

In Fig. 3 can be seen the result of the traffic light optimization of the entire city. Our tool generates a sequence of optimal TLPs, that is the result of optimizing the current plan continuously. This search process stops when the algorithm is unable to find more accurate plans or by demand of the operator.

Every time the user selects an optimized plan, the application shows the differences with respect to a base plan, also selected by the user. As this tool is aimed at helping to make changes in the traffic light phase duration that benefit the traffic flow, the differences between the base plan and the optimized plan are highlighted in different colors. When there are big differences between the phase time of an intersection, the marker which represents the intersection is colored in red, a medium difference is represented in yellow, and a small or null difference is represented in green color. This color scale might help decision makers to focus on a subset of intersections looking for possible problems in the programming of those traffic lights, in which differences in time were longer.

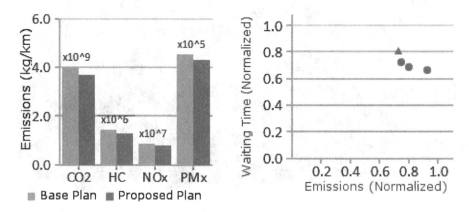

Fig. 4. Results of the execution of HITUL. On the left, the comparison between the based plan and the selected optimal plan, for several pollution indicators ($CO2$, HC, NOx, and PMx). On the right, the set of optimized plans proposed is shown, using a triangle mark to highlight the plan selected for the comparison with the base plan.

Using HITUL, the decision maker could generate traffic light schedules to minimize waiting time, journey time, and emissions. The improvement achieved with HITUL in solution quality with respect to the expert's solution is remarkable. In Fig. 4 left, it can be seen a comparison of the emissions of the base plan generated by the expert's algorithm and an optimized solution using HITUL. This optimized solution is highlighted in Fig. 4 right by using a triangle mark. In this case, it represents the plan that produces less pollution to the environment at the expense of a longer waiting time for drivers. Finally, the HITUL system allows the user to select the non-dominated solutions to compare with, which is a very useful functionality for decision-makers to match occasional traffic needs in terms of the two optimization criteria selected.

The TLP problem is, in fact, a multi-objective problem since the drivers want to minimize the waiting time and journey time, meanwhile the municipality wants lower gas emissions. For this reason, HITUL is able to run a multi-objective algorithm which provides a Pareto front with non-dominated solutions considering two objectives at the same time. In Fig. 4 right, it is shown a Pareto front taking into account waiting time and gas emissions as equally important objectives. Then, the decision-maker could pick one non-dominated solution up from the generated Pareto front.

5 Conclusions

In this paper, we present a decision support system, named HITUL, that helps traffic managers to generate optimal TLPs for actual cities, leading to high potential benefits in terms of energy consumption, traffic flow management, pedestrian safety, and environmental issues.

The proposed system addresses most of the drawbacks of current existing systems considering very large zones and realistic information. Also the system provides some facilities for making easier the decisions of the traffic managers, such as allowing the comparison between traffic plans, highlighting the importance of each individual traffic light in the final plan, or allowing to restrict the zone to be considered, the traffic profile used or even the main goal that s/he wants to optimize. The validation of the system in Málaga, a medium-large spanish city, has demonstrated that HITUL is able to provide real support for decision makers regarding the planning of the city traffic light network.

As future work, we plan to extend the study to other cities, aiming to address different types of network topologies and traffic densities. Also, new optimization algorithms will be applied, as well as hybrid approaches built for selecting the algorithm that best solves the traffic problem for the real city characteristics. Finally, we plan to integrate our tool with other systems that provide us with more city data in real time (e.g., based on sensors) for more accurate solutions.

Acknowledgements. The authors have been partially funded by project number 8.06/5.47.4142 in collaboration with the VSB-Technical University of Ostrava, the University of Málaga (Andalucá Tech), and by the Spanish MINECO project TIN2014-57341-R (http://moveon.lcc.uma.es).

References

1. Alba, E., Blum, C., Asasi, P., Leon, C., Gomez, J.A.: Optimization Techniques for Solving Complex Problems, vol. 76. Wiley, Hoboken (2009)
2. Aldridge Traffic Controllers: SCATS. Technical report, Australia (2015)
3. Bäck, T., Fogel, D.B., Michalewicz, Z.: Handbook of Evolutionary Computation. Oxford University Press, New York (1997)
4. Behrisch, M., Bieker, L., Erdmann, J., Krajzewicz, D.: Sumo-simulation of urban mobility. In: The Third International Conference on Advances in System Simulation (SIMUL 2011), Barcelona, Spain (2011)
5. Bodenheimer, R., Brauer, A., Eckhoff, D., German, R.: Enabling GLOSA for adaptive traffic lights. In: 2014 IEEE Vehicular Networking Conference (VNC), pp. 167–174. IEEE (2014)
6. Boussaïd, I., Lepagnot, J., Siarry, P.: A survey on optimization metaheuristics. Inf. Sci. **237**, 82–117 (2013)
7. Zin, C.: eDaptiva: full-featured urban traffic management center. Technical report, Czerch republic (2015)
8. Deb, K., Pratap, A., Agarwal, S., Meyarivan, T.: A fast and elitist multiobjective genetic algorithm : NSGA-II. IEEE Trans. Evol. Comput. **6**(2), 182–197 (2002)
9. Garcia-Nieto, J., Olivera, A.C., Alba, E.: Optimal cycle program of traffic lights with particle swarm optimization. IEEE Trans. Evol. Comput. **17**(6), 823–839 (2013)
10. Glover, F.W., Kochenberger, G.A.: Handbook of Metaheuristics, vol. 57. Springer Science & Business Media, New York (2006)
11. Goldberg, D.E.: Genetic Algorithms in Search, Optimization and Machine Learning, 1st edn. Addison-Wesley Longman Publishing Co, Boston (1989)
12. Guerrero, J., Damian, P., Flores, C., Llamas, P.: Plataforma para gestión de la red de semáforos de zonas urbanas. Sistemas, Cibernética e Informática **1**(7), 12–18 (2010)
13. Haklay, M., Weber, P.: OpenStreetMap: user-generated street maps. IEEE Pervasive Comput. **7**(4), 12–18 (2008)
14. Krajzewicz, D., Erdmann, J., Behrisch, M., Bieker, L.: Recent development and applications of sumo-simulation of urban mobility. Int. J. Adv. Syst. Meas. **5**(3–4) (2012)
15. Lozano, M., Molina, D., Herrera, F.: Soft Computing: special Issue on scalability of EAs and other metaheuristics for large-scale continuous optimization problems. Technical report (2011)
16. Nebro, A.J., Durillo, J.J., Vergne, M.: Redesigning the jMetal multi-objective optimization framework. In: Proceedings of the Companion Publication of the 2015 Annual Conference on Genetic and Evolutionary Computation, GECCO Companion 2015, pp. 1093–1100. ACM, New York (2015)
17. OMRON Group: Sustainability report 2004. Technical report, Japan (2004)
18. Wen, W.: A dynamic and automatic traffic light control expert system for solving the road congestion problem. Expert Syst. Appl. **34**(4), 2370–2381 (2008)
19. Zhu, Y., Liu, X., Li, M., Zhang, Q.: POVA: traffic light sensing with probe vehicles. IEEE Trans. Parallel Distrib. Syst. **24**(7), 1390–1400 (2013)

Stakeholders Approach to Smart Cities: A Survey on Smart City Definitions

Victoria Fernandez-Anez(⊠)

Transport Research Centre, TRANSyT,
Universidad Politécnica de Madrid, Madrid, Spain
victoria.fernandez.anez@upm.es

Abstract. The concept of Smart City is not yet statically defined, and thus, in the last years, several scientific articles and papers have been written focusing on the subject. The main objective of this research is to identify and compare the different discourses that stakeholders involved in Smart City projects build around the concept. The definition of the Smart City concept has been the key element selected to be analyzed, being used to stablish the conceptual basis that structures the different points of view that stakeholders have about the topic.

The research about the Smart City definition has consisted in the analysis of 32 different Smart City definitions in which 404 terms have been tagged or classified following a methodology that is divided in 3 steps of definition regarding stakeholders, key issues and text analysis. As a result, a comprehensive definition and different strategies have been developed.

Keywords: Smart City · Discourses · Definitions · Text analysis · Stakeholders · Governance

1 Introduction

The concept of Smart Cities has been extending since the 90s in parallel with the liberalization of telecommunications and the development of services through internet. The term Smart City has become in recent times synonymous with extensive use of information technology cities, although a Smart City means much more than that [1].

The first public draft of the Operational Implementation Plan for the European Consortium for Innovation in Smart Cities focused efforts in 3 main fields: energy, mobility and ICT [2]. But the scientific literature on the subject was already widening the limits of the concept including other topics that are core in the city, as well as integrating them in a holistic approach. The concept of Smart City is not yet statically defined, and thus, in the last years, several scientific articles and papers have been written focusing on the subject. In the scientific literature, the emphasis on social and environmental capital distinguishes the concept of "Smart Cities" of pure technology-centered approaches, and drives the new goals of ICT as a vehicle to promote the objectives of cities from the multidimensional perspective.

At a theoretical level, methodologies that attempt to correlate the basic parameters of the Smart City concept are being developed. Triple Helix methodologies are used to analyze the dynamics of knowledge-based systems, taking into account three pillars:

© Springer International Publishing Switzerland 2016
E. Alba et al. (Eds.): Smart-CT 2016, LNCS 9704, pp. 157–167, 2016.
DOI: 10.1007/978-3-319-39595-1_16

university, industry and government, in a highly related interaction with the concept of Smart City with respect to their global positioning [3].

Which are the discourses of the different stakeholders regarding the Smart City concept? The main objective of this research is to identify and compare the different discourses that stakeholders involved in Smart City projects build around the concept. It will provide conclusions about the differences and similarities existing among the points of view of stakeholders, providing information that is key to understand the interaction among them. The definition of the Smart City concept has been the key element selected to be analyzed. Being an open concept which does not have a static character, the Smart City definition is being used to stablish the conceptual basis that structures the different points of view that stakeholders have about the topic. It includes the main goals and the most important topics and describes the role that technology plays in the approaches of the different stakeholders.

2   Methodology

The research about the Smart City definition has consisted in the analysis of 32 different Smart City definitions in which 404 terms have been tagged or classified following a methodology that is divided in 3 steps:

Definition of the main stakeholders participating in the Smart City through literature. Firstly, the main stakeholders that take part of the Smart City have been defined. Smart city has been identified as a knowledge based system [1] and thus, the model that has been used is the knowledge-based triple helix models. Four stakeholders groups have been defined: universities, private companies and governmental institutions, both at local level and large scale.

Civil society is defined by several authors as one of these groups [4, 5] but it was not possible to find their provided definitions in this study up to this point. Examples of Smart City definitions have been selected through documents produced framed in each of these groups (Table 1).

Definition of the key issues to classify the Smart City concepts: Smart City action fields, Smart city main goals and technological approach. These key issues have been defined through the analysis of the existing literature on the topic.

On a first step, the Smart City projects have been divided into the six main fields that Smart City strategies are considering in the city: *governance, economy, environment, mobility, people and living* [33]. This classification has been chosen being the most used in the literature by different authors and adopted by the European Commission in the report Smart cities in the "Mapping Smart Cities in the EU".

A second step consisted in identifying the main goals of the Smart City, which have been synthesized into three main goals: *sustainability, quality of life* and *efficiency*.

Technologies play a key role in the development of the Smart City, but there exist different points of view about the role technology play in the city. It can be seen as a *tool*, as a way of *connection* or as a goal, and it is seen whether as a wide concept

Table 1. Stakeholders definitions reviewed

Academic institutions	Governmental institutions	Local governments	Private companies
Politecnico di Milano, Universita degli Studi di Milano (Italy) and VU University, the Nederlands [6]; Institution of Engineering and Technology (UK) [7]; Technical University of Lisbon [8]; State University of New York, U.S. [9]; University college, London [10]; Bartlett School of Architecture, London [11]; TEI of Larissa and Aristotle University of Thessaloniki, Greece [12]	European Commission [2], Conseil des Communes et Regions d'Europe Council of European Municipalities & Regions [13], and European Innovation Partnership on Smart Cities & Communities. [14] United Smart Cities [15], Intelligent Community Forum [16]	European cities: Amsterdam [17], Barcelona [18], Zaragoza [19], Manchester [20]; Non-European Cities: Boston [21], New York [22], Singapur [23], and Medellín [24]	IBM [25], CISCO [26], Telefónica [27], Ferrovial [28], Indra [29] and Siemens [30]. Boyhugues [31], GE-Allstom [32]

including every kind of *technology* used within the city, or reduced to the use of *ICT*, even sometimes just as the management of *information*.

Analysis of Smart City concepts through text analysis techniques. The Smart City definitions have been studied using text analysis tagging techniques, a methodology frequently used in social sciences research. Definitions key words have been separated and analyzed according to the defined key issues. The definitions have been tagged and grouped according to their correspondence with the issues according to cited literature. Excel tables have been used to classify the main words in the definitions to obtain the first outcomes in a non-automatic process.

A total number of 404 terms have been extracted from the 32 definitions and analyzed. Some of them appear several times. Analysis provided an overview of the different terms used to make reference to the categories defined. In the analyzed definitions, terms are not only directly mentioned, but are also referenced through element that configure its identities and structure (i.e. in the analyzed definitions, *governance* is mentioned not only as the term itself, but also referenced through elements that configure governance systems (citizens, stakeholders, leaders, government, agencies, etc.).

3 Definitions by Stakeholders

In a first stage of this research, definitions from a first selection of stakeholders have been analyzed separately (Fig. 1).

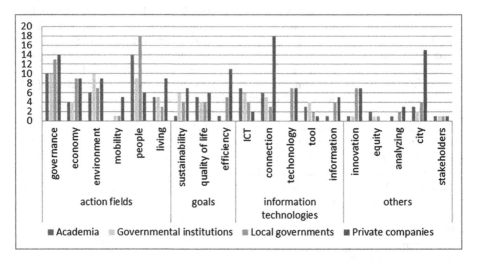

Fig. 1. Classification of terms in academic Smart City definitions.

Smart Cities from the point of view of Academia. (See Fig. 1) Among the concepts that appear in the academic papers, the ones related to people present a higher number of mentions. Concepts related to *people* are the key element in Smart Cities, appearing in 6 of the 8 definitions analyzed, appearing in several occasions. "Mobility" does not appear as a topic in any of the analyzed definitions.

Regarding the goals of Smart cities, to reach a higher *quality of life* is highlighted as their main objective (5 terms), being *efficiency* and *sustainability* mentioned each in just one of the analyzed definitions. Another conclusion is that in this kind of definitions, objectives are being focused on the processes more than in the goals.

The theoretical point of view of technology within the Smart City is mainly focusing in *ICT* (7 times mentioned) as a *tool* (3 times) for *connection* (6 times) within the city. *Connection* and *tool* are also important in the definitions, whether directly mentioned or implicitly expressed. For the academic institutions researched, the topics selected are the main ones, and urban and city concepts are the only ones slightly outstanding among the other concepts included in the classification.

Smart City approaches by Governmental Institutions. (See Fig. 1) Concepts related to *governance* and *environment* are the main ones highlighted by the analyzed definitions of Smart Cities provided by institutions followed by concerns about *people*. The city as a services provider, in the *living* action field, does not appear to have such as important role in the definitions provided by Inter-governmental institutions. *Economy* appears to be less important, becoming the social aspect the part of sustainability enhanced in these definitions. Finally, *mobility* appears just once.

The main goal of Smart Cities, as described by inter-governmental institutions analysed definitions, is related to the enhancement of more *sustainable* cities, but besides *quality of life* also appear to have a key role in Smart City definitions. Concepts related to *efficiency* do not have any relevance in the definitions proposed by the Inter-governmental entities.

Definitions of Inter-governmental entities do not consider *technology* from a wide point of view to become as part of the Smart City, but understands *ICT* as the main technological element to be considered. Supporting this focus in *ICT*, its role as a *connection*, becoming a *tool* in the approaches of 4 of the definitions and not and objective itself.

Innovation, equity and *stakeholders* are other terms mentioned in this set of definitions.

Local governments and Smart Cities. (See Fig. 1) Local governments Smart Cities definitions are mainly focused in concepts related to *people* (society and citizenship), even though governance concepts also play a key role. Other aspects of sustainability (*economy* and *environment*) appear mentioned in a smaller number of occasions. *Mobility* is mentioned in only one of the analyzed definitions.

Local governments approach of Smart cities is almost equally driven by the goals of *sustainability, quality of life* and, mainly, *efficiency*. But it is also important to highlight that the definitions local government provide are not highly focused in the objectives, but in the elements that compose a city and in the citizens that inhabit it.

Local governments definitions have a wider perspective of *technology* within the city, mentioning any type of technology as key for a city to become Smart. Despite this fact, *ICT* is also appearing in 4 of the 8 analyzed definitions. The use of technology and ICT as a *tool* is appearing a smaller number of times than in the definitions previously analyzed. *Innovation* for local governments is a key topic, appearing in 6 of the 8 definitions and being as important as technology, and even being a substitute of this concept considering technology to be the element behind the term of innovation.

Private companies defining Smart Cities. (See Fig. 1) Concepts related to *governance* are the most highlighted by private companies among the ones referring to the different action fields. *Economy* and *environment* terms appear in 7 of the 8 analyzed definitions, being also an important element. Terms related to *people* and services that can be provided (*living*) do not play and important role. *Mobility* appears as a topic in the half of the analyzed definitions. The goals are mostly focused on *efficiency*, which appears in all definitions, but *sustainability* and *quality of life* also appear in 7 and 6 of the analyzed definitions respectively.

While in the previous analyses the most important concepts where *people* or gov*ernance*, included in the action fields, in the Smart City definitions provided by private companies, the term that is mentioned a higher number of times is a technological one. *Connection* is the most important aspect highlighted by Private companies in their definitions about Smart Cities. *ICT* only appears in 2 of the definitions, not limiting the scope of private companies to a type of technology. It is important to highlight that technology is not understood as a *tool*, this concept only appearing in one of the analyzed definitions.

The definition of the Smart City they provide emphasizes the *city*, the urban aspects. They define the Smart City from the point of view of providers of *management* solutions aiming to improve the efficiency of the city, and present a strong relationship with the local governments definitions. *Innovation* is also important, appearing in 5 of the 8 analyzed definitions and being mentioned more than once in some of them.

4 Comparative Analysis

The final step is to compare the results of the semantic analysis of the Smart City definitions provided by Universities, Institutions, Local Governments and Private Companies. These comparisons aim to help understanding the differences and the common approaches among the different stakeholders taking part in the Smart City.

Classification of topics (Fig. 2) is distributed in a similar way in the definitions of Academia, Institutions and Local Governments paying special attention to the action fields, composed of more elements and thus of more terms. Private companies definitions include a more balanced approach to the topics. In their definitions, weight is less placed in the variety of action fields and more in other concepts.

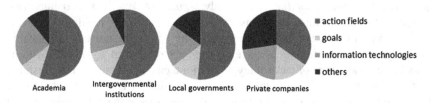

Fig. 2. Distribution of concepts among the analyzed aspects

Secondly, key words have been classified into the defined Smart City dimensions (*governance, economy, environment, mobility, people and living*) (Fig. 3). Regarding the definitions provided by Academia and local governments, *people* is the most mentioned element of a Smart City. The analyzed definitions of Inter-governmental Institutions focus in *environment, governance* and *people*, while for private companies, *governance* concepts play a major role, followed by the *economy* and environment.

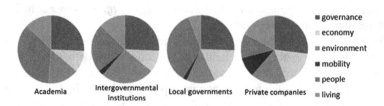

Fig. 3. Comparison among approaches regarding Smart City action fields

Environment is not such an important element, even if it is the focus of great investments and the concepts of the initial definitions of Smart City where highly related to this field [2]. *Mobility* appears mainly in the discourses of companies, and it is mentioned once in definitions of Academia and Local governments.

Regarding the main goals of the Smart Cities (Fig. 4), in analyzed academia definitions, the *quality of life* is the most important objective of a Smart City, while governmental institutions state that *sustainability* is the key goal of a Smart City, followed by *quality of life*. Local Governments and Private Companies focus on *efficiency* as the main issue that the Smart City concept should address, local governments having a slightly more balanced vision of the goals of the Smart City. *Efficiency* does not play a key role on the definition of the Smart city provided by institutions, and has the same importance as *sustainability* for Universities.

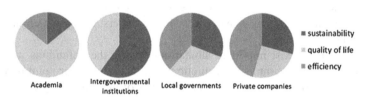

Fig. 4. Comparison among approaches regarding Smart City goals

In definitions of Academia and Governmental Institutions, a Smart City is defined by the use of *ICT* (Fig. 5). Regarding *technology, connection* is the principal issue for them. On the other hand, Local Governments and Private Companies approaches to *technology* are wider and include many other possibilities. Understanding technology as a *tool* to reach the Smart city goals does not appear as an important issue to Local Governments and Private Companies, but is one of the main approaches presented by Institutions.

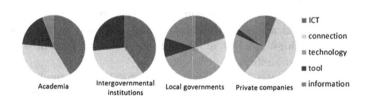

Fig. 5. Comparison among approaches regarding technology in Smart City definitions

5   Conclusions. Defining Smart City: A Cooperation and Agreement of Stakeholders

One of the basis of the Smart City concept as defined by the European Commission [2] is to be a "multi-stakeholder, municipally based partnership". The approach of the different stakeholders varies in the fields to act in, the objectives and their point of view about technology. Only understanding the differences and providing guidelines for the connection of the different stakeholders to include all points of view it will be possible to get the holistic approach that is essential to the Smart City, providing this multi-stakeholder partnership. A comprehensive definition that involves all the approaches must be stablished.

However, this definition means that multiple stakeholders have to be involved in the smart city, but local governments have the role of stablishing the basis for the development of the concept. Local government analyzed definitions, when compared in the analyzed fields, show a close approach between the objectives of municipalities and the ones of private companies. This can seem obvious regarding the customer-provider relationship they have, seeming that private companies are being better able to understand local governments needs, but poses two questions. First of all, it is not clear who is influencing who and remarks the danger of municipal investments being driven by market interests. But it also highlights the challenge that Academia and Inter-governmental institutions must face in better understanding which are the real needs of municipalities.

Meanwhile, there exist important similarities among the definitions provided by universities and inter-governmental institutions, presenting a wider point of view that places the citizen and the *quality of life* in the center of the Smart City concept. In the analyzed definitions, all stakeholders focus in *governance* and *people* as the main action fields in which a Smart City must be based and focus on, leading to citizen centric approaches.

Results also show independence between the results of Academia and Inter-governmental institutions and the ones of private companies in all the analyzed fields.

However, regarding technology, the definitions of these three groups of stakeholders understand connection as key, while municipalities definitions express a wider need of technology implementation and is thus not so focused in the idea of integration.

As a conclusion, a definition is provided aimed to set the basis for future works in the field of Smart cities:

A Smart City is a system that enhances human and social capital wisely using and interacting with natural and economic resources via technology-based solutions and innovation to address public issues and efficiently achieve sustainable development and a high quality of life on the basis of a multi-stakeholder, municipally based partnership.

This definition includes the main action fields (governance (multi-stakeholders, municipality)), economy, environment, people and living (services and public issues). Technology appears in the definition following the wide idea of analyzed municipalities definitions, but also as a tool for connection and in a wide perspective that include several kinds of technologies. Innovation is an important vector mentioned by definitions by all groups of stakeholders. Finally, the goals of the Smart City (Sustainability, quality of life and efficiency) must be included in a balanced way (Fig. 6).

This research has a limited scope including only a small part of existing definitions, and will be extended by automatizing the research through software to reach a wider number of definitions. However, some guidelines for the future are already suggested by the results.

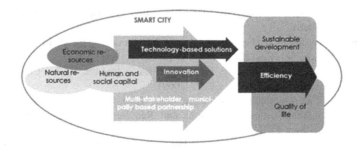

Fig. 6. Proposed Smart city definition

Firstly, tools for assessment are necessary to enhance a balanced implementation of Smart City strategies and initiatives, specially tools that allow local governments and local decision makes trace the guidelines for the development of their cities if they are supposed to lead the way to a smarter city. This approach would avoid a strong influence of market interests driving municipal investments.

Another conclusion if that to get the citizen centric approach that can be extracted from definitions, awareness and participation of citizenship and civil society should be enabled, creating and promoting their own visions.

Besides, inter-governmental institutions must be able to reach municipalities in order to materialize their policies. Economy plays a key role for municipalities according to this analysis. Financing provided according to criteria of Governmental Institutions like UN or EU through their financing entities (World Bank, European Investment Bank) can play a key role in the development of Smart Cities through the projects they support, getting a more balanced approach to the Smart City concept aligning local projects with policies that these institutions develop.

Finally, a close research about municipalities and their needs can help to align Academia objectives with the ones of municipalities, helping to improve the benefits that research can have in the whole society, in a world that is increasingly urbanized.

Acknowledgements.   This work has been possible through my participation in ASCIMER project developed in TRANSyT (Transport Research Centre of Universidad Politécnica de Madrid) and funded by the EIB Institute. Special thanks to Yara Falakha, Daniel Sarasa, and Jesus Leal, partners and professor at MCS that gave together with me the initial steps of this research.

References

1. De Santis, R., Fasano, A., Mignolli, N., Villa, A.: Smart city. fact and fiction. MPRA Paper No. 54536. Munich, Germany (2014)
2. European Union. Mapping Smart Cities in the EU. European Parliament. Directorate General For Internal Policies. Policy Department A: Economic and Scientific Policy (2014)
3. Leydesdorff, L., Deakin, M.: The triple helix model and the meta-stabilization of urban technologies in Smart cities (2010)

4. Etzkowitz, H., Zhou, C.: Triple Helix twins: innovation and sustainability. Sci. Public Policy **33**(1), 77–83 (2006)
5. Lombardi, P., Giordano, S., Farouh, H., Yousef, W.: Modelling the smart city performance. Innov.: Eur. J Soc. Sci. Res. **25**(2), 137–149 (2012)
6. Caragliu, A., del Bo, C., Nijkamp, P.: Smart cities in Europe. In: 3rd Central European Conference in Regional Science – CERS (2009)
7. Harrison, C., et al.: Foundations for smarter cities. IBM J. Res. Dev. **54**(4), 1–16 (2010)
8. Correia, L.M.: Smart Cities Applications and Requirements, White Paper. Net!Works European Technology Platform (2011)
9. Nam, T., Pardo, T.A.: Conceptualizing smart city with dimensions of technology, people, and institutions. In: The Proceedings of the 12th Annual International Conference on Digital Government Research (2011)
10. Batty, M., et al.: Smart Cities of the future. UCL Working Paper Series, Paper 188 (2012). ISSN: 1467-1298
11. Haque, U.: Surely There's a Smarter Approach to Smart Cities?, Wired, 17 April 2012. http://www.wired.co.uk/news/archive/2012-04/17/potential-of-smartercities-beyond-ibm-and-cisco. Accessed July 2013
12. Anthopoulos, L., Fitsilis, P.: From digital to ubiquitous cities: defining a common architecture for urban development. In: Proceedings of the 6th International Conference on Intelligent Environments, Kuala Lumpur, Malaysia, 19–21 July 2010
13. Schweiker, M.: Smart Cities. Conseil des Communes et Régions d'Europe-Council of European Municipalities and Regions. Presentation (2010)
14. European Union, European Innovation Partnership on Smart Cities and Communities. European Union (2013)
15. UN. United Smart Cities (USC). https://sustainabledevelopment.un.org/partnership/?p=10009. Accessed 3 Apr 2016
16. Kinnunen, T., Majava, J., Kess, P., Deering, B.J., Gillette, J.: Drive for intelligence: transformative factors in smart city development. In: 2015 IEEE First International Smart Cities Conference (ISC2), pp. 1–6. IEEE (2015)
17. Amsterdam Smart City. http://amsterdamsmartcity.com/. Accessed 15 Apr 2015
18. Ajuntament de Barcelona. Barcelona Smart City. http://smartcity.bcn.cat/. Accessed 17 Apr 2015
19. Ayuntamiento de Zaragoza, Estrategia de Gobierno Abierto Ciudad Digital 2012–2015 (2012). http://www.zaragoza.es/ciudad/sectores/tecnologia/tecno/ciudad-inteligente.htm. Accessed 16 Mar 2016
20. Manchester City Council. Manchester Digital Development Agency. http://www.manchester.gov.uk/. Accessed 16 Mar 2016
21. City of Boston. Digital strategy. http://www.cityofboston.gov/DoIT/strategy/. Accessed 15 Mar 2016
22. Ringness, Isabelle: What are Smart Cities?, 19 June 2014. New York International. http://nyintl.net/2014/06/what-are-smart-cities/. Accessed 15 Mar 2016
23. Infocomm Development Authority of Singapure. Intelligent Nation 2015 (2015). Singapore Government. http://www.ida.gov.sg/Tech-Scene-News/iN2015-Masterplan. Accessed 17 Mar 2016
24. Alcaldía de Medellín. Medellin Ciudad Inteligente. http://www.mdeinteligente.co/. Accessed 16 Mar 2016
25. IBM. Smarter cities. http://www.ibm.com/smarterplanet/us/en/smarter_cities/overview/. Accessed 21 Mar 2016
26. CISCO. Smart + connected communities. http://www.cisco.com. Accessed 21 Mar 2016

27. Telefónica. Smart Cities. https://m2m.telefonica.com/smart-cities/smart-cities. Accessed 22 Mar 2016
28. Ferrovial. Ciudades. http://www.ferrovial.com/es/lineas-de-negocio/ferrovial-servicios/centros-de-competencia/ciudades/. Accessed 22 Mar 2016
29. Indra. Smart Cities. http://www.indracompany.com/sector/administraciones-publicas/oferta/smart-cities. Accessed 22 Mar 2016
30. Transforming cities for the better through sustainable technology. Siemmens. http://w3.siemens.com/. Accessed 22 Mar 2016
31. Une ville durable, connectée et intelligente. Bouygues Enegies and sercices. http://www.bouyguesenergiesservices.com/une-ville-durable-connectee-et-intelligente. Accessed 4 Apr 2016
32. GE-Allstom. Smart cities. http://www.gegridsolutions.com/. Accessed 4 Apr 2016
33. Giffinger, R.: Smart Cities Ranking of European Medium-Sized Cities. Centre of Regional Science, Vienna UT (2007)

Author Index

Printed in the United States
By Bookmasters